The Gaited Horse Bible

BUYING, TRAINING, AND RIDING NATURALLY

GAITED HORSES—HUMANE TECHNIQUES FOR

THE CONSCIENTIOUS HORSEMAN

Brenda Imus

Creator of the Best-Selling *Gaits from God* DVD Series

T
TRAFALGAR SQUARE
North Pomfret, Vermont

This book is dedicated to all my friends and supporters who have never stopped believing. Thank you.

First published in 2011 by
Trafalgar Square Books
North Pomfret, Vermont 05053

Printed in China

Disclaimer of Liability
The author and publisher shall have neither liability nor responsibility to any person or entity with respect to any loss or damage caused or alleged to be caused directly or indirectly by the information contained in this book. While the book is as accurate as the author can make it, there may be errors, omissions, and inaccuracies.

Library of Congress Cataloging-in-Publication Data

Imus, Brenda.
   The gaited horse bible : buying, training, and riding naturally gaited horses — humane techniques for the conscientious horseman / Brenda Imus.
      p. cm.
   Includes index.
   ISBN 978-1-57076-417-2
   1. Horses--Paces, gaits, etc. 2. Horses--Training. I. Title.

   SF289.I68 2011
   798.2'3--dc22

                          2010036226

All photos by Brenda Imus except: pp. x, 1, 6, 7, 8, 10, 55, 57, 92, 93 *bottom*, 97, 103, 194 (Belinda Penegor); pp. 21, 49 (Debbie Pye); p. 22 (Jane Jacobs); p. 25 (Brooke Jacobs); p. 32 (Maggie McCallister); p. 37 (Lisa Gunnoe, provided by Andrew Hendrix); pp. 41, 44 (courtesy of the Icelandic Horse Farm, Vernon, BC); p. 69 (Karen Heltzel); p. 74 (Mimi Busk-Downey); pp. 80, 84, 125, 145, 162, 192 (Kris Robards); p. 93 top (Elizabeth Kopplow).

Illustrations courtesy of Brenda Imus except: pp. 4, 109, 110, 113, 118, 121, 177 (by Joan Muller); pp. 91, 210, 236, 237 (Robin Peterson); pp. 102, 104, 106, 107, 108, 122, 178, 224 (Brita Barlow Johnson); pp. 187, 188 (used by permission from *Better than Bombproof* by Rick Pelicano).

Book design by Lauryl Suire Eddlemon
Cover design by RM Didier
Typefaces: Minion; Giovanni

10 9 8 7 6 5 4 3 2 1

Contents

Acknowledgments

THIS BOOK WOULD NOT BE IN THE READER'S HANDS IF IT weren't for the assistance, and patience, of a number of individuals. The first people I would like to thank are Martha Cook, Managing Director, and Caroline Robbins, Publisher and my editor at Trafalgar Square Books. I was assigned to write this book in 2004, and it was to be completed the following year. Events in my life forced me to postpone the writing several times, yet these women were unflaggingly patient, and adjusted my deadline not only on several occasions, but for several years. This is unheard of in the publishing industry, and I cannot begin to thank them enough for continuing to extend the opportunity to complete this work. I believe that I learned enough in the interim to have redeemed the time well.

Writing the book was only half the story, as illustrations in a "how-to" book such as this are just as important as written instructions. A couple of illustrators I planned to work with also had fateful events occur and weren't able to come through for me when the time came to get down to business. Martha was kind enough to allow me to use a number of illustrations done by Brita Barlow Johnson from previous works. Brita agreed to allow me reprint rights and graciously took time from her busy schedule to help me shoot some last minute photography—you'll see her and her talented, handsome gray American Saddlebred, "Pendleton" (aka William Pendleton Grey) on several pages of this book. Joan Muller and Robin Peterson, two very accomplished professional equine illustrators, also stepped up to the plate at the last minute, and provided some wonderful illustrations. Joan's creative cutaway drawings that allow the reader to view the internal structures of the horse's mouth are amazing, and her enthusiasm for natural barefoot trimming sent me on an exciting new journey. Robin's background as a veterinarian is evident in her precise anatomical drawings. A special thanks to both of them!

Photographer Belinda Penegor came to a clinic held near Memphis, Tennessee, to shoot photos of horses performing the exercises described in this book, as well as several conformational shots. She has a keen eye, and was able to get several nice "before-and-after" photographs that, I hope, will encourage readers, proving that remarkable progress can be had in a relatively short time. Belinda worked in an arena under less than optimal lighting conditions, so the results are a testimony to her skills—both with the camera and computer software. Kris Robards worked with me in Missouri, and provided other off-site photos, and I owe her a huge debt of gratitude for her contribution. A number of other horse trainers and owners graciously provided photographs, so this book is enriched by a wide variety of illustrations.

Equally important are those persons who enabled me to get on with my work during, and following, a challenging time of life. Bobby Beech, owner of National Bridle Shop, helped me keep my line of products—and livelihood—when he chose to feature them in his store, catalogs, and on his Web site. We also worked together to find reputable, talented, and reliable producers of those products—his experience in the business has been invaluable. Thank you, Bobby. My friend and cousin, Brenda Wehrenburg, has been a faithful and reliable source of encouragement and help. I wish her and Richard the long, happy life they deserve!

Of course I'm grateful to my four grown children—Tonia, Charlie, Zack, and Jamie—for their unflagging faith in me (to say nothing of their insane practical jokes that always helps keep me on my toes).

I also want to thank Jake Royek, my partner and soul mate, for keeping things running on the farm as this book took on a life all its own. His 4:00 A.M. mornings, and cheerful willingness to take on new tasks and obligations, are appreciated more than he will ever know or imagine.

All of the above people, and others too numerous to mention, helped restore my faith in a patient, accepting, and all-loving God—to whom I owe the greatest "thank you" of all.

Thank you, Lord.

Preface

GAITED HORSE OWNERS FREQUENTLY BECOME FRUSTRATED by the scant number of horse trainers who are familiar working with these types of horses. And, when they do find one, they are concerned that "traditional" gaited-horse training methods and devices may be employed— not necessarily in the best interests of the horse.

The good news is that once your horse has been green-broke to ride, the best person to develop his smooth saddle gaits is you! That's because, whether you or someone else starts this part of his training, you're going to have to learn how to ride the horse to maintain that training, or there's a like-lihood the horse will eventually fall out of form and "lose" his gait. Then, you'll be right back where you started, searching for a trainer to help retrain the horse.

You need to learn only a few basic principles to develop and then main-tain your horse's gaits. As you do you will build an important relationship with him (as well as saving trainer's fees). It's a "win-win" situation all the way around.

This book will be a useful guide for anyone who plans to school gaited horses, but it is geared specifically to the everyday trail and pleasure rider. I've attempted to take what may seem like a complex topic and make it eas-ily understandable to horsemen at every level. The tools and techniques I suggest are effective for every kind of gaited horse, whether a Tennessee Walking Horse, Missouri Fox Trotter, Peruvian Paso, Gaited Morgan, Paso Fino, Mountain Horse—the list of recognized breeds goes on, and grows longer every year. The gaits these horses perform may differ because of vary-ing conformation and inborn gait inclination, but they can—and should— be developed using the same simple methods.

The majority of people buying gaited horses now are a far cry from pre-vious generations. Gaited horses used to be considered the flashy "Cadillacs" of the horse world, and were used primarily for showing. People's desire to enhance their gaits for the show ring, giving them an excessively "spirited" look, has led to abuse—some of it extraordinarily severe. While the Tennessee Walking Horse has typically received the lion's share of negative press, training and show ring abuse has certainly not been limited to this breed. Fortunately, there are owners today who actively seek more humane and practical ways to train.

Baby boomers started fueling the market for smooth-gaited, pleasure horses in the late 1980s. Because of increased discretionary income and fewer family responsibilities as their children matured, the number of these adult horse owners began to soar in the 1990s. With their aging bodies, it was only natural for this generation to discover—and prefer—the gaited horse's easier ride. As the popularity of all kinds of gaited breeds increased exponentially, breeders rushed to meet the demand of this new lucrative market. Mares that might have been bred infrequently, if at all, became foal-production machines. Such casual breeding practices resulted in a plethora of horses that possess less natural smooth-gaiting ability than their predecessors.

This generation of adult horsemen is more likely to question the status quo than their counterparts of 30 or 40 years ago. As the popularity of horse expos, instructional clinics, books, and DVDs prove, today's typical equestrian hobbyist is thirsty for knowledge. Their goals are often different, as well. Whereas horse owners used to have horses to show and compete, now in our increasingly fast-paced, competitive world, people today are more inclined to buy horses for sheer relaxation and pleasure, and to enjoy the process of schooling their own animals.

Brenda Imus

Introduction

I STARTED SERIOUSLY RESEARCHING GAITED HORSES IN 1992 and published *Heavenly Gaits: The Complete Guide to Gaited Riding Horses* in 1996. This was followed, two years later, by *Gaits of Gold: Selecting, Fitting and Training the Naturally Gaited Horse*. It seemed like a reasonable assumption at the time that I would move on to new topics, as I thought these combined titles contained all the information necessary for a person who wanted to buy or train a smooth-gaited riding horse. After all, I'd done several years of extensive research, often using older, out-of-print published sources and the wisdom of well-known trainers. I'd also purchased and trained a few gaited horses of my own, and helped my circle of friends work out problems with theirs. I never suspected my education was still in its infancy!

After *Gaits of Gold* was published, I began conducting training clinics across the United States and Canada. The horses and riders I worked with usually taught me as much as I taught them. At the same time, my personal herd expanded as I entered into a period of buying and retraining gaited horses—and quickly discovered there was always an abundance of them on the market who *needed* retraining. This offered me the advantage of working with several types on a day-to-day basis, and being confronted by many issues typically found in gaited horses of all breeds.

While most of the training techniques I advocated in *Gaits of Gold* are still useful and effective, I've since discovered that a few—gleaned primarily from traditional gaited-horse trainers, magazines, and old breed-related books—are not in the long-term best interests of the horse, and in fact, are based on flawed concepts. Likewise, the information I shared regarding equitation, hoof care, and tack has undergone a dramatic transformation as I've gained a wider range of personal experience, keeping my eye focused on the horse as the final authority.

My work led me to ask a number of questions that seemed to have never before been specifically addressed. For example, it was—and is—

often stated that gaited horses commonly suffer from soundness issues, particularly in their hocks and stifles, at a relatively young age. I discovered this to be all too true, all too often. As many as a quarter of the animals I worked with demonstrate some problems with their stifles, yet no one could tell me why this was so.

I was also told it was a "fact" that gaited horses couldn't perform their smooth saddle gaits when ridden "round" through the back and giving softly at the bridle as many horses in other disciplines, such as dressage, are today. It became evident to me this was the reason why so many animals were high-headed and hollow backed.

My early experience with basic dressage made me aware that horses ridden in such poor form were likely destined for trouble, sooner or later. I wanted to know why these horses, capable of performing their physically

There's nothing inherently wrong with occasionally allowing a horse to gait "full out" like this Tennessee Walking Horse for short periods of time. It can be fun for both horse and rider. But if a horse is encouraged to gait with a high head and hollow back too often—or for too long—it almost surely will result in eventual soundness issues.

complex smooth saddle gaits, couldn't be trained to become "soft" and "round" through their back. I had also noticed that my own horses were capable of gaiting at liberty across a field with impulsion generated from their hindquarters. I wondered why this energy couldn't be "gathered" on the bridle while the horse was being ridden in gait.

Another common problem is the gaited horse's temperament. I was often presented with animals that were spooky, herd bound, barn sour, lazy, stumblers, rushers, rearers, buckers—or just plain *no fun* to ride. How could this be so universally true among so many different types? What common factors contributed to these problems? I embarked on a quest to find the answers.

While some of these issues could be attributed to the way gaited horses were being trained, saddled, and ridden—which often caused them to develop a hollow back—I began to suspect *other* factors not yet generally understood were also at play. In my mind it seemed like a "chicken or egg" question: Were these animals hollow-backed and bady behaved because of poorly fitted saddles (it became glaringly apparent to me that gaited horses are especially challenging to fit to a saddle) and outdated training principles, or were the principles and the saddles a natural consequence of other, as yet unidentified, issues?

I noticed that many of the horses I worked with suffered from physical discomfort—even outright pain. I began to focus on ways to make them more comfortable in order to improve their behavior and performance, as well as the relationship between horse and rider. This proved to be a multi-faceted, life-changing, and extraordinarily rewarding task.

Perhaps the most daunting challenge I faced over the past few years has been demonstrating to "old-school" gaited-horse trainers that gaited horses can and should be taught how to be ridden in a softly "rounded-up" and functionally correct frame. Old ways die hard. Some trainers have been more than a little discomfited by the seemingly sudden presence of a hitherto unknown, middle-aged woman from (of all places!) New York State—where gaited horses have never been considered a "way of life"—who has the nerve to publicly question all the tried-and-true methods passed down from generation to generation. What's more, this "upstart" has designed and marketed a line of gaited-horse products from which she profits. Can her motives be pure?

The answer to the last question is an unequivocal "Yes," though I certainly understand their skepticism.

Nevertheless, the old ways leave much to be desired from the horse's perspective. Thanks to well-known teacher-and-trainer clinicians such as Ray Hunt, Bill and Tom Dorrance, Pat Parelli, John Lyons, Clinton Anderson, Lynn Palm, Jane Savoie, and a score of others, the general equestrian world has undergone a revolutionary change in understanding and implementing more humane ways to successfully work with horses. It is finally time for our gaited horses to also benefit from this more enlightened point of view.

This book is offered in an ongoing attempt to help other horse lovers understand the process of working with gaited horses in a way that allows the animal to be ridden in good "rounded-up" form, using humane training principles that enable him to live a long, useful, and sound life.

It is my heartfelt desire that those who consider themselves "horsemen" (myself included) never stop being open to learning more about the nature of horses.

CHAPTER 1

Gaited Horses 101

What Is a Gaited Horse?

T HE TERM *GAITED HORSE* IS NOT A PRECISE TERM, because every horse performs some gait or another. Historically we've associated the walk, trot or jog, canter or lope, and gallop to horses in general. The trot, in particular, is the working gait of the general horse population, as it is ground covering and can be performed over long distances. The trot, however, is often jarring and difficult to ride. For this reason, breeders have long sought to produce horses that naturally perform a substitute gait for the trot (known as a *smooth saddle gait*) that is faster than the regular walk, smoother and easier to sit than the working trot, and can be sustained for longer periods of time than a canter or gallop. Breeds of horses that resulted from these efforts came to be referred to as *gaited horses*.

While all gaited horses can perform some easy-to-sit gait in place of the trot, there are nonetheless differences among these smooth saddle gaits based on the horse's breed, individual conformation, and training.

GAIT TERMS CREATE CONFUSION

Over the years many people, even those who own gaited horses, have expressed frustration over their inability to understand the horse's smooth saddle gaits. It seems to be a complex subject, though the basics are actually quite simple. Confusion is caused because there is a wide assortment of breeds of gaited horses, with each one claiming to possess unique signature gaits, called by breed-specific names (see sidebar, p. 15). When you count all these various gaits, breed by breed, you come up with an array of supposedly "unique" gaits. One work I referenced named 32 "different" gaits, and another claimed over 100! Actually, if you consider some breeds originating from diverse regions such as South America or India, you could add many more (see chapter 2, p. 59, for more breeds of gaited horses).

On the other hand, some people use a single term, such as *ambling,* or *single footing,* to describe *all* smooth saddle gaits.

People are surprised when I inform them there are actually only five smooth saddle gaits. These are the *fox trot, flat walk, rack, running walk,* and *stepping pace.* Most of these gaits are performed within a certain range of speed, and a few of them are called by a slightly different term when the horse is moving in a faster or slower speed range, when his head is high or low, or when the motion of the legs is more or less animated (see sidebar, p. 8). All five gaits are interrelated, so it becomes easy to identify them once these relationships are understood. I will help this process by introducing the Gait Spectrum. (Note: I do not include the canter and gallop in the Gait Spectrum since they do not fall within its parameters. However, I do describe these gaits on p. 14.)

DIAGONAL GAITS			Slightly Diagonal Intermediate Gaits	INTERMEDIATE (SQUARE) GAITS	Slightly Lateral Intermediate Gaits	LATERAL GAITS	
				Speed Rack 12-20+ mph		**Speed Pace** 12-20+ mph	
				Rack 7-12 mph			
Fox Trot 7-12 mph				**Running Walk** 7-10 mph			
				Flat Walk 5-7 mph			
Fox Walk 4-7 mph	**Trot** 4-12 mph			**Working Walk** 3-4 mph		**Pace** 4-12 mph	**Stepping Pace** 4-8 mph
				Dog Walk less than 3 mph			

1.1 The Gait Spectrum: At one end of the Spectrum are the diagonal gaits where diagonally paired legs move in synchrony—or nearly so—and at the other end are the lateral gaits, where laterally paired legs move in synchrony—or nearly so. When neither lateral, nor diagonal pairs of legs move closely together, the gait is called "intermediate," or "square." Note that some horses perform the intermediate gaits more toward the diagonal or lateral or ends of the spectrum and have a slight inclination toward diagonal or lateral timing.

The Gait Spectrum

WHAT DETERMINES GAIT?

The timing of the hind legs as they relate to the motion of the forelegs determines the basic nature of any gait, that is, whether the gait is *diagonal, lateral,* or *intermediate* (fig. 1.1). Horses that move *diagonally* opposed pairs of legs in two-beat synchrony (or near synchrony) are said to be *diagonally oriented.* Those that move *lateral* or "same-side" pairs of legs in synchrony (or nearly so) are *laterally oriented.* Horses that are neither strongly lateral nor diagonal are performing what is known as an *intermediate* or *square gait*— one that requires each leg to move completely independently of every other leg. The changing relationship between hind legs and forelegs all along the spectrum between these two extremes of diagonal and lateral is what creates all gaits unique to the gaited horse (figs. 1.2 A–G).

Therefore, all gaited horses' legs move either in a *diagonal* (trot/fox trot) orientation, a *lateral* (pace/stepping pace) orientation, or in one of the *intermediate* gaits (walk, flat walk, running walk, or rack). These differences can be likened to people who are right handed, left handed, or ambidextrous.

1.2 A–G The trot is a two-beat gait where the horse works diagonal sets of legs in perfect unison (A).

The fox trot is similar to the trot and sometimes is referred to as a "broken trot" because the forefoot lands an instant before the diagonally opposed hind foot (B). This eliminates the trot suspension and consequent concussion to the rider.

Drawing C illustrates an evenly timed four-beat walk. Each foot picks up and sets down independently of every other. The gait is performed with varying degrees of energy and speed. A very slow, uncollected walk is called a "dog walk." A slightly more energetic and faster walk (3–4 mph) is called a "working walk," and the next fastest and more collected walk (5–7 mph) is called a "flat walk."

While the footfall pattern of the running walk is the same as the dog walk, working walk, and rack, the running walk has a much greater length of hind stride, which results in an "overstride" (the hind foot steps beyond the print of the front) and increased head nod (D).

The rack has the same footfall patterns and even four-beat timing as the dog walk, but is performed with much greater speed and impulsion from behind (E). Some horses can rack at very high speeds.

The stepping pace is performed so that lateral pairs of legs work together, but the hind leg sets down a split instant before the same side foreleg (F).

The pace is performed with lateral pairs of legs working in perfect synchrony (G). There is a moment of suspension between one pair of feet picking up and the other setting down. This can be a most difficult, jarring gait to ride as it is not possible to post to the pace, and the motion in the saddle is both up and down as well as side to side.

I've coined the word "quadridextrous" to describe horses that perform smooth saddle gaits because they can move all four legs independently even when traveling at speed, unlike non-gaited horses that only move diagonal or lateral pairs of legs in unison when traveling faster than a walk. As with ambidextrous people who are able to use each hand independently but still prefer to primarily use their left or right hand, some gaited horses have a minimum degree of "quadridexterity" and strongly prefer a diagonal or lateral gait. Others are extremely quadridextrous by nature, and can perform most of the gaits along the Gait Spectrum with ease, even at fast speeds.

Diagonal Gaits

TROT

A horse that is strictly diagonally oriented performs the *trot*, moving diagonally opposed sets of legs in *perfect* two-beat synchrony (right hind/left front; left hind/right front) with a moment of suspension between the time one pair of feet picks up and the other pair hits the ground (fig. 1.3). It is

1.3 This American Saddlebred is trotting, with two sets of diagonal legs working together.

1.4 This multi-gaited Tennessee Walking Horse mare is performing a fox trot, where the forefoot lands slightly before the diagonally opposed hind foot. This gives the impression that the horse is "walking in front and trotting behind."

this "hitting the ground" that causes a jolt or concussion to the rider. Horses usually trot at speeds from 4–10 mph, though some can trot more slowly—the Western jog, for example—while longer-limbed horses may reach a ground-covering 15 mph. Because the trot is an evenly timed two-beat gait, with a moment of suspension and resulting jolt, it is not considered one of the saddle gaits.

FOX TROT

The other diagonal gait is the *fox trot* (fig. 1.4). It is the smooth saddle gait related to the ordinary trot. When a horse moves diagonal pairs of legs together but the timing is such that the forefoot lands a *split second* before the opposite hind foot, the horse is performing a fox trot. (You can remember this by equating *forefoot/fox trot*.) This gait has uneven, *four-beat* timing. (You can hear the cadence if you say the sentence, "Hunk 'o meat and two potatoes," to the sound of the footfalls.) The fox trot is smoother than a trot because there is always at least one forefoot on the ground at any time, which eliminates suspension and subsequent concussion. The hind legs are also used like springs, which reduces the impact of the hind feet hitting the ground. The fox trot can be very smooth to ride, and is generally performed at speeds from 7–12 mph. Again, some horses may fox trot at greater or lesser speeds, depending on their conformation and innate quickness.

I once used a GPS to clock one of my fast fox-trotting mares, and she executed her gait at an amazing 14 mph. Because I could not believe she maintained a true fox-trotting footfall pattern at that speed, a friend later shot a video of me riding her and proved she had. On the other hand, some horses perform the fox trot at exceptionally slow speeds—even 4 mph. Old-timers used to refer to this as the *fox walk*.

A fox-trotting horse moves with a long, sweeping stride in front, a minimum amount of lift from the knees, and with one forefoot always on the ground (with the exception of some fast show-ring versions of the gait, where there may be a brief moment of suspension in front). The hind legs lift high at the hocks and there is a moment when both hind feet are off the ground, which gives the appearance of a horse that is "walking in front and trotting behind." The head moves in a quick up-and-down noddng motion, in time with the hind legs.

An "aberration" of a fox trot is known as the *slick trot*. This gait occurs when the diagonally oriented horse's hind foot lands an instant *before* the opposite forefoot. The result is an uncomfortable jar at the back of the saddle that is extremely hard on the rider's seat bones and back. (I discuss this variant gait and how to correct it in chapter 9—see p. 232.)

1.5 This horse is pacing—moving lateral sets of legs in perfect synchrony (note the pink bell boots on the left side). It's a particularly jarring gait for the rider.

Lateral Gaits

PACE

Like the trot, the pace is an evenly timed, two-beat gait, has suspension between footfalls, and is therefore not usually considered a true saddle gait (fig. 1.5).

1.6 A pretty Missouri Fox Trotting Horse doing a stepping pace—a gait usually comfortable for the rider and easy for the horse to execute, but with the downside that it contributes to early unsoundness (see more about this on p. 226).

Types of Gaited Horse Walks

The type of walk a horse performs is defined by his speed and the amount of energy he generates. A horse slowly walking across a pasture or moseying down the trail is performing a *dog walk*. When he picks up his speed to 3-4 mph and there is some energy generated from his hindquarters, he is performing a *working walk*. When the rider asks him to distribute more weight rearward and collect on the bridle, and he reaches speeds of 5-7 mph, he has transitioned into the *flat walk*, which may be likened to the "first gear" of smooth saddle gaits.

Horses that pace are laterally oriented and move same-side pairs of legs together in perfect two-beat synchrony (right hind/right front and left hind/left front). This results in a distinctive side-to-side motion in the saddle and, like the trot, because there is a moment of suspension between the pairs of feet picking up and setting down, there is also concussion transmitted from the ground through to the horse's back and the rider's seat. This combination of side-to-side and jarring up-and-down action makes the pace a particularly difficult and uncomfortable gait to ride.

Most horses pace at speeds from 4–12 mph, but there are exceptions to the rule. Some horses pace at the same slow speed others perform a basic four-beat dog walk. It used to be said of these horses that they could "pace all day in the shade of a tree."

STEPPING PACE

Just as the fox trot is the smooth saddle gait related to the trot, so the *stepping pace* is the smooth saddle gait related to the pace (fig. 1.6). In this case, two same-side pairs of legs (right hind/right front and left hind/left front) move in synchrony, but the hind foot lands an instant *before* the same side forefoot, creating an unevenly timed, *four-beat* gait. This timing eliminates the suspension and concussion created by the pace, making it more comfortable to ride.

Horses *step pace* at speeds ranging from 4–8 mph, but when they go faster than this, they commonly convert to an uncomfortable and jarring *two-beat* pace. Besides most horses' inability to remain smooth at higher rates of speed, there are other drawbacks to allowing a horse to perform the pace and stepping pace. I discuss these later in this chapter (see p. 16).

Intermediate (Square) Gaits

WALK

Exactly at the center of the Gait Spectrum, between the trot and the pace, is the walk, whereby neither diagonal nor lateral pairs of legs move in unison. Instead, each foot moves independently of the other feet in an evenly timed, four-beat gait. The walk is the gait from which the intermediate (square) saddle gaits originate (fig. 1.7). This is why the French call it "the mother of all gaits."

The footfall pattern and timing of the *dog walk* and *working walk* are the same as those seen in the *flat walk, running walk,* and *rack.* Which of these

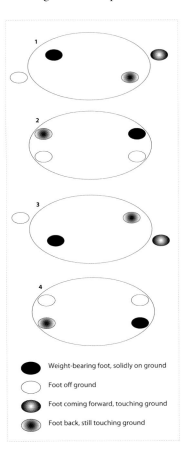

1.7 The footfalls of the walk: The basis of all the intermediate or square gaits. The walk is neither lateral, nor diagonal, and is called a "square" gait because the legs at all four corners move entirely independently of one another. The sequence is: left hind, left front (1); body carried forward on the left laterals (2); right hind, right front (3); body carried forward on right laterals (4). There are always two or three feet on the ground at any given point of the gait movement.

● Weight-bearing foot, solidly on ground

○ Foot off ground

◑ Foot coming forward, touching ground

◐ Foot back, still touching ground

square gaits the horse performs once he is moving faster depends upon his conformation, speed of travel, and how he is "wired"—that is, whether he is diagonally or laterally oriented, or is strongly quadridextrous.

FLAT WALK

When a horse is asked to "work the walk" (walking fast with increased impulsion from the haunches and a light degree of contact on the reins), he usually speeds up naturally into a *flat walk* (fig. 1.8). While this term is most often used in connection with the Tennessee Walking Horse, it is a good description of the gait that is transitional between a simple walk and whichever gait is the individual horse's faster gait, regardless of his breed. The flat walk develops the horse's ability for faster gaiting by conditioning both his muscles and his neurological memory for working a four-beat gait

1.8 A flat walk being performed by a Tennessee Walking Horse with great energy and engagement. Horses can usually flat walk at speeds from 5–7 mph.

with increased speed and collection. The flat walk's speed is between 5–7 mph, and the flat-walking horse transmits a relaxed rolling motion through his body that results in a moderate head nod.

RUNNING WALK

The *running walk* possesses the same evenly-timed, four-beat footfall pattern as the ordinary walk, but is faster—generally from 7–10 mph, though an occasional horse can maintain a running walk as fast as 12 mph. A horse that can perform a running walk must be conformed so he is able to generate a long, deep stride from behind, resulting in *overstride* (figs. 1. 9 A & B).

Overstride is attained when the track of the hind foot lands 4 or more inches in front of the track of the forefoot. A running-walk horse with good conformation may overstride by as much as 12–20 inches. While some trainers claim overstrides of 24 inches or more, such animals are usually not performing in a manner intended by nature, but have instead been trained using mechanical and/or chemical "enhancements." As said in my introduction (see p. ix), these methods are detrimental to the long-term physical and mental soundness of the horse.

A signature move of the running walk is the horse's head nod. Humans

1.9 A & B The leading horse, a Walkaloosa, is doing a rack, while the black horse, a Tennessee Walking Horse, is doing a smooth running walk (A). The footfalls of these gaits are the same, but the racking horse has a quick, short stride, while the running-walk horse's hind leg reaches deeply beneath his body so that the track of the hind foot overstrides the track of the forefoot by several inches (B).

use swinging arms to balance themselves when walking or running. When we take a short stride, our arms take a short swing; the longer our stride, the longer the swing of our arms. If you take very fast, long strides and hold your arms down tightly to your sides, you'll begin using your upper body and head for balance—and will develop a head nod! Since horses have no arms to swing, they use their neck and head as a fulcrum for balance. The longer the stride of the running walk, the more distinct the up-and-down action of this fulcrum.

Not all horses that perform the running walk—even those with an inborn long overstride—possess a natural deep head nod, and this is because of their overall conformation. An exaggerated head nod has become a show-ring standard for Tennessee Walking Horses, so over the years trainers have discovered mechanical means of "developing" this trait. This is a mistaken notion, as it forces the horse into an unnatural body frame and detracts from his ability to perform his gaits comfortably.

The long hind legs of a horse capable of performing the running walk demonstrate a minimal amount of lift, and there's always one hind foot on the ground. The forelegs have a higher lifting, rolling action with a moment of suspension between the forefeet picking up and setting down—people used to say the horse was "catching some air" when his speed picked up and there was suspension between the action of the forelegs. It is this action that signals when the horse has transitioned from a flat walk to a running walk. The overall appearance of the running walk is one of a horse that is "walking in back, and trotting in front."

RACK

The fastest of the intermediate gaits, the *rack* shares the timing and footfall patterns of the running walk, but features a shorter length of stride (see figs. 1.9 A & B). This means the hind foot may "cap" the track of the same side forefoot—land on top of, or 1 to 3 inches in front of the track of the forefoot—or land *behind it*, where it is called an *understride*. Show-ring standards for various breeds of horses have established "ideal" tracking specifications for different show-ring gaits. A Paso Fino, for example, should

Rack Semantics

The pattern of footfalls in the rack is identical to the walk, the primary difference between them being that of speed, though horses perform the rack in different ways. Some horses perform the rack so quickly that there is only one foot on the ground at any given time—this is called the *single foot*. Other horses pick up lateral pairs of legs together, but the footfall pattern is an evenly timed, four-beat gait. This is commonly called the *saddle rack* or *step rack*.

demonstrate understride when performing his *fino gait,* but may exhibit some overstride with the *paso largo.*

As discussed previously, a horse nods or shakes his head as an aid in balance, and the longer the hind foot strides, the more the horse nods or shakes his head. Because of the rack's shorter hind stride, this gait does not produce as much head nod or shake as that demonstrated in a running walk.

A note about the running walk and rack: Horses that can perform a running walk always possess the ability to shorten stride, so can invariably perform a rack as well. Not all racking horses, however, have the conformation to be able to achieve overstride, so may be physically incapable of executing a good running-walk gait. I discuss these conformational issues more thoroughly in chapter 4 (see p. 87).

SPEED GAITS

The rack and pace are the two gaits that can be executed at great speed. It takes time to achieve overstride combined with the head nod of the running walk, so a horse performing a correct running walk at higher speeds naturally shortens his stride for greater efficiency of motion, the head nod disappears, and the evenly timed four-beat gait becomes a rack. A horse performing a rack at higher speeds usually maintains the footfall pattern and timing of the rack. It is possible for a horse to rack over 20 mph, though it is rare for one to exceed 15 mph. Once that speed has been exceeded, the gait is commonly called a *speed rack.*

Some very laterally oriented horses will transition into a very fast pace, rather than a rack, when gaiting at speed. This is true of some of the so-called speed-racking horses popular in the Southern United States, as well as of Icelandic Horses who perform what is known as the *flying pace.*

It should be understood that just as most people are not capable of champion race speeds, most gaited horses do not possess the ability to gait at very high speeds—they will top out at 10–12 mph. Animals that are capable of speed gaiting should not be expected to do so until their bodies are mature enough to withstand the rigors, and they should then be well conditioned for the extremity of their sport. Riders who expect too much speed too soon place their horse's soundness at risk.

Riding a very fast gaited horse is a lot of fun, and a primary reason why some people own smooth-gaited horses. But if speed work is overdone, the horse will likely develop physical issues over time. Fast gaiting should be limited to 10 minutes or so, with lots of slower work performed in good form—as I describe on p. 180—to help keep the horse's body strong enough to bear the stress of faster gaiting.

VARIATIONS OF GAIT

While an ideal running walk or rack are perfectly timed *four-beat gaits,* in reality many horses perform them slightly on the lateral or diagonal ends of the Gait Spectrum (see p. 3). What this means is that one horse might perform his running walk or rack halfway between a lateral gait, such as the stepping pace, and a true intermediate gait, while another might execute it halfway between a diagonal fox trot and a true intermediate gait. The difference in timing, especially considering the speed of gaiting horses, is so miniscule that trying to section and cross-section the Gait Spectrum in such a way as to delineate more than the six essential gaits is pointless. The truth is, most horses will tend to slip from one "gear" to another, especially early in schooling. As training progresses the rider's goal is to develop consistency of timing.

Gaits "Off" the Gait Spectrum

Most gaited horses can also execute the canter (or lope), and gallop, though horses with a strong lateral orientation may be "canter challenged." Because the training described in this book improves their ability to move lateral pairs of legs more independently, their ability to perform these other gaits usually improves as well.

THE CANTER AND GALLOP

The canter (referred to as the "lope" in Western riding) is an unevenly timed three-beat gait whereby one pair of diagonals works in unison, while the

A Gait by Any Other Name

While every breed of gaited horse claims a unique set of gaits, the gaits on the Gait Spectrum are the only true gaits a horse will perform—unless he bounces down the road on his head, or develops an additional pair of legs! However, various breeds do have a slightly different appearance when gaiting due to variants in conformation and training, and breed associations have developed different names for these gaits:

- Tennessee Walking Horse: *walk, flat walk, rack, running walk*
- Missouri Fox Trotting Horse: *walk, fox walk, flat walk, fox trot*
- Icelandic Horse: *tolt* (rack or running walk) and *flying pace* (speed pace or stepping pace)
- Paso Fino: *paso fino* (very short-strided rack or stepping pace), *paso corto* (rack or stepping pace with average length of stride), *paso largo* (running walk), *trocha* (fox trot)

- Peruvian Horse: *paso llano* (stepping pace or rack), *sobreando* (stepping pace), and *hauchano* (pace)
- American Saddlebred: *rack* (very fast rack), and *slow gait* (highly animated stepping pace performed at slow speed)
- Single-Footing Horse: *single foot* (fast rack performed with only one foot on the ground at any given time)
- Florida Cracker Horse: *coon rack* (stepping pace or rack)

OTHER GAIT TERMS

- The *Indian shuffle:* A stepping pace performed by horses with foundational Appaloosa breeding in their background. It is performed in such a way that the hind foot slides, or shuffles, under the horse as it sets down, thus acting as an excellent shock absorber. Unlike most horses with a strong lateral orientation, most Indian-shuffling horses easily perform a smooth, rocking-chair canter and can remain supple and slightly collected in their gait.
- The *amble:* Sometimes used to describe any smooth saddle gait, it commonly describes the stepping pace.
- The *saddle rack:* A gait whereby lateral pairs of legs pick up at nearly the same time, but each leg strikes the ground independently in an evenly timed, four-beat gait. This is possible because the horse's forelegs have a greater amount of lift than the hind legs, and there-

fore require more time to complete the pick-up/set-down sequence. This gait is also known as the *step rack.*
- The *slick trot:* This gait occurs when a diagonally oriented horse's hind foot lands an instant ahead of the opposing forefoot. The result is an uncomfortable jar at the back of the saddle that is hard on the rider's seat bones and back. (I discuss this variant gait and how to correct it in more detail on p. 232.)
- *Termino:* This name describes the unique outward rolling action of some Peruvian Horses' forelegs. The motion begins in the shoulder, and though the entire foreleg is smoothly rolled outward, the foot lands squarely on the ground. Peruvian Horses use this motion for balance, which means they require less head nod, even when they are performing with a very long length of stride.

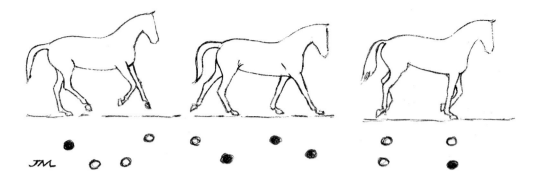

1.10 In the canter, the horse springs off his non-leading hind leg onto his leading hind leg and diagonally opposed non-leading foreleg. From these, he moves onto his leading foreleg. He then balances on this leg as the non-leading hind comes forward to repeat the sequence.

other pair works in opposition (fig. 1.10). The direction of travel dictates which lead (leading hind and foreleg) the horse takes to maintain his balance, as there is a greater proportion of the horse's weight borne on the inside of a circle. When traveling to the right on a circle, for example, the two inside legs will move farther forward and bear more weight than the outside legs. When traveling straight the horse can take either a right or left lead, depending on the rider's cues.

The canter begins as the horse sets the outside non-leading hind foot beneath him and uses it to spring onto the diagonally opposed leading front foot. Then the inside leading hind foot sets down in unison with the outside non-leading front foot, which serves to steady and balance the horse. Thus, the order of footfalls for the canter (on a right lead) is: LH—RF—**RH/LF**—LH—RF—**RH/LF**. The familiar cadence is 1—2-**3**—1-2-**3**—1-2-**3**.

The gallop is similar to the canter, except it is performed at greater speed and the diagonals that work together aren't perfectly synchronized. When it is a right hand lead, the order of footfalls is: LH—**RF**—**RH**—LF—LH—**RF**—**RH**—LF. This results in a very fast four-beat gait with emphasis on two beats: 1-2-**3-4**—1-2-**3-4**—1-2-**3-4**.

Detrimental Effects of Specific Gaits

Many gaited horses perform a pace or stepping pace as their preferred gait. While it is always our intent to encourage the horse to perform his most natural gait, bringing the laterally oriented horse as close to the center of the Gait Spectrum as possible is wise for his welfare. While a stepping pace is often smooth for the rider, the horse is going in a strung-out manner that encourages a *ventroflexed*—hollow-backed—frame. This can cause long-term soundness concerns.

Over time a horse ridden in a ventroflexed frame is weakened throughout his entire body. Weight is "improperly" distributed on his hind legs and forelegs, creating excessive stress, which lead to problems such as arthritis, bone spavin, bowed tendons, and locking stifles. This inverted frame causes negative permanent changes in the spinal column as the edges of the vertebrae begin to impinge upon one another, while the muscles of the topline also deteriorate. This makes it difficult for the horse to cope with the weight of a saddle and rider, and finding a saddle that will correctly distribute the rider's weight becomes especially difficult.

Horses ridden in a ventroflexed frame often develop an "upside-down" neck, with a bulge on the underside of the neck and a dip on the top. Such horses are resistant to the bridle, and often have a difficult time negotiating hills and rough terrain because they cannot arch their neck downward to clearly see where they are placing their feet.

Most gaited horses prefer the "pacey" gaits because they are by far the easiest. The weaker the horse, the more he prefers these more damaging gaits—and consequently, he becomes even weaker and more damaged. To pace or step pace, all he has to do is stiffen up that large back muscle that runs all along his topline and "shuffle" his lateral legs underneath himself: back and forth, back and forth, and back and forth. The action is hypnotic to the point of being addictive. Furthermore, performing a correctly executed intermediate gait, or the diagonal fox trot, requires him to put out a great deal more effort as his large back muscle needs to be put entirely to work.

What Gait Is My Horse Performing?

Identifying the gait your horse is performing under saddle can be a challenge. It's important to be able to ascertain, at minimum, when the animal has fallen into a pace or stepping pace so you can *square* it up to a more functionally *intermediate,* sound gait.

It can be very helpful to have a friend record you riding on video so you can study it carefully to observe your horse's gaits. Watch just *one set of legs* at a time, first lateral and then diagonal pairs. When you observe lateral pairs of legs moving together, you've got a pace or stepping pace, and failing that, carefully observe one pair of diagonal legs to see if they synchronize. If not, then watch one hind foot come up under the horse—just one, or you'll quickly get confused! Should it appear that the hind leg comes up under the horse's body and *meets* the diagonally opposed foreleg, then you have a rack or running walk.

OBSERVATION IS THE BEST TEACHER

Besides watching video recordings of yourself on your horse, make it a habit to observe the footfall patterns of other people's gaited horses at every opportunity. You'll note that while the footfall patterns of a particular gait are the same, the way different horses appear when performing it may be quite dissimilar. If you practice the skill of recognizing the various gaits by training your eye to recognize their footfall patterns, it will soon become possible to identify them with merely a glance.

Trot

- *From the Ground:* Observe one set of diagonals. When that pair pick up and set down at the same time, your horse is *trotting.*
- *From the Saddle:* You'll note that the head is upright and shaking slightly. You'll also feel a distinct jarring from the saddle to your seat and the motion will be strongly up and down.

Fox Trot

- *From the Ground:* You will observe the horse picking up and setting down one set of diagonals nearly together, but the forefeet strike the ground noticeably sooner, and there is one forefoot always on the ground. Both the head and tail bob in time with the action of the hind feet, and the horse's ears may flop. The horse appears to be "walking in front and trotting behind."
- *From the Saddle:* The *fox trot* has a back-to-front feeling and a slight

If you practice the skill of recognizing the various gaits by training your eye to recognize their footfall patterns, it will soon become possible to identify them with merely a glance.

"bump" is felt through the cantle to your pockets because there is more lift in the hind legs than in the forelegs, and also a moment when both hind feet are off the ground, creating a slight amount of concussion upon set-down. The sound of a fox trot is very distinctive, and as I've said, it mimics the cadence of the phrase, "Hunk o' meat and two potatoes."

Pace

- *From the Ground:* When you see a pair of diagonal legs and notice they do not move in synchrony or nearly so, observe a pair of lateral legs. If one set of laterals picks up and sets down at precisely the same time, and the horse is moving in a stiff high-headed frame, he is performing a *pace*.

- *From the Saddle:* There is both side-to-side *and* up-and-down motion. It's difficult if not impossible to get "with" your horse's action, and you may feel like you've been dropped into a clothes dryer! Watch your horse's neck and head to see if it swings from side to side because this is a telltale sign of the pace.

Stepping Pace

- *From the Ground:* The *stepping pace* will appear to be similar to the pace, except that you'll see the horse's hind foot set down an instant before the same side forefoot. Again, the horse appears stiff and high-headed.

- *From the Saddle:* The stepping pace may be difficult to identify because it often feels smooth to the rider. Don't take it for granted that a smooth gait is the rack, running walk, or fox trot. As I discussed earlier, many horses will choose the stepping pace if given the chance, simply because it requires so little physical effort. You may see a slight side-to-side motion of the horse's neck and head, and feel a rolling, side-to-side motion as the horse works off lateral sets of legs.

  Stepping pace horses may hold their head very high, or conversely, be overflexed into "false collection"—a forced headset but little or no rounding of the back and impulsion from behind (fig. 1.11). Often

1.11 Too much contact on the reins without good impulsion from the hindquarters results in "false collection," which in turn encourages a pace or stepping-pace gait.

these horses are so stiff it feels as though one is riding a stick horse rather than a flesh-and-blood animal! Their hind end drifts to the outside when being ridden around corners. One good indication of this gait is that, when cued for more speed, the horse immediately jumps into a jarring, straight pace.

Running Walk

- *From the Ground:* The *running walk* horse demonstrates noticeable overstride and a head nod that originates with a rolling motion through the shoulders. Many people believe a running walk horse has to have a very high headset, but this is not true. Instead, he carries his poll at, or slightly above, the withers.
- *From the Saddle:* This gait gives the rider a fluid, rolling, "gliding" sensation. There's a sense of power as the long hind legs propel the horse and rider forward. If the horse performs the gait a bit on the lateral (many do), there will be a *slight,* side-to-side motion of the neck and head. This motion is "V"-shaped as the horse lowers and then raises his head, unlike a stepping pace horse, whose neck will simply move from side to side and not up and down.

Rack

- *From the Ground:* How a racking horse appears depends on his manner of performing the gait. Some racking horses exhibit a great amount of leg lift and animation both hind and fore, while others have less lift and reach. A racking horse may have a slight overstride, may cap his strides, or demonstrate understride, depending upon his conformation (see fig. 1.9 B, p. 11). When you observe the horse and note that neither the diagonal nor the lateral pair of legs move in synchrony, the hind legs are not producing overstride but appear to come under the horse to meet the opposite side foreleg, and there is little or no head nod or shake, the horse is performing a rack.
- *From the Saddle:* You will experience a very smooth ride with no side-to-side or hind-to-fore motion, and the horse's head will move only slightly in time with his hind feet—at very fast speed there will be no head motion at all.

CHAPTER 2

Breeds of Gaited Horses

Gaining in Popularity

THE INCREASED POPULARITY OF SMOOTH-GAITED horses has resulted in more horses available for sale and registered with the different breed organizations. Until the early 1990s, the only North American breeds with significant numbers were the American Saddlebred, the Tennessee Walking Horse, the Missouri Fox Trotting Horse, the Peruvian Horse, the Icelandic Horse, and the Paso Fino.

Since then registries have formed for other types of gaited horses. These include the Rocky Mountain Horse, the Kentucky Mountain Horse, the Spotted Saddle Horse, the Racking Horse, gaited horses with Appaloosa coat patterns, and the Standardbred (although this breed existed much earlier, they were generally used for race driving rather than riding), and many others—see the list at the end of this chapter.

Some of these organizations now boast more registered horses than do the original breed registries. Several smaller registries cater to "pockets" of certain types of horses found in localized regions of the country and off-shoot types from the earlier breeds—for example, concentrations of certain bloodlines. There are also breeds that count a small percentage of gaited stock amongst their number, but those numbers are not high enough to permit the breed to be counted as smooth-gaited, as a whole.

The United States isn't alone in its appreciation of smooth-gaited riding horses as there are dozens of gaited-horse breeds in countries around the world (see list, p. 59).

AMERICAN SADDLEBRED HORSE

HISTORY

In the early seventeenth century, pacing stock from Scotland *(Galloways)* and Ireland *(Hobbies)* were imported by breeders into Virginia and the Narragansett Bay area of Rhode Island. Breeders crossed these horses—as well as Morgans and other types common to their regions—and within 50 years had produced a horse that came to be known as the *Narragansett Pacer.*

While the Galloways and Hobbies were two-beat pacing horses, Narragansett Pacers became popular for their easy-to-sit saddle gait (called either a "pace" or "amble" at the time), as well as their strength and docile temperament. They usually stood around 14 hands and were sorrel in color, with many of them being "piebald" (spotted). By the eighteenth century, the Narragansett Pacer was one of the most popular riding horses in the Colonies, and was reputed to be the horse Paul Revere rode when he took his famous ride in 1775.

By that time, however, the diminutive horse was already on its way to being bred out of existence. In 1706, Colonists began importing Thoroughbred horses from England and crossing them with Narragansett Pacers (as well as Morgans, Arabians, and other common Colonial stock). Crossing small ambling stock with larger non-gaited horses produced a

2.1 This American Saddlebred Horse stallion, Joe Fabulous, demonstrates the beauty, strength, and style that typifies the breed.

larger horse that was originally called *America's Horse.* Because of the increased percentage of trotting blood, many of these horses were non-gaited or had only an innate aptitude for learning the easy saddle gaits. This seemed inconsequential at the time because rustic roads and rough bridle paths had been replaced by sophisticated roadways, so a horse was used at least as much for pulling a carriage as for riding.

America's Horse came to be widely known as the *Kentucky Saddler,* and was used for riding, working farms, and participating in regional horse shows, where he excelled. Owners took great pride in the beauty, power, and presence of their horses.

Gaines Denmark

Denmark, a Thoroughbred sire, was bred to a gaited mare that subsequently produced the gaited stud colt Gaines Denmark in 1851. The American Saddlebred Horse Association, founded in 1891, was the first American horse-breed registry, and Gaines Denmark became such a popular sire that more than 60 percent of the horses listed in the Association's first three registry volumes trace back to him—making him largely responsible for retaining a strong line of gaited blood among American Saddlebred Horses.

BREED CHARACTERISTICS

The American Saddlebred Horse stands between 15 and 17 hands, and has a long, arched neck set into a deeply sloping shoulder and well-defined withers. He has a high-set head with a finely chiseled appearance, and close, gracefully shaped ears. His topline is short and straight, with rounded, well-sprung ribs, a level croup, and smooth, strong muscles.

While most American Saddlebred Horses do not exhibit a natural smooth gait at birth, many retain the innate ability to be trained for it. The smooth gaits performed in the show ring include a fast, animated rack, and a slow, animated, and highly collected stepping pace called the *slow gait.* American Saddlebred Horses are expected to perform a slow, collected, "rocking-chair" canter with an easy-to-ride, gliding, and up-and-down motion.

USES

Besides being a popular show horse, the American Saddlebred Horse is also used for driving, jumping, endurance, and pleasure trail riding. With the exception of racing, this versatile and athletic horse generally excels at any sport for which he is trained.

COMMON SHOW RING TACTICS

The "peacocks" of the horse world, American Saddlebred Horses have long been expected to exhibit extremely animated show-ring gaits and to have a long "waterfall" tail carried in an upright position. To enhance this image, trainers began to resort to "show stacks" and "tail sets." Show stacks are shoes with high pads and wedges that may also carry toe weights, with chains commonly placed around the front pasterns (see photo on p. 234). These devices cause a higher lifting action of the forelegs. A tail set, or brace, is used on a horse that has had tendons on the underside of his tail cut so he cannot lower it. The trainer then braces the tail upright to stretch the muscles and obtain the high tail carriage required in five-gaited classes. In addition to this, some trainers "ginger" horses before a class—that is, they insert hot ginger in the horse's anus. Pain from this is severe enough to cause the horse to reflexively raise his tail as high as possible.

It says much about the American Saddlebred Horse's accommodating nature that most of them tolerate these practices at the hands of their "care-

2.2 A & B Courageous Lord, the 2009 World Grand Champion Five-Gaited American Saddlebred Horse, shows off his blazingly fast rack during his victory round (A). Note the four-beat gait—each foot lands independently of the others. Here you also see him performing the American Saddlebred's animated two-beat diagonal trot (B).

takers." There are now some pleasure classes that do not require high-set tails or show stacks, though unfortunately, this is still not the case for five-gaited show classes.

Tennessee Walking Horse

HISTORY

In the year 2000, the Tennessee Walking Horse was designated the state of Tennessee's official horse, as the breed originated in that state and has enjoyed a long, rich history there.

Riding and racing trotters or pacers was a popular sport in Canada and the United States during the 1800s. Originally, men raced trotting horses because it was nearly impossible to ride a fast pacing horse. As roadways improved, men started hooking their racehorses to wagons, sleds, and carts; ultimately, the lightweight racing cart became the norm. Once racehorses no longer had to be ridden, pacing horses became widely accepted because of their faster speeds, or "standards." In the mid-nineteenth century, the standard length of time most racehorses could "run" a mile was established at 2 minutes and 30 seconds. Horses that met or exceeded this standard—whether trotters or pacers—were eligible for registry in the U.S. Trotting Association and were called "Standardbreds."

Black Allan

Middle Tennessee had several popular racecourses where both trotting and pacing races were run. Standardbreds, Thoroughbreds, Morgans, and Canadian Pacers (developed from Narragansett Pacer lines—see p. 22) were all imported into the area to compete. Out of this rich pool of trotting and pacing race blood emerged Black Allan, an important progenitor of the Tennessee Walking Horse.

Though Black Allan was an extremely handsome and well-built pacing horse, he was not a popular sire during most of his lifetime because he was smaller and not as fast as other sires in the region. Consequently, he passed through many hands before being purchased by James R. Brantley of Coffee

Creek, Tennessee. Mr. Brantley acquired Black Allan (who came to be called simply "Allan") as a byproduct of a donkey-buying deal with J.A. McCulloch. Brantley purchased a black Jack donkey from McCulloch for $400, and McCulloch offered Allan for an additional $110. McCulloch called Allan "The Old Teaser" because he used the stallion to tease mares in preparation for breeding them to his Jack—a more humbling circumstance could hardly be imagined for a stallion.

Brantley was an astute student of horse genealogy, and before agreeing to the offer he went to great lengths to trace Allan's pedigree. He discovered that Allan was an equine "blueblood," tracing to outstanding breeding horses of every discipline and type—some were renowned for beauty, some for speed, and still others for extremely smooth saddle gaits. He sealed the deal with McCulloch and brought Black Allan home to Tennessee, where for the first time Allan was put to use as the fine breeding stallion he was. Brantley bred him to his best mares, including his favorite, Gertrude.

The 1904 product of this union was Roan Allen (no one is sure why the spelling of the name changed), who proved to be a popular and prepotent sire and show horse that naturally performed the entire spectrum of saddle gaits. He also inherited his sire's gentle temperament, intelligence, and versatility, successfully competing in children's classes, harness classes, and under saddle.

Walking Horses Gain National Popularity

Unlike those people involved in developing the American Saddlebred Horse, who line-bred for horses that could be *trained* to perform smooth saddle gaits, Tennessee breeders bred to a wide variety of horses, and were highly focused on producing horses that *naturally* performed smooth saddle gaits—especially a gait that was called the "running walk" (see p. 11). These horses came to be called *Walking Horses,* and because all the top breeders were located in middle Tennessee, this was eventually expanded to *Tennessee Walking Horses.*

The first official registry for the Tennessee Walking Horse was founded in 1935, eventually settling on the title Tennessee Walking Horse Breeders' and Exhibitors' Association (TWHBEA), and in 1939, the first National

> Tennessee breeders bred to a wide variety of horses, and were highly focused on producing horses that naturally performed smooth saddle gaits.

Show and Celebration was held in Shelbyville, Tennessee. Shortly thereafter, Tennessee Walking Horses became extremely popular all over the United States. The famed Midnight Sun was foaled in 1940, and awarded World Grand Champion (WGC) at the 1945 and 1946 Celebrations. Merry Go Boy was born in 1943, and was WGC in 1947 and 1948.

During this time artificial insemination (AI) was still permitted in the Tennessee Walking Horse industry, and the contributions of these two stallions were in demand by hundreds of mare owners. Breed association officials, concerned at the prospect of too much inbreeding, prohibited AI in 1952 (it is once again permitted). Nevertheless, Midnight Sun and Merry Go Boy appear on the pedigrees of a large percentage of Tennessee Walking Horses.

The Beginning of Change

The Tennessee Walking Horse was developed by breeders with a depth of understanding and knowledge, and a commitment to the horse second to none. Unfortunately, this high level of horsemanship did not persist on a wide scale as these unique horses increased in popularity, and a cloud of controversy and scandalous practices cast a long, dark shadow over the breed's history.

Unlike the American Saddlebred Horse, bred for a highly animated, lifting stride, Tennessee Walking Horses originally demonstrated an efficient, ground-covering, low-slung gait. During the late 1940s and the 1950s, it was common for American Saddlebred Horses and Tennessee Walking Horses to compete at the same shows. Attendees wildly applauded the fast, animated rack of the American Saddlebred, preferring it to the less animated running-walk gait, and judges responded to their appreciation by pinning the horses with the most action. So, trainers of the Tennessee Walking Horse began to breed and train show horses for those qualities. Because champion show horses were the most popular breeding stock, overall breed standards began to change to favor the new style and "way of going."

BREED STANDARDS

The Tennessee Walking Horse typically stands between 15 and 16 hands. His head has a straight, noble profile with a large, prominent, and expressive eye, and ears in good proportion to the size of his head. He has a well-shaped, medium-length neck set into a shoulder with an upright to medium angle and well-defined withers. His back is either short or medium in length with strong, smooth coupling to hindquarters with a long, well-angled hip. His croup should be even with, or slightly below, the height of his withers. He boasts sufficient yet refined bone with long hind legs and large, strong hocks.

2.3 Tennessee Walking Horse stallion Champagne Watchout is owned, trained, and ridden by Jennifer Jackson of Walkin' On Ranch. Watchout is a fine example of a Tennessee Walking Horse that can do it all—including competing at gaited dressage.

From the 1940s to the late 1990s, black and bay were the most common colors because "Big Lick" show breeders bred for these colors—dark legs make it more difficult to see signs of "soring" (see more on this in Common Show Ring Tactics, below). Since the early 1990s, there has been an increased number of Tennessee Walking Horses with spotted coat patterns, including tobiano, overo, and sabino (leading to the origins of the Spotted Saddle Horse—see p. 58), as well as chestnut, sorrel, palomino, buckskin, and roan. Heritage breeders, especially, value horses with roan and sabino coats, as these colors were widespread among early foundation horses.

The Tennessee Walking Horse's signature saddle gaits include the flat walk and the running walk (see pp. 10 and 11). Some Tennessee Walking Horses execute an exceptionally smooth "rocking-chair" canter, while others perform only the walk, flat walk, and running walk.

Tennessee Walking Horse trainers who wanted to win show classes with minimally talented horses took the abuses practiced by American Saddle-bred show trainers to a new level.

USES

This gentle, sensitive, athletic and versatile horse is an appropriate choice for virtually any equestrian activity. Besides being excellent flat-shod and bare-foot show horses, they are a favorite choice of people who enjoy "Field Trials"—the sport of horseback riders competing hunting dogs against one another. Their smooth, ground-covering gaits enable them to excel at both competitive and pleasure trail riding, and the sport of gaited dressage is gaining a strong foothold within the breed. The Tennessee Walking Horse may be enjoyed as a flashy yet docile parade horse, a reining horse, a driving horse, or be used for game competitions.

COMMON SHOW RING TACTICS

Beginning in the early 1950s and continuing nearly to the present time, Tennessee Walking Horse trainers who wanted to win show classes with minimally talented horses, or who didn't want to take the time necessary to develop talented horses to a high level, took the abuses practiced by American Saddlebred show horse trainers (see p. 25) to a new level. They started by adding high pads between the front foot and the shoe, causing the horse to appear to be built "uphill" with his croup lower than his withers, and to have a higher lifting stride in front. One excess led to another until it became common to install very heavy shoes and weights on the forefeet, changing the timing of the gait and adding exaggerated lift and animation.

"Soring" to Produce Gait

Most disturbing of all, trainers eventually devised various ways to "sore" a horse so he executes his gaits in such an exaggerated manner that no horse being shown naturally could possibly compete with it. When a Tennessee Walking Horse transitions to a nice running walk, it is common to hear people comment that he is "hitting his lick." So, show-ring horses with the exaggerated gaits became known as "Big Lick" Walking Horses.

Big Lick show horses are bred to pace rather than perform the running walk—the gait is then altered using various methods (see below). As I mentioned earlier, beginning in the early 1950s, the entire breed's type and gait were dramatically changed because of the increased percentage of pacing blood used to produce top show-ring horses—those most in demand for breeding.

To sore a horse, a trainer (from here on I will refer to these people as "handlers") places kerosene, hot mustard oil, diesel fuel, or another caustic agent on the horse's pasterns and covers this with clear plastic wrap and an outside wrap to allow the substance to "cook," or burn deeply into the horse's flesh. Chains are then placed on the front pasterns so whenever the horse picks up a front foot the chain hits the sored area, causing him to snap the foot up as high as possible to avoid the contact.

Some Big Lick handlers "pressure shoe" the horse, placing golf balls, tacks, and other pain-causing objects between the show stacks and the sensitive bottom of the horse's foot. Every time the horse's weight transfers to a front foot he experiences searing pain, so he quickly snaps his forefeet off the ground to shift as much weight as possible to his hindquarters in a futile attempt to alleviate that pain—his hind stride then lengthens, creating exaggerated overstride (see p. 11), as he attempts to keep weight off his tortured forefeet for as long as possible.

A Big Lick horse may have both forefeet cut to the quick, so that contact with the ground is painful; some handlers go so far as to deliberately

2.4 Tennessee Walking Horse Papa's Royal Delight demonstrates a smooth, ground-covering flat walk that consistently "takes home the blues." Anita Howe of Howe They Walk Farm is up.

founder the horse in their efforts to create the unnatural and pain-ridden "Big Lick" show gait.

Backlash against Big Lick Begins

Somewhat ironically, the very observers whose preferences originally created the demand for Big Lick horses eventually began to decry these inhumane practices, and during the late 1950s and 1960s a storm of controversy rose over the subject. Unfortunately, the Big Lick culture was by then so ingrained, and the handlers who sored horses so adamant at denying it, that all attempts to eliminate the practice were ineffective. In response to increased public outrage, in 1970, the United States Congress passed the Horse Protection Act that established humane training standards and made Tennessee Walking Horse handlers submit horses to pre-show and post-show inspections by a "Designated Qualified Person," or DQP—self-policing agents provided by Walking Horse organizations, as well as by agents of the United States Department of Agriculture (USDA).

The nefarious practice of soring horses continued in spite of these concerted efforts to have it stopped. Judges and DQPs were often Big Lick handlers themselves, so having a horse evaluated by one was akin to asking a fox to guard the henhouse, and the USDA simply didn't have enough personnel to effectively police thousands of horse show classes every year. Even when a conscientious inspector checks a horse, soring can be difficult to spot and to prove. Handlers routinely "steward" sored horses by palpating the horse's sored pasterns and severely punishing the horse for flinching or otherwise exhibiting symptoms of pain. Some trainers create pain in another part of the horse's body so it won't respond to palpation on the sored limb. A pressure-shod horse may have hard acrylic packed between his stacks and hoof to prevent him from responding to a hoof tester. Various topical and internal anesthetic agents may be administered to the sored horse before a show class to mask the pain during an inspection, with the effect wearing off in time for his "performance."

Alternative Choices

Though in 2005 the Tennessee Walking Horse Breeders' and Exhibitors' Association instituted strict new guidelines regarding sored horses, many people became disillusioned with the seeming lack of commitment to ending the problem and banded together to find solutions and offer alternative venues for people who want to ride and show natural, sound Tennessee Walking Horses. These include (see p. 239 for contact information):

• Tennessee Walking Horse Heritage Society

The Tennessee Walking Horse Heritage Society's membership is made up of stalwart, dedicated owners of Walking Horse farms that never gave in to the trend of producing Big Lick style show horses during the decades when a naturally docile, correctly gaited utility horse was thrown by the wayside in favor of padded-up, pacing show stock. This organization's goal is to breed, use, and promote the type of Walking Horse that was originally bred by the early horsemen of Middle Tennessee. The goal of the Heritage Society is to restore the original, natural, smooth saddle gaits to the breed, and preserve important bloodlines that have become rare by making the wide variety of foundation Walking Horse blood retained by their families available to other breeders. Members also selectively breed old bloodlines to contemporary lines that still exemplify the breed's original qualities.

• The National Walking Horse Association

The National Walking Horse Association (NWHA) was founded in 1998. NWHA goals include:

- To preserve and foster the natural abilities of the Walking Horse.
- To promote a wider understanding of Walking Horses.
- To stand against abusive and inhumane treatment.

Members of the organization accomplish these goals by promoting educational and recreational programs, and providing horse show affiliations that use knowledgeable, conscientious DQP's and judges who are committed to maintaining compliance with the Horse Protection Act. Members of NWHA may register their Walking Horses with this non-profit organization's "tracking registry."

• Friends of Sound Horses (FOSH)

An organization founded for the sole purpose of eliminating the practice of soring horses is Friends of Sound Horses (FOSH). FOSH is proactive on behalf of all gaited horses, with a primary focus on the Tennessee Walking Horse. FOSH provides a variety of information and resources for gaited-horse owners, including sound shows, inspection services, clinicians, and books.

Horse-show managers have the opportunity to follow FOSH principles at their show, and/or hire judges and inspectors trained by FOSH. FOSH administers a national judging program known as the Independent Judges Association (IJA) that trains judges how to evaluate the natural Tennessee Walking Horse and many other gaited breeds. The IJA rule book sets the standards by which IJA officials mark cards, and these judges are available for shows. FOSH is also licensed by the USDA to provide well-trained DQPs for show-class inspections.

FOSH not only denounces Big Lick practices but also disapproves of "Plantation" show classes, where horses are shown with very long feet and large, heavy shoes. This organization only promotes the use of naturally trained, flat-shod and barefoot Walking Horses.

One of FOSH's primary tools for ending soring is education, and to this end they sponsor the Sound Horse Conference. This conference, hosted every 18 months, includes presentations by veterinarians, trainers, government enforcement leaders, attorneys, professors, humane association professionals, and individual volunteers and horse people on topics from current soring observations, cultural objections to the practices, technologies and methods for enforcement, and initiatives in progress to end soring.

FOSH affiliates with various clinicians and trainers who promote sound training principles, and teaches judges and DQPs how to determine if a horse's gait has been achieved by natural or artificial means. The organization has published the names of all persons ever suspended from showing horses because of violations of the Horse Protection Act (HPA) so that a person who wants to hire a "sound" trainer can check to see if someone they use, or are planning to use, has ever been a violator. This is quite a bold

> FOSH not only denounces Big Lick practices but also disapproves of "Plantation" show classes, where horses are shown with very long feet and large, heavy shoes.

move, as rumors of barn burnings and intimidation tactics— even death threats—have been directed toward those who dared defy the network of people involved with the sore horse industry.

Perhaps equally important is the influence FOSH has had on bringing people with this worthwhile common cause together to pool information and resources. Whereas previous efforts had been loosely organized and fragmented, once a dedicated and efficiently run organization using effective tools and speaking on the topic with authority came into existence, people—including officials of the USDA—were bound, sooner or later, to begin to listen and act upon their recommendations.

FOSH's concerted and well-organized efforts toward ensuring strict adherence to HPA regulations have been combined with a focused campaign to make sure the public is aware of the facts about soring abuses, and how they can help end this disgrace. FOSH publishes articles and press releases, and maintains a Web site, which includes all press—including articles and television features—addressing this issue.

AN ONGOING PROBLEM

One of the events that has had the biggest impact on public awareness happened on August 25, 2006, when a large number of USDA inspectors showed up at the annual Tennessee Walking Horse National Celebration in Shelbyville, Tennessee (the largest capstone show of the year for this gaited breed). Six of the ten contenders for the final World Grand Championship class failed to pass inspections and were disqualified from showing, causing the class to be cancelled for the first time in the Celebration's 68-year history and creating an unprecedented storm of controversy.

Following the 2006 Celebration, there was great hope among Tennessee Walking Horse fans that the era of sored horses was finally winding down to a close, but this has not been the case. In 2007, there were 103 citations for sored horses at the annual Celebration. That number increased to 180 in 2008, and in 2009, the number of violations leaped back up to over 400, proving there is still a need for greater effort and diligence on the part of everyone who cares about the welfare and future of these wonderful horses.

2.5 The Missouri Fox Trotting Horse Southern Sunrise's Romeo shows off the fox trot that won this 2009 Southern Classic Championship class.

MISSOURI FOX TROTTING HORSE

HISTORY

Missouri gained statehood in 1821, and from the time it was first settled it was known for its fine horses. Many of the nation's top breeders populated Northern Missouri as well as the nearby states of Virginia, Kentucky, and Tennessee.

The Missouri Fox Trotting Horse is Missouri's officially designated state horse, and was developed by men who managed large herds of cattle in the rugged foothills and hollows of Missouri's Ozark Mountains. These men routinely rounded up and herded these cattle over treacherous, heavily forested terrain. They spent many long days in the saddle and their horses had to be sensible, surefooted, and possess stamina as well as "cow sense."

Besides working cattle, horses that served families living in the Ozark Mountains needed to be strong enough to plow their farms, haul their wood, and pull their buggies to church on Sunday. Since there were no "super highways" through the Ozarks, fox trotting horses also carried the local doctor, midwife, and sheriff quickly and safely to where assistance was needed.

There was a preponderance of the blood used to develop the early American Saddlebred Horse in Missouri and surrounding regions in the early nineteenth century that went into the foundation blood of the fox-trotting horse. At the time, these were simply called *Saddle Horses,* and they were crossed with Morgan Horses, Canadian Pacers, and Thoroughbreds. Cattlemen regularly converged on the stockyards, giving them the opportunity to hold impromptu races and haggle over sales, trades, and breedings.

Missouri horsemen developed a fine eye for good horse flesh, and though many of them never traveled far from home to breed their mares to the most famous sires of the era, they were experts at perceiving whether two local horses would make a "good nick," or cross. By the middle of the nineteenth century, the easy-to-sit, surefooted fox trot gait had become especially popular for navigating the "hills and hollers" of the Ozarks, and Missouri breeders bred specifically for that gait.

Contemporary Missouri Fox Trotting Horse Established

In the 1930s, fox-trotting horse breeders began to cross their horses with Walking Horses from nearby Tennessee in an effort to extend and improve their horse's flat walk. This cross became so popular that a high percentage of today's registered Missouri Fox Trotting Horses carry the blood of foundation Tennessee Walking Horses. There are actually a few rare lines of horses that are "double registered," or officially registered with both the Missouri Fox Trotting Horse Association and the Tennessee Walking Horse Breeders' and Exhibitors' Association.

Popular American Saddlebred sires of this era also made significant contributions to the breed. One of these, Rex McDonald, competed in thousands of horse shows over a ten-year period, and was declared officially "unbeatable" in the show ring. Rex McDonald was also the last horse to be crowned Grand Champion at the last St. Louis Horse Fair ever held, in

1903. This outstanding horse was great-great-grandsire to the fox trotter mare Betty Fox, who produced three World Champion Missouri Fox Trotting Horses: Lucky Strike (1962), Red Warrior (1964), and Golden Rawhide (1966).

Breed Association Founded

The Missouri Fox Trotting Horse Breed Association (MFTHBA) was founded in 1948 in Ava, Missouri, for the purpose of preserving this unique breed. By 1955, a number of horses had been registered—a precise figure was never determined—but a fire engulfed the secretary's home in 1955, destroying the Association's records and stud books. The Association was reformed in 1958, and the founders oversaw the breed's first National Show and Celebration the following year on September 26, 1959, in Ava (where the Association is still headquartered).

Stud books of the MFTHBA were open until 1982 and horses of various breeding were examined and certified eligible for registration as a Missouri Fox Trotting Horse. In 1982, it was required that at least one parent of a registered horse be registered with the Association. The following year the stud books closed completely, and both parents of a registered horse had to be previously registered.

This policy of keeping the stud books open for an extended length of time allowed fox-trotting horses to be out-crossed to horses of other breeds, guaranteeing a diverse genetic pool that produces horses with an array of talents.

BREED CHARACTERISTICS

The Missouri Fox Trotting Horse stands between 14 and 16 hands, is strong-boned and well-muscled. He has an attractive, fine head with a tapered muzzle, large, expressive eyes, and "foxy," or alert ears. The neck is high-set into deeply sloping shoulders and well-defined withers. He has a short back that is tightly coupled to substantial, well-muscled hindquarters. He has good bone with flat knees and large, well-formed hocks. The overall appearance is one of solid strength and good balance. He comes in a wide array of colors including black, bay, chestnut, sorrel, buckskin, and pinto—gray and palomino are especially prevalent colors within the breed.

The Missouri Fox Trotting Horse's signature gaits are the fox walk, flat walk, and fox trot.

USES

The Missouri Fox Trotting Horse's calm, unflappable nature, good sense, and surefootedness make him a popular choice for mounted police and forest rangers. This stylish horse excels in the show ring, where absolutely no action devices, tail sets, or special shoeing is permitted. More than 90 percent of fox trotters are used for trail riding, and over the past decade they have become increasingly favored by competitive and endurance trail riders.

ICELANDIC HORSE

HISTORY

Icelanders take great pride in their horses, who boast the purest equine blood in the world because they have been bred in Iceland without outside influence for over 1,000 years. Though small in stature the Icelandic Horse is hardy, independent, and fearless.

Vikings from Norway originally landed in Iceland in the year 874, when sailors fled the tyrannical rule of King Harald Fair Hair in ships that carried household goods and livestock—including their best horses—in their holds. Nordic people had a long history of both horsemanship and seamanship, calling their massive ships "horses of the sea." It is believed their horses originated from Asia, whose roots lay in the ancient Mongolian Horse.

In 98 A.D. Roman Historian Tacitus wrote in his book *Germanus* that German people possessed horses that were the aim of young men and much indulged by old men. The horse was considered sacred, and a culture of mysticism existed around him. Some Icelandic settlers released a horse upon landing on shore, settling wherever the horse stopped to graze. This culture of "mystical horsemanship" continued in Iceland for many centuries, and remnants of it are still evident.

Later settlers to the island originated from the Western Isles of Scotland, Ireland, and the Isle of Man—all regions known for fine horsemanship. The

deeply rooted equestrian traditions shared by all of Iceland's early settlers produced a people dedicated to producing and preserving top quality horses.

A Breed Shaped by Its Environment

Iceland is a basalt (volcanic) rock island located in the North Atlantic Sea. Its inland topography is varied and rugged, with volcanoes; quicksand bogs; hot water springs and geysers; treacherous rivers with changing currents; boiling mud craters; large desert areas; massive glaciers; and craggy, ice-capped mountains. What Iceland does not have is deep, rich soil, and (with

2.6 Like their early predecessors, today's hardy Icelandic Horses come in an array of colors, and are still sometimes raised in large herds on inhospitable terrain.

rare exceptions) trees. This environment limits road development and makes much of the island uninhabitable. From the time it was originally settled, only horses could provide inland transportation—and the animals that did so had to be extraordinarily sensible, strong, and surefooted.

Developed in Isolation

Iceland's first government assembly (Althing) was held in the year 930 (making it the oldest democracy in the world). Having no exposure to the outside world made the horse the Icelandic people were so dependent upon extremely vulnerable to outside disease. To avoid a devastating loss of horses to foreign diseases, at that first Althing, the further importation of horses was declared illegal. This ban continues to the present, so that the genetic qualities of the Icelandic Horse are solely attributable to horses that were already in existence between the eighth and tenth centuries—a period of time when strong, compact, laterally gaited horses were the norm. While that type of horse was out-crossed to other types in the rest of the world, which resulted in change, Iceland's horses carried this unique heritage into the present age.

Early Horse Management

Iceland is also known for its genetically pure breed of Icelandic sheep, which outnumber the country's human population two to one. Every year in mid-September Icelandic horses are used to round up sheep for the trip to market. The roundup lasts about a week. Until early in this century several selective bands of 15 to 25 broodmares and one carefully chosen stud were turned out after the annual roundup to fend for themselves on large tracts of land located slightly inland from the coast. Forced to forage for food in an inhospitable environment during brutally cold winters, the horses became hardy, strong, and independent—only smart, naturally "easy-keeping" horses survived. Mares settled easily and had few problems with unassisted foaling because the process of natural elimination ensured that animals with inherent breeding or other physical weakness would not survive to pass them on to future generations.

Horses have also traditionally been a primary source of red meat for the

Forced to forage for food in an inhospitable environment during brutally cold winters, the horses became hardy, strong, and independent.

Icelandic population. To the present day Icelandic horses are raised as meat for exportation and domestic use. Riding horses judged as inferior are simply slaughtered for food.

Contemporary Breed Management

During the 1900s, Iceland's government began to manage the country's horse-breeding program, and the animals began to be bred and raised on farms rather than in the wild. The Agricultural Society of Iceland developed strict guidelines for judging horse stock and maintains detailed records on every horse produced.

The first Icelandic breed organization was formed in 1904, and the first registry established in 1923. In the mid-twentieth century they were exported to Germany and Great Britain, and since then have enjoyed increased popularity around the world. The International Federation of Icelandic Horse Associations (FEIF) was founded in 1969 and serves as the breed's international governing organization. FEIF has established stringent judging guidelines for conformation, temperament, and smooth saddle gaits.

BREED CHARACTERISTICS

Though the Icelandic Horse is small, standing on average between 13 and 14 hands, he has exceptionally good bone and a strong, compact body. These characteristics combined with his cheerful "can do" attitude make it possible for him to carry a disproportionate amount of weight for his size, handling adult riders with ease. The Icelandic Horse (there is no word for "pony" in Iceland) has a medium length muscular neck set high into a moderate to deeply sloped shoulder, and low but well-defined withers. His head profile is straight, with a wide flat forehead and small alert ears. His back is long as is his croup, which is also steeply angled and tightly coupled. Because of his naturally high headset, even when ridden in good form, his nose will be slightly above the vertical.

Icelandics are hardy, easy-keeping horses that are late maturing and long-lived. They are not started under saddle until their fourth or fifth year, but are commonly ridden into their late twenties, and mares are safely bred into their mid-twenties. They grow a double coat and long "beards" in the

2.7 Melodja, an Icelandic mare, shows off her smooth tolt—the gait for which the breed is known. Amanda Pretty is riding.

winter months, and—with the exception of Appaloosa patterns—are available in every imaginable color. The Icelandic Horse is a highly sociable animal that bonds well with people and other animals. Because of his social nature it is advisable that he be housed with at least one other herdmate—preferably another Icelandic Horse.

The Icelandic Horse is either four- or five-gaited. All can perform the walk, tolt (running walk or rack), trot, and canter, and some can execute the flying pace (speed pace), as well (see below). When being judged, 60 percent of a horse's score is based on his saddle gaits and 40 percent on his conformation, so Icelandic Horses are not judged until they are trained to ride.

USES

The Icelandic Horse has no natural predators in its native country, but had to adapt to dangerous terrain where he confronted rock slides, mud bogs, dangerous river crossings, and unexpectedly tempestuous weather. Therefore, rather than spooking and fleeing perceived danger, the horse learned to carefully evaluate a situation to determine the safest course of action. These conditions, combined with a long history of selective breeding, created a bold, intelligent, surefooted horse that enjoys a uniquely close partnership with his rider.

Icelandic Horses are often raced either over flat ground or in steeple-chases. They are shown in a variety of disciplines, including speed-gaiting (flying pace) classes and those that determine which horse has the smoothest, most correct tolt; driving classes; and exhilarating synchronized gaited riding drills performed at blazingly fast speeds. An Icelandic Horse has an uncannily accurate sense of direction, and is a great trail-riding mount, safely and smoothly navigating even the most challenging terrain. Horsemanship and judging clinics are a popular pastime, where entertainment is as important as education. These smooth-gaited, fast, sturdy little horses are notorious for being a lot of fun!

PERUVIAN HORSE

HISTORY

The Peruvian Horse is another breed that was developed exclusively in one country and whose blood remained untainted from outside sources for centuries. Beginning in 1531 when Francisco Pizarro landed in Peru, Spanish Conquistadors brought both "Chargers" (trotters) and "Hackers" (smooth-gaited horses) to the New World, all with pure Spanish heritage. After the wars ended, farmers began to breed horses specifically for smooth saddle gaits.

By the middle of the seventeenth century, importation of horses into the country ceased, and intensive line-breeding produced a smooth-gaited, athletic, docile yet energetic animal—though each of three regions of the country produced horses with characteristics slightly different from one another, depending on their primary use.

Northern Peru

Northern Peru boasted the vast sugar plantations called *haciendas* that covered hundreds of square miles of land. Plantation horses were ridden for many miles a day, and possessed great endurance and smooth saddle gaits, as well as strength. These Northern Peruvian horses were known for exhibiting *termino* (see p. 15), and were docile and somewhat coarse in appearance.

Southern Peru

Southern Peru had less agricultural production than Northern Peru because of the Andes Mountain range and the surrounding arid desert climate. Farming was limited to small pockets of fertile oasis that formed where rivers flow down from the mountains to join the Pacific Ocean. These farmers needed horses that were surefooted over all kinds of terrain.

Southern breeders focused on producing horses with great *brio*, or "fire-under-control" type of spirit. Their horses had long, flowing manes and tails, exhibited less termino, and their gaits were less consistently "locked-in" than Northern horses. These horses tended to be rather plain-headed.

Central Peru

The city of Lima is located in Central Peru, a region of the country that was more densely populated than Northern and Southern Peru. There was less emphasis placed on agricultural pursuits, and more on commercial ones. Horses originating in Central Peru had long, graceful necks and beautiful, well-shaped heads. They were very well conformed and had consistently good saddle gaits, but demonstrated less brio than Southern horses, and less termino than Northern ones.

Establishing a Single Type

Though all Peruvian breeders valued common qualities—beauty, animation, brio, termino, and smooth saddle gaits—for decades they were too proud to cross horses from their region with horses from another in order to improve and strengthen these desirable qualities.

Starting in 1942, all this changed when a Lima businessman and professional animal husbandman named Carlos Luna de la DeFuente opened La Agricola, Lima's first animal supply store. Luna de la DeFuente was extraordinarily well-informed and passionate about Peruvian Horses, and encouraged breeders from all over the country to congregate in a back room of the store to exchange information and arrange for sale, trade, and breeding deals among them.

First National Breed Show and Organization

Though provincial horse shows were popular throughout Peru, the first national horse show wasn't organized until 1945. The first two National Peruvian Paso Horse Shows were held in Lima, Peru, and were sanctioned by the Club Hipico, a well-respected national horse club. Because members of Club Hipico were more familiar with trotting horses than with gaited stock, in 1947, at one of the meetings held at La Agricola the country's preeminent breeders of gaited Peruvian Horses collaborated to form the Asociación Nacional de Criadores Propietarios de Caballo Peruanos de Pasa (ANCPCPP)—the National Association of Owners of Peruvian Paso Horses.

> For decades Peruvian breeders were too proud to cross horses from their region with horses from another in order to improve and strengthen desirable qualities.

Brought Back from the Edge

In the 1930s the Pan American highway was built across Peru, and riding horses were replaced by automobiles. At the same time farmers began to rely more on modern machinery than on horses. All this caused smooth-gaited riding horses to lose value. Beginning in the late 1940s political upheavals plagued the country, seriously endangering the remaining Peruvian breeding operations. Horses were in such low demand, especially in Southern Peru, that breeders sold them cheaply to peasant farmers who populated the canyons, or *quebradas,* of Southern Peru. Many of the country's finest bloodstock virtually disappeared into those canyons.

The Story of Sol de Oro ("Viejo")

In the late 1940s and early 1950s horse shows became popular and horses from Northern and Central Peru invariably claimed top honors, though Southern breeders had previously taken great pride in producing the nation's best Peruvian Horses. One Southern breeder by the name of Gustavo de la Borda especially mourned the lack of fine Southern bloodlines, and began to scour the *quebradas* in an effort to locate their descendants. His efforts eventually paid off richly in the form of a small, nondescript, crippled stallion by the name of Sol de Oro (also called "Viejo," which translates to "The Elderly One").

The stallion had a crippled foreleg that had been broken in a roping incident when he was three years old. Following that his owner gave the horse very little care—and it showed. But Gustavo de la Borda's practiced eye saw the potential for greatness, and appreciated the little scrub stallion's brio, so he paid the farmer who owned Sol de Oro $200—a great deal of money for a seemingly worthless, lame stallion of undetermined age and lineage.

His faith was not misplaced, as Sol de Oro was destined to become the most influential Peruvian Horse sire of all time, with his get winning every National Champion of Champions show class in Peru since 1961, and a majority of the United States Champion of Champions classes since 1973. Gustavo de la Borda was exceptionally generous, allowing anyone who wanted to breed a mare to Sol de Oro to do so. Though the little horse was at first under-appreciated by other breeders, when his offspring started dominating

2.8 The Peruvian Horse's strength, presence and beauty are a result of exacting breeding standards that go back more than 200 years.

the show ring, demand for his services skyrocketed, resulting in a significant improvement of the entire Peruvian Horse population.

Exportation to North America

Because Peruvian Horses were considered a national treasure, breeders were reluctant to export them to other countries, so during the time when the population of Peruvian Horses decreased in its native land, the breed as a whole was in danger of becoming rare and little known. In the 1960s, Verne Albright, a devoted Peruvian Horse aficionado from Canada, began to promote the Peruvian Horse to people in North America. He rode across North and South America on Peruvian Horses and ultimately wrote dozens of articles and several books on the subject. Largely in response to his efforts, demand for these horses from people in the United States and Canada increased dramatically. Peruvian breeders wisely rethought their position on exporting good breeding stock, and sent large numbers of horses from Peru to North American breeders, who greatly increased their numbers.

BREED CHARACTERISTICS

The Peruvian Horse stands between 14.1 and 15.2 hands high. He has a heavy, medium-length, elegantly shaped neck set high into a deeply sloped shoulder, and moderately sized, well-muscled withers. He has a long, flowing mane and tail, with the tail set low and carried quietly tucked between his legs. His head is refined with large, expressive eyes, a broad forehead that is flat or slightly concave, and medium-sized ears with a fine inward curve at the tips. His torso should be as deep as his legs are long, with a very round, short-to-medium length back with broad, tight coupling to a well-muscled croup that sits level with, or lower than, his withers.

The Peruvian Horse has refined yet substantial bone, with clean, well-defined joints, short cannons, and discernible angulation of the hocks. When evaluating a Peruvian Horse it is especially important to avoid one with wind puffs or exceptionally long, over-angulated pasterns, as this may be an early indication of degenerative suspensory ligament desmitis (DSLD), a condition prevalent in some lines of the breed.

This horse may have many different colors, including bay, chestnut, black, brown, roan, dun, palomino, or gray; though solid-colored horses are preferred, white markings on the face and legs are acceptable.

The Peruvian Horse is noted for exhibiting *termino,* the smooth outward rolling motion of the forelegs that helps him navigate easily through sand and assists in balance, which may be why he demonstrates less head nod than other gaited horses. A Spanish characteristic of the breed is *brio,* a term that describes an animal that has great energy, vitality, presence, and willingness, combined with a docile, easy-to-train, unflappable temperament.

The Peruvian Horse is said to be the smoothest riding horse in the world; thanks to centuries of selective breeding, this may be true. He performs the *paso llanno* (a laterally oriented running walk—see p. 11), which can be sustained over very long distances, and the *sobreando,* a faster stepping pace (see p. 9). These gaits are performed with a proud, high headset and several inches of overstride.

A horse with excellent "thread" makes smooth transitions from the walk all the way up to his fastest gait, and one with *pisos* performs his gaits with good timing, animation, elegance, and good forward motion. *Gateado* is a term that describes an agile, cat-like motion—a horse that possesses this quality transfers no action at all to his rider's seat.

USES

The Peruvian Horse's primary use is that of a smooth-gaited riding horse suited to showing, exhibition, parades, and trail riding. He is becoming a popular choice for endurance and field-trial riders, but is seldom if ever driven, jumped, or used for hunting or dressage. Peruvian breeders coined the term "Peruvian horsepower" to describe a horse that can carry 220 pounds over 30 miles in only five hours; one that can do twice that distance in ten hours is called a "round-trip horse."

In the show ring judges look for correct gaits, beautiful conformation, brio, and great endurance. Show classes may last an hour or more, and the horses are required to warm up for several hours prior to a class.

PASO FINO

HISTORY

The Barb, Andalusian, and Spanish Jennet horses that the Spanish Conquistadors brought to the New World beginning in the early sixteenth century were the forebears of today's Paso Fino horse. Though the Paso Fino was bred on Caribbean islands as well, breeding was most concentrated in Colombia and Puerto Rico where the majority of today's horses originates. Breeders from these countries produced individual, yet closely related, types of smooth-gaited riding horses.

Though the early horses used to develop the Paso Fino were the same Spanish horses used in the development of the Peruvian Horse (see p. 46), these two breeds are not to be confused, as they have different and unique standards. The Peruvian Paso—later called simply the Peruvian Horse in an attempt to prevent people from confusing the two breeds—was bred for *extension of stride* and purity of gait in a geographically isolated country without outside influences for hundreds of years. *Paso Fino* means "fine step" in Spanish, and describes the smooth, *short-strided gait* that became the breed's signature show gait. Also, unlike its Peruvian distant cousin, the Paso Fino breed was influenced by a wide variety of blood imported into its original homelands, causing the breed to be more varied in type and sometimes less "locked in," or innately established, in its gaits.

Colombian and Puerto Rican horses exerted the strongest influences on the breed, and the two distinct types of horse developed in these regions still exist and are separately recognized by breeders who specialize at producing the Paso Fino.

Puerto Rican Paso Fino

Paso Fino horses originating in Puerto Rico were not out-crossed to horses from other areas as much as those developed in Colombia and other regions; therefore, those who promote this horse claim they breed truer to type and have more consistently locked-in natural gaits than do those originating from other places.

> Though the early horses used to develop the Paso Fino were the same Spanish horses used in the development of the Peruvian Horse, these two breeds are not to be confused, as they have different and unique standards.

Paso Fino horses from Puerto Rico first arrived in the United States in the 1950s and 1960s when military personnel purchased them while stationed on the island. Many of these soldiers arranged to have their horses imported to the States rather than sell them when they were transferred home. These were the first Paso Finos to be used for pleasure and breeding stock in the United States.

U.S. Paso Fino Horses

Beginning in the 1960s Paso Fino horses were imported from various regions into the United States, and there was a great deal of cross-breeding among these animals, as well as to Puerto Rican stock already here. The Colombian Paso Fino, in particular, exerted a strong influence on the type of horse that evolved in North America. In 1973 the Paso Fino Horse Owners' and Breeders' Association was founded, and the name was eventually shortened to the Paso Fino Horse Association (PFHA).

In 1974 the new breed association designated six stallions as Foundation Sires in an effort to create appropriate, high standards for the breeding of Paso Finos in North America. While other individual horses and bloodlines were also used for breeding, and the importation of breeding stock goes on to the present time, these six horses placed their significant stamp upon the breed. Three of the foundation sires originated in Colombia: Mar de Plata LaCE, El Pastor, and Hilachas. Two—Bolero LaCE, and Faeton LaCE—were imported directly from Puerto Rico, and a third, Lucerito, was a Puerto Rican stallion imported into the Dominican Republic before later being purchased by the owners of a breeding farm in the United States. (LaCE stands for LaHood's Champion Equines, and is a suffix for horses imported or owned by George LaHood, Jr., an avid U.S. breeder and promoter of the breed.)

BREED CHARACTERISTICS

The Paso Fino stands between 13 and 15.2 hands high, with the average horse standing 14 to 14.2 hands. He has a smooth, stocky, and well-muscled build, with a well-arched, medium-length neck set very high into sloping shoulders, and defined, but not prominent, withers. His head is finely chiseled with a wide, flat, or slightly convex forehead, large, expressive eyes, and petite ears that curve gracefully inward at the tips. He has a long and luxurious mane and tail. His back is short with broad, tight coupling to a rounded and slightly sloped croup. The legs are short and refined, exhibiting strong, clearly defined tendons, clean, flat knees, and strong, unblemished hocks.

Like other Spanish horse breeds, the quality of *brio* is valued, and some of them also demonstrate *termino* (see p. 51). This horse's coat color includes black, bay, brown, chestnut, palomino, buckskin, gray, and dun. Spotted horses may have sabino or tobiano coat patterns.

The Paso Fino gaits, besides the walk, trot, and canter, are the *paso fino,* the *paso corto,* and the *paso largo.* The *paso fino* cannot be performed by all Paso Fino horses but is a specialized, evenly-timed, four-beat racking gait used primarily for show and exhibition. The gait is performed with a maximum amount of collection at a speed much slower than a walk, executed with an extremely fast, short stride. When exhibiting the gait the horse is ridden over a narrow wooden platform that allows the audience to hear the staccato-like sound of his footfalls and observe the piston-like action of the legs and feet as horse and rider demonstrate perfect timing and control while progressing forward, only inches at a time.

The *paso corto* is an evenly-timed rack performed with a moderate degree of collection at speeds ranging from 4–8 mph. It is considered the Paso Fino horse's "working gait," and many can maintain it over long distances.

The *paso largo* is a speed rack, speed pace, or stepping pace (depending on how the individual horse performs it), executed at very high speeds.

In Colombia, some Paso Finos are bred to perform the *trocha,* or fox trot. This gait is acceptable—even valued—in Colombia, but highly faulted among breeders in North America.

2.9 A Paso Fino performing a paso corto in beautiful form, contradicting the untrue but common adage that a horse is unable to gait when "rounded" through the back and collected on the bridle.

Paso Fino horses are versatile and compete in a variety of show classes, including gaited riding, driving, competitive trail, reining, gymkhana, and versatility. Some have a great deal of "cow sense" and are used for team penning and on working cattle ranches. Many enjoy careers as competitive, pleasure, or trail riding mounts.

Recently Founded Breed Registries

Some of the more recently founded breeds are closely related to a longstanding breed, while other newcomers originate in different parts of the world. A few of the breed organizations exist for the purpose of preserving and promoting horses that were long recognized as a "type," with particular qualities, but with no official registry or standards.

MOUNTAIN HORSE

Mountain Horses were originally bred by inhabitants of the Appalachian Mountains of Eastern Kentucky during the early twentieth century. They remained relatively obscure until the 1980s, when several breed registries were formed to preserve and promote this type of horse.

The Mountain Horse is known for his docile, willing, and easily trained temperament, surefootedness, and easy-to-ride, low-slung rack. He is compact in size, with a medium build that is neither slight, nor heavily muscled. This type of horse often possesses the "silver dapple" gene, which is expressed through chocolate coat colors with flaxen manes and tails, but a Mountain Horse can be any solid coat color, and may have white on his face and on his legs below the knees and hocks. Palomino is a prevalent color among Kentucky Mountain Saddle Horses, and Spotted Mountain Horses may boast sabino, tobiano, or overo coat patterns. Following is a list of types of Mountain Horses:

- Rocky Mountain Horse
- Kentucky Mountain Saddle Horse

2.10 A double-registered Mountain Horse displaying the breed's compact body style and "silver dapple" gene, which is expressed as a chocolate coat with flaxen mane and tail. Mountain Horses are generally known for their calm, unflappable nature and friendly disposition.

- Mountain Pleasure Horse
- Spotted Mountain Saddle Horse

SPOTTED SADDLE HORSE

The Spotted Saddle Horse is a smooth-gaited horse that boasts a tobiano, overo, or sabino coat pattern. This horse is represented by two breed registries—the Spotted Saddle Horse Breeders' and Exhibitors' Association (SSHBEA), and the National Spotted Saddle Horse Association (NSSHA). The former organization has had soring issues similar to those experienced by Tennessee Walking Horses (see p. 26), and the NSSHA was formed as an alternative organization to promote horses that perform without the use of inhumane training devices, substances, or practices.

Many of these horses look like "lit up" Tennessee Walking Horses because that breed has had the largest influence on their bloodlines—indeed, many Spotted Saddle Horses are double-registered with TWHBEA and one of the Spotted Saddle Horse organizations. But most Spotted Saddle Horses owe their coloration to breeds other than the Tennessee Walking Horse. None of the foundation or "old time" Tennessee Walking Horses had overo or tobiano coat patterns.

All of this "miraculously" changed in the late 1980s and early 1990s with the burgeoning popularity of spotted horses of every breed when, within a few short years, a breed that had never had spotted colors began to produce spotted foals! In their efforts to please customers, wily breeders were breeding their Tennessee Walking Horse mares to stallions with pinto coloration and then fraudulently registering the foals as pure Tennessee Walking Horses. (TWHBEA eventually required DNA testing to verify Tennessee Walking Horse ancestry, but previously registered spotted horses were essentially "grandfathered" into the breed since there were no DNA records of their parents on file.)

Because many types of horses were used to create the Spotted Saddle Horse, they come in a variety of sizes and body types. Spotted Saddle Horses usually stand between 14.2 and 15.2 hands high, have substantial bone, and a quiet temperament. They perform a variety of gaits, including the flat walk, running walk, and rack—including, at times, the speed rack (see p. 13).

Other Gaited Breeds

Afrikan Saalperd (South Africa)

Albanian Myzeqea (Albania)

Alter Horse (Portugal)

American Gaited Pony (United States)

American Walking Pony (United States)

Asturian (Spain)

Basuto or Basoto (South Africa)

Breton (France)

Campolina (Brazil)

Canadian Horse (Canada—not all are gaited)

Canadian Pacer (Canada)

Cape Horse (South Africa)

Cayuse Indian Pony (United States)

Chamurthi or Spiti Pony (India)

Costeño (Peru)

Criollo (Argentina—not all are gaited)

Datong (China)

Deliboz (Eurasia)

Florida Cracker Horse (United States)

Gaited Morgan Horse (United States)

Galiceño (Mexico)

Lac La Croix Indian Pony (Canada—not all are gaited)

Mangalarga Marchador (Brazil)

Marwari or Malani (India)

McCurdy Plantation Horse (United States)

Montana Traveler (United States)

Nakota Horse (United States)

National Show Horse (United States)

Nez Perce Horse (United States—not all are gaited)

North American Single Footing Horse (United States)

Racking Horse (United States)

Spanish Mustang (United States and Canada—not all are gaited)

Standardbred (United States)

Tiger Horse (United States)

Virginia Pocket Horse (United States)

Orlove Trotter (Russia)

Pantaneiro (Brazil)

Tacky Horse or Marsh Horse (United States)

Tennuvian (United States)

Walkaloosa (United States)

CHAPTER 3

How to Choose the Perfect (for You) Gaited Horse

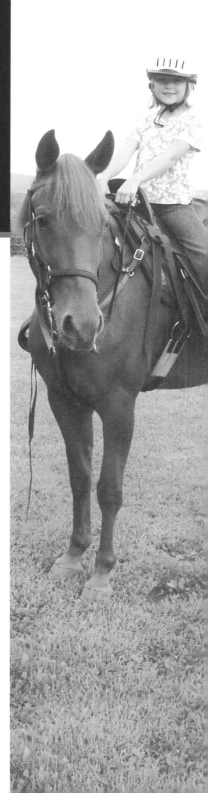

A Common Scenario

MANY YEARS AGO I ACQUIRED A BRIGHT RED ROAN sabino Tennessee Walking Horse gelding that proved to be as quirky and undependable as he was big, well-gaited, and beautiful. (The irregularly white-spotted sabino coat pattern is very common among "old style" Tennessee Walking Horses, which was the type of horse I hoped to find.) When I evaluated him for purchase, it was apparent he was a real character. He handled acceptably well from the ground, though he attempted to push into my personal space more than I prefer. Under saddle he was quick, strong, spirited—and just a hair more willful than what I liked. Still…he was so good looking, the price was right, and I had faith in my ability to reform a difficult horse, so I made the impulsive decision to take him home with me. It was a decision I would regret for several years.

I dubbed the horse "Winston," and every time I planned to ride—and I rode often—I did so with my heart in my mouth. I never knew if I was going to saddle up the "good" Winston (the "winner"), or the "bad" Winston (the "wiener"). One day he would be as good as gold, going over, under, or through anything I asked, and the next day, he would nearly rear up over backward to avoid an inconspicuous rock by the side of the road.

In spite of the problems, the eternal optimist in me kept believing that one day Winston would wake up and decide, due to his overwhelming love for me, to become the poster child for truly *great* horses. Boy, was I dreaming!

I had a real problem on my hands, since I had become attached to Winston. I knew a few very good riders who were willing to buy him from me, even knowing the difficulties I'd had, but I was reluctant to pass on a horse with serious issues.

After five years—and getting dumped three times during one riding season—I finally made the decision to sell him to an eager buyer, someone who could ride a "tornado." I had expected his departure from my barn to be heartrending; but instead, it was a tremendous relief. No more "gutting up" for a ride. No more walking on eggshells when another horse acted up, or wondering if he was going to do one of his "rear up high, do a fast 360-degree turn, duck low and swerve to the left, then go for an all-out bolt" at the sight of a small downed tree by the trail. While riding is always an adventure, this had been more excitement than I ever cared to experience.

My fears about selling a problem horse were unfounded. The buyer rode and loved Winston until he passed on to "horse heaven" in his later years. All this only goes to demonstrate that a nightmare for one person may well be another's dream horse.

Stories like mine are all too common. A horse can be a bad "actor" due to his past training (or "untraining"), a pain issue, or poor breeding. Problems may be rooted in the rider's lack of skill or experience, or her inability to determine what type of horse is most appropriate for her.

Some horses are simply not honest—or at least not honest all of the time. The most dangerous horses are those "95-percenters": just when you

think you can trust them, they invent something to do that's more stupid and dangerous than ever. Such horses are always more interested in playing games than in forging any sort of partnership with a human.

It is important to make an honest assessment of your riding skills, motivation for buying a particular type of gaited horse, and overall riding interests before going horse hunting (fig. 3.1). Do you want a horse you can both take to shows and ride on the trail, or are you strictly interested in one aspect or the other? Your size, physical condition, and level of confidence and skill should also help determine the animal you choose. Make a list of all the

3.1 A confident, experienced rider does best with a horse that has a lot of natural "get-up-and-go." This Walkaloosa mare (Purim Moon) is full of energy. While that energy is apparent in this photo, the rider's relaxed demeanor helps the mare remain calm and focused.

Primary Purchase Considerations

When looking to buy a gaited horse, you should consider the following (which I explain in detail on the pages ahead):

- Temperament
- Soundness
- Size and conformation
- Manners under saddle
- Smooth gaiting ability
- Training and experience
- Type and talent
- Price

While these are all important for any buyer, their order of importance varies from person to person. Someone who doesn't mind a "hot" horse may be more concerned with the horse's soundness than with his temperament. A confident, experienced trainer may be more interested in the horse's innate talent, or the quality of his smooth saddle gaits, than with his current training and experience.

Notice I place "price" last on this list. Unfortunately, too many people put price as their number one priority. While this is understandable, buying the wrong horse cheaply costs far more in the end—not only in dollars, but in emotional and perhaps physical turmoil. So it is worth stretching your budget or saving up for the right horse.

qualities a horse must possess to be seriously considered for purchase, then no matter how inexpensive, pretty, or personable a horse may seem, be determined to purchase him only if he specifically meets your most important criteria.

Stick to the plan, and take your time. Hurrying into buying a horse frequently leads to problems further down the road. Since you are committing to own an animal with a life span of 20-plus years, consider all aspects. And please, don't place a high premium on a particular color. Trust me, that pretty red roan coat of Winston's wasn't nearly so impressive when viewed from under his belly!

On the pages that follow, I list some of the primary issues you should consider when purchasing a gaited horse.

Temperament

There are few things more disappointing or counterproductive than purchasing a horse temperamentally unsuited to you. This scenario can take several forms, but I'll start with the most common. Take the buyer who is a beginner or just slightly more skilled—perhaps with good balance and adequate communication skills, but not necessarily very confident. Often this person has had a bad experience or two in the saddle making her a bit tense and nervous when mounted.

The rider looks at a horse at the seller's establishment, rides it on a trail there in familiar tack and accompanied by someone on one of the horse's pasture buddies. All goes well, and the horse is purchased.

Once home, however, things change—sometimes quickly, sometimes over a period of time. The horse may become barn sour, buddy sour, or spooky. He may begin to rush, bolt, or rear as the problems escalate. Every incident makes the new owner more tense and fearful. These feelings are inevitably communicated to the horse, who in turn becomes more intractable.

In addition to their financial investment, by this time many owners have an emotional one too, and are reluctant to give up. Though few admit it, the root of this is often simple embarrassment at admitting their equestrian limitations. The underlying problem is that buyers often purchase horses that are too willful, spirited, or green for their level of ability.

This is why it's essential to be completely honest about your level of experience and riding ability (see sidebar, below). The majority of people looking to purchase smooth-gaited riding horses are middle-aged, or older. While they may still occasionally picture themselves speed racking down a country road with the wind whipping through their hair, this probably isn't advisable as their reflexes have slowed, their body may be stiff from nervousness and the effects of old injuries and aging, and they just don't bounce as well as they once did!

When deciding what kind of horse is right for you, ask yourself the following questions:

- Is my riding up to a quick, agile horse?
- Do I become tense in challenging circumstances?
- Am I comfortable handling a temperamental horse?
- Do I clue in quickly to a horse's communications, or am I often at a loss?
- Do I prefer a "quirky" horse with some emotional complexity, or an uncomplicated, easygoing animal?
- Am I experienced, perceptive, and patient enough to take things slowly and calmly with a nervous, young, or less experienced horse?

MANNERS ON THE GROUND

You'll also need to determine a horse's ground manners in all kinds of circumstances—after all, you're going to be off his back more than on it. I always watch the way the seller responds to the horse. Does he seem apprehensive? While the problem could be with the owner, it is probable the horse has a behavior issue.

When you approach the horse, does his eye remain "soft"? Is he willing to have his ears handled? Feet? Mouth? Tail? Sheath or udder? (Have the current owner handle sensitive areas before you try.) Does he pin his ears or swing his hind end toward humans or animals when they approach?

Does the horse lunge or work in a round pen? If so, ask to see him go. Does he respond quickly and willingly without pinning his ears, or does he show willful disobedience or other signs of disrespect and aggression?

Lead the horse to see if he is respectful of your space and walks along at the speed you set. Does he pay attention to you, or is he distracted by other horses or your surroundings? It's surprising how many horses have not been well schooled for proper leading. This can be taught if you're willing to take the time, but your ultimate purchase price should be determined partially by how much additional training—especially in the basics—the horse requires.

AVOIDING VICES

Horses can develop a number of common vices, some of them minor annoyances, some destructive of property, and others downright dangerous either to the horse, the human, or both. Some of the most common follow.

Halter Pulling

Some horses refuse to be tied and pull back strenuously until their halter, lead rope, or the tie post gives way. Such horses are known as "halter pullers." They wreak havoc on tack and equipment, and may exert enough force to damage their neck trying to escape. Halter pullers are not only difficult to manage but are dangerous for the unsuspecting person who ties the horse to a trailer or post and suddenly finds himself underneath a powerful, frenzied animal that has literally "lost his mind" trying to break free.

Horses can develop a number of common vices, some of them minor annoyances, some destructive of property, and others downright dangerous either to the horse, the human, or both.

One such horse I evaluated seemed placid during our initial introduction. I took him into a large tack building and tied him to one of the building's supportive posts while I turned to get his tack. He nearly pulled the building down on top of me before I managed to locate a knife and cut him loose. I risked injury getting close enough to do so, but as he had the only exit blocked, it was my only available course of action. I never again "assumed" a horse would tie, nor have I ever since walked under the neck of a tied horse!

Ask to see the horse tied in a variety of places and under varying circumstances—away from other horses, within eye and earshot of loud equipment, and to a horse trailer. While he is tied in a safe, secure spot, try to spook him by waving your hands or a piece of cloth around. What triggers one halter puller might not faze another, so you'll want to test him thoroughly.

Cribbing, Wind Sucking, and Wood Chewing

A horse that cribs compulsively grabs with his teeth onto any available solid object (such as a wooden fence or manger), arches his neck and sucks in air. Wind sucking is essentially the same habit, except the horse has learned to grab onto his own tongue, rather than an outside object. Wood chewing is similar, but rather than sucking air, the horse actually chews and eats wooden objects.

These behaviors develop because of boredom, and are more common among horses kept in stalls with little or no turnout. Show horses deprived of turnout with other herd members are especially prone to these vices. If you are buying an ex-show horse trained for the "Big Lick," or the "slow gait," or any horse that wore show-ring "stacks" (weighted and/or heightened shoe packages), or other action devices, be aware that many handlers who train for these kinds of classes use methods and devices that take a high emotional toll on the horse. Stressed horses have a higher likelihood of developing these vices.

Cribbing and wood chewing are damaging to physical objects, as well as to the horse. Wooden fencing and stalls quickly show signs of wear-and-tear as the horse works them with his teeth, or incessantly chews on them. The animal's teeth wear down unevenly and excessively, and horses with these habits are highly prone to colic. Horses who demonstrate these behaviors use them to "tune out" their owners. Aside from all this, most people find these vices extraordinarily annoying.

When evaluating a horse, see if he wears a "cribbing strap," a leather collar fit snugly around his throatlatch. This is used to prevent the horse from arching his neck in order to crib or wind suck. If he doesn't wear a collar, check for a worn strip of hair at the top of the neck, which will indicate a collar exists but has been removed. Examine wooden surfaces in the stall where your potential purchase is housed. Are they badly worn or chewed at the top? If any of these signs are apparent, continue your search for a horse elsewhere to avoid the frustration and expense of dealing with a horse with one of these vices. While cribbing can be managed, and may even be reduced if the horse is kept where he gets regular turnout, most people prefer not to bring such an animal into contact with other horses, as these habits may be learned.

Stall Weaving, Fence Pacing, and Circling

Other vices to avoid are stall weaving, fence pacing, and circling. These are all compulsive, repetitive motions that create excessive stress on the horse's body, leading to unsoundness. When the horse is a stall weaver he stands and shifts his weight from side to side while weaving his head back and forth over his stall door. When turned out to pasture a fence-pacing horse runs back and forth along the fence line. A circling horse continually seems to "chase his own tail." Besides developing soundness issues, horses with these vices are difficult to keep in good condition because of excess calories burned.

Stall Kicking

Some horses develop the habit of kicking their stall walls, which is hard on stalls, doors, and horse trailers, to say nothing of the horse's back feet and legs. Kicking frequently leads to *capped hocks,* a condition where there is swelling or puffiness at the point of one or both hocks. In fact, capped hocks can be a sign of a stall kicker—that, and hoofprints on stall surfaces. A stall

kicker can be dangerous, as the vice is compulsive, and the horse might inadvertently kick a human or other animal, with disastrous results.

One such story involves a friend who was repairing a stall door that had been damaged by a stall kicker, and the offending stall kicker was with him in the stall. Fortunately for him, I happened to stop by and glanced into the stall just as the mare prepared to let loose with both hind legs. I yelled out a warning and he jumped aside, barely avoiding a kick to the head.

In my experience stall kickers tend to be stubborn, temperamental, and impatient—poor qualities for any kind of riding horse.

3.2 Observing a horse in his pasture can indicate whether he is spirited or docile. This Tennessee Walking Horse mare is demonstrating a lot of energy—and, on occasion, she is known to show this same quality when under saddle!

Pasture Behavior and Dynamics

If possible, spend time watching the horse in the pasture when he is loose to get some idea of his temperament (fig. 3.2). Also see how he relates to other horses. Is the horse driven away from food or water? Does he exhibit signs of being very low on the pecking order, with lots of bite or kick marks? If so, he will be difficult to manage when you turn horses out together. At the other end of the scale is the animal that is aggressively dominant toward others. I prefer a horse that seems to get along with herdmates but can defend himself when necessary.

Soundness

While a vet exam (see p. 73) is an essential step in evaluating a horse you are serious about purchasing, you will most likely look at several before becoming interested enough to make the monetary investment involved in scheduling one. For this reason, it's important to be able to spot common unsoundness issues for yourself during your initial evaluation. Primarily, you will want to determine that the animal's legs, feet, and breathing are not compromised.

LEGS

Be sure to check over the horse's legs for serious conformational flaws and signs of unsoundness. (Conformational flaws are covered at greater length in chapter 4—see p. 88.) Signs of unsoundness in the legs include swelling and lumpy protrusions or scars. These are particularly alarming if they appear at the joints as they may be a precursor or indication of existing arthritis or other joint problems.

Take the following steps to evaluate the horse's legs:

1. Ask the owner to lead the horse *toward* you, first at a regular walk, then at a faster walk. Can you detect any limping or excessive head bobbing to one particular side? While a gaited horse should demonstrate head bobbing or nodding when walking fast, the motion should be identical on each

side. Otherwise, the horse is rebalancing his weight off one leg to compensate for discomfort.

Do the front legs swing noticeably inward or outward at the lower leg? With the exception of *termino,* exhibited by Peruvian Horses (see p. 15), the action of the forelegs should be straight forward. If it is not, then the bones of the horse's forelegs are not straight from shoulder to hoof. This lack of a straight "pillar"-type foundation causes excessive stress on the joints of the forelegs. Since horses naturally carry 60 percent or more of their weight over their forelegs, it is important to determine if their legs will stand up to this task over time.

2. Now have the horse led *away* from you at a walk, and then a faster walk. Does either hind leg twist at the hock or pastern with each stride? This places excess strain on the joints, leading to future problems. The horse's footprints should track straight forward directly underneath his body and exhibit the same tracking pattern from one side to the other (see p. 11).

Do the forefeet interfere with the hind feet? A long stride is desirable with some breeds of gaited horses, such as the Tennessee Walking Horse, but excessive interference indicates a conformational defect and may cause the horse to stumble or fall down, a very dangerous situation.

3. Ask the owner to walk the horse in a *tight circle in each direction.* Is there any sign of a "hitch" in the stifle area as the horse raises his inside hind leg? An upward fixated patella (locked stifle) is a common problem for gaited horses. While it can usually be dealt with appropriately, you'll want to decide if you're willing to work it out—and whether this particular animal is minimally, or seriously compromised. When the horse is circled, check to see that there is no stiffness or short-striding on either hind or foreleg in either direction. This, too, indicates discomfort and possible unsoundness.

FEET

The old saying "No hoof, no horse," is true if you plan to buy a horse for anything other than an expensive pet. So thoroughly evaluate all four feet. Are they worn evenly? Do they show other signs of appropriate farrier care? Or are there long cracks or splits in the hoof wall? Cracks originating at the

The old saying "No hoof, no horse," is true if you plan to buy a horse for anything other than an expensive pet.

coronary band at the very top of the hoof are especially troublesome, as they are difficult to eliminate and may allow bacteria to pass into the foot, causing internal infection and compromising the foot's overall health and structural strength.

Are there signs of previous founder such as flaring at the toe or horizontal rings on the horny part of the foot? Foundered horses rarely come back to full usefulness, and a gaited horse's foot needs to be able to withstand an increased number of footfalls when the horse is gaiting.

The additional stress of increased footfalls when the horse is gaiting is also why it's of particular importance that the feet be large enough to support the horse's weight. It's impossible to offer exact criteria for determining appropriate foot size, as some blocky, tough feet can withstand more shock than other, larger feet with weaker hoof walls. In general the foot should appear to be in proportion to the overall size of the horse's body—you don't want to see the equivalent of a sumo wrestler standing on top of a ballerina's foot.

Some horses develop extremely large "pancake" hooves, with flat soles. This is to be avoided, as the bottom of the foot should be concave in order to absorb concussion. If you acquire such a horse, proper trimming and conditioning should correct his feet over a year's time (see p. 234).

LUNGS

Watch the horse breathe and count his respirations for 15 seconds. Multiply this by four to find his per-minute resting respiration rate. A horse's normal resting respiration is between 8 and 15 breaths per minute—the lower the rate, the more fit the animal. His breathing should not appear labored, and the nostrils should flare only slightly with each breath.

Heaves

When the nostrils flare significantly with each breath and are red inside rather than a light pink, you should be wary of Chronic Obstructive Pulmonary Disease (COPD) also known as "heaves." With this condition you see the sides of the horse noticeably expanding and contracting hard when he breathes, and this extra effort eventually causes the development of a ridge of hard muscle that extends along both sides of the barrel. Heaves is usually caused by allergies, and though there are some stopgap measures that may prolong the horse's useful life, this is an incurable, chronic condition that should eliminate the horse from your list of possible purchases.

THE PRE-PURCHASE VETERINARY EXAM

While some people insist that the exam be performed by a veterinarian not associated with the current owner, my experience indicates that a veterinarian who is familiar with the animal is your best choice. I have never known one who was so fearful of losing a customer that he or she would misinform a potential buyer about an animal's health: Pre-purchase exam forms are quite exacting, and as a rule a veterinarian will be cautious and warn the buyer of even the slightest possibility of health issues—current and potential. I know that my vet, for example, does not hesitate to point out his concerns to a buyer, which I expect him to do, as a conscientious professional.

A few years ago I traveled several hundred miles to look at a seven-year-old Tennessee Walking Horse gelding. Most of my herd consisted of youngsters, broodmares, and stallions, and I needed a horse to help train young stock and fulfill the role of the "anybody-can-ride-him" horse on the farm. The gelding was ridden by an 11-year-old girl, who was obviously heartbroken over selling him. The girl's mother told me that her daughter needed a more challenging horse: They had found a promising prospect, but needed to sell this horse before buying the other. It sounded plausible.

I checked out the gelding carefully and watched the little girl ride before taking him for a spin myself. It was a cold and windy day, but he was a perfect gentleman. Better yet, when I cued him for gait he transitioned upward into a nice flat walk, an equally smooth running walk, and at his fastest speed he performed an evenly timed four-beat rack that was a *lot* of fun to ride. I put some leg on him to see just how much he knew and he responded easily with side-passes, turns on the forehand and haunches, and rein backs. I'd discovered a gem!

Once home, I arranged for who I thought would be an objective vet in their area (*not* theirs) to do a complete evaluation, which the horse passed

3.3 This Peruvian Horse is short-backed, tightly coupled, and strongly-muscled. He has good bone and is built close to the ground. Horses such as this can carry more weight than a taller, "willowy" animal.

with flying colors. I purchased him and made the long trip to trailer him to his new home.

The weekend following his arrival, I took him on a trail ride with friends. It wasn't a particularly vigorous ride, but I sensed him tiring before long and rode back to camp alone. After a few days' rest, I saddled him up again, this time for a very short ride. His behavior was nothing like it had been! He kicked out to the side and crow-hopped so badly that I took him back to the barn to make sure he didn't have a problem with his saddle or bit.

To make a long story short, the horse suffered from Equine Protozoal Myeloencephalitis (EPM), a neurological disease brought on by exposure to

Determining a Horse's Weight-Bearing Capacity

How can you accurately determine a horse's weight-bearing capacity? Most animals can comfortably carry 20 percent of their own weight. A well-conformed (see chapter 4—p. 87) and highly conditioned horse may carry as much as 25 percent of his body weight, and a few well-built horses with heavy "bone" and the right kind of body structure may surpass that.

"Bone" is the measurement of the circumference of the foreleg cannon bone, just below the knee. One useful formula for determining if a horse can handle your weight is to add the weight of the horse, rider, and tack together, divide this number by the cannon bone's circumference, then divide that figure by 2; the result should be between 75 and 85. When the number is higher than this, you are too heavy for the horse.

Contrary to popular opinion, a tall horse isn't necessarily the best weight-bearing one as he has a high center of gravity, making it easy for a heavier, less agile rider to throw the horse off balance. (Compare this to riding piggyback with your legs low around someone's waist, or high up on his shoulders. Which is the more secure position?) For optimum weight-bearing ability, the horse should have good bone, stand between 14 and 15.2 hands, have low-set knees and hocks, wide loins, and a short back (fig. 3.3).

The fitness level and balance of the rider is an important consideration when determining weight-bearing ability. A horse can more easily carry a well-balanced, agile rider than an unfit, uncoordinated person. Therefore, if you are a heavy rider, it is greatly to your advantage to work at staying as fit as possible.

The type of riding is also a factor when considering weight. If you trail ride long and often over rough, mountainous terrain, you don't want to be on a horse at the very edge of being able to handle your weight comfortably. On the other hand, if you ride easy trails for an hour or so , or only show in the occasional pleasure class, you may do fine on a horse with less capacity for carrying weight.

If you are seriously considering a horse but are not certain he can handle your weight on your type of rides, ask if you can take him on a trial basis—or at least a trial ride—before purchase. Does the horse "lug" up hills, seem to fall clumsily into transitions, stumble frequently, or otherwise feel as though he is being physically overburdened? When this is the case, or you are unable to thoroughly evaluate the horse before buying, *keep looking.*

opossum feces. I spent $2,000 giving him two rounds of very expensive treatment, to which he did not respond. Some investigative work led to the name of the previous owners' veterinarian, and I discovered there had been intermittent signs of the disease—albeit no definitive diagnosis—prior to my initial visit to their farm. In other words, the owners knew there was the possibility this horse suffered from a debilitating neurological disease, and decided to dump him on an unwary buyer rather than take the loss themselves. Had I contacted *their* vet, rather than the "objective" one who had no previous history on the horse, I would have saved thousands of dollars, days of time, and great emotional trauma. After several months in my barn, I had to make the heart-wrenching decision to have this nice horse euthanized.

Size and Conformation

If you find mounting a bit of a challenge you should search for a gaited horse that's not too tall—taking your own height into consideration—and will stand completely still for mounting. A person with very short and/or heavy legs may get sore thighs riding a horse with an extremely wide back, while someone with very long legs might have trouble giving effective leg aids while astride a small, narrow-bodied animal. A diminutive rider who has limited strength in her arms and back may not be able to properly keep a "bull-necked" horse (see p. 100) with a thick throatlatch on the bit. When test riding a prospective purchase, try to get a real "feel" for whether you and the horse are a good physical match.

Manners under Saddle

Watch the horse being ridden to determine if he's mannerly under saddle. If he is, mount up yourself to get a personal feel for the horse. I'm amazed how often people purchase horses and bring them home without ever riding them. Trust me, if you're too intimidated to ride him at the seller's facility, you'll only get more fearful after you've brought him home.

Is he responsive to your seat, legs, and hands? Is he soft and supple, or does it feel like you're riding a board of lumber on four legs? Is he obedient to your cue for stopping? Backing-up? Standing still in one spot? Does he stay focused on you, or is he easily distracted, and seem to "tune you out"?

Is he calm and placid, or does it feel as though he could "blow" at any time? Of course rearing, strong balking, or bucking eliminates a horse from consideration.

Smooth Gaiting Ability

When you're observing the horse being ridden by someone else, watch to see which smooth saddle gaits he performs. Since his current gaits may not be perfected, you'll also want to analyze his conformation to determine which his best natural gait or gaits will be once he's been fitted, trained, and ridden responsibly (see p. 87).

Saddle up and ride him to experience his gaits for yourself. Is he smooth at the regular walk? Many horses with a strong natural overstride have a rolling motion through their back at the walk that is uncomfortable and hard on the rider's back, and this cannot be "trained out" of them. If you have a bad back or hips, and often spend hours just walking on the trail, you'll want to avoid a horse with this characteristic.

Are his upward transitions smooth or does he leap directly from a slow walk to a faster gait? Does he move with good impulsion from the hindquarters, and collect softly on the bridle while maintaining his gait? Will he sustain one speed and one gait, or does he "shift gears" without being asked?

If you really want to enjoy your new gaited horse, it's important to match the horse to your expectations and experience.

Training and Experience

If you really want to enjoy your new gaited horse, it's important to match the horse to your expectations and experience. I touched on this topic in the story on p. 73. Since I was in the market for a horse that was finished enough to let me "pony" youngsters off him—sometimes over rough, narrow

3.4 A quiet, child-safe horse such as this Missouri Fox Trotter is worth his weight in gold!

trails—I was looking for one that already knew how to yield to leg aids and was unflappable and soft in the bridle. I knew exactly what I wanted, and considered only horses that would meet my particular needs.

As a rule of thumb, unless you are a patient and experienced horse person, it is wise to invest in an animal that is already trained in whatever discipline you plan to practice. If you're going to be trail riding in rugged mountains, don't purchase a horse that has only been exposed to flat arenas and show rings. Instead, look for an easygoing, surefooted animal—ideally one that has been raised and trained in the mountains.

If you're hoping to compete in small regional gaited-horse classes that require smooth gait transitions and fast responses, it makes no sense to adopt an off-the-track pacing Standardbred that has never learned to respond to a mounted rider's aids, let alone how to perform a correct canter. In this case, hunt for your gaited horse among breeders and trainers who produce good quality show horses.

If you plan to learn to drive your horse, then that well-trained and experienced driving Standardbred makes perfect sense, and of course you can work at teaching him other disciplines over time if you like. (The beauty about driving Standardbreds is that they are tractable and easy to train, and many of them can be taught to perform very nice saddle gaits.)

Type and Talent

It's important to consider intrinsic talents that have been bred into various breeds and types of gaited horses. (I will briefly discuss this from the buyer's point of view here, but for more information about gaited breeds and types, please refer to chapter 2, p. 21.)

- Spanish-type gaited horses such as the *Paso Fino* and *Peruvian Horse* tend to be "hot" and spirited. They possess great stamina and heart but may intimidate a more timid or less experienced rider. This is especially true of horses possessing *brio*. Horses with great brio are most suitable for experienced riders who plan to compete in the show ring. Some

3.5 This diminutive rider is well matched to her
spirited Spotted Saddle Horse.

of these horses are more mild-mannered and docile, but you will want to ride one several times to be certain that is the case before making a commitment to purchase. (For more on these breeds, see pp. 46 and 52.)

- *Missouri Fox Trotters* have placid temperaments, are sturdy and big-boned, and early lines were used extensively for working cattle in the Ozark Mountains (fig. 3.4). If you are a heavy rider, or if your goal is to trail ride or learn team penning, the search might begin with Missouri Fox Trotting Horse farms. (For more on the breed, see p. 37.)

- *Tennessee Walking Horses* are sensitive, attuned to their rider, and willing to please. They usually do well with a calm, sensitive rider. Horses bred for the "Big Lick" have a "big engine." These horses often endure physical and emotional abuse when being trained for show. Those who fail in the show ring are culled for sale to the pleasure and trail-riding market. Well-meaning people who try to "rescue" them may discover they have acquired a horse with too much energy and too many complex problems for their level of experience. Less experienced riders should be wary of former "Big Lick" horses, and look for those bred specifically for pleasure riding. (For more on the breed, see p. 26.)

- *Spotted Saddle Horses* are sturdy and dependable, and some have a talent for speed as well (fig. 3.5). If you enjoy the fast gaits and want a sane and surefooted horse, then these are worth checking out. (For more on the breed, see p. 58.)

- The various breeds and types of *Mountain Horses*—the *Rocky Mountain, Kentucky Mountain, Mountain Saddle Horse,* and *Kentucky Natural Gaited Horse* are just what their name promises: surefooted mountain horses. They have a calm, quiet nature and efficient ground-covering gaits. Their exceptional docility makes them an appropriate choice for beginning or nervous riders. (For more on these breeds, see p. 56.)

The Right Price is a Fair Price

Reputable horse dealers—and contrary to popular opinion, there are many of them out there—can hardly afford to sell a horse at the price most buyers expect to pay. People who sell horses commonly hear something like this: "I need a safe, mature, well-trained, calm horse that I will use only for trail riding. I have a bad back and need a horse that has good smooth gaits. I really love a palomino color (or buckskins and spotted horses), and prefer a gelding. I'll give the horse a *very* good home, but can't afford to spend more than $1,500."

Potential Problems to Avoid

Hardly a month goes by when I don't hear from someone who is attached to a problem horse and eager to give him to a good home where he will be appreciated and properly retrained.

More than once a desperate horse owner has contacted me because she has "rescued" a former show horse, only to discover she isn't prepared to retrain such a horse on her own, and can't find, or afford, an appropriate trainer in her area. Even if she locates a trainer, she now realizes after trying to work with the animal that she isn't experienced enough to handle and ride a spirited show horse—even if he is retrained.

I also hear from people who get a "real deal" at an auction, only to discover the horse has a serious vice, or vices. They buy the horse cheaply, but then find that keeping him is anything *but* cheap—the horse is too dangerous to ride without extensive retraining, and it's going to be extremely costly to have him retrained by a competent professional.

Then there's the person who wants a smooth-gaited riding horse she can relax and enjoy riding, but she impulsively purchases an untrained or green youngster instead. She quickly discovers she's over her head, and the training she's attempted to do with him created problems she doesn't know how to fix. Now she's scared to ride him, and is looking for someone to help.

It is better to err on the side of caution when deciding if a horse is within your capacity to train, or retrain. Problem horses are beyond the ability of most casual riders, and finding a suitable new owner for one is nearly impossible because a person experienced enough to retrain a problem horse is usually smart enough not to acquire one!

Now let's look at this scenario for just a moment. A breeder either pays the (high) price of keeping a breeding stallion, or else pays the (high) price of breeding his good quality mare to a good quality stallion. Not only has he invested a considerable amount of money by the time the foal arrives, but he's spent countless hours tending to the mare to ensure she stays healthy and sound.

Once the foal arrives, that workload doubles. If you've never had the experience of raising a foal, you probably cannot imagine how much strenuous and time-consuming labor goes into socializing him and training him

3.6 The breeder and owner of this Peruvian Horse foal will have a great deal of time, labor, and money invested in him before he is sold. (Peruvian Horse mare owned by Sandra van den Hof, Belgium.)

3.7 People who look to purchase a horse cheaply because it is "only" for trail riding have little understanding how well-trained a good trail horse like this Spotted Saddle Horse ought to be. Trail horses have to negotiate tricky terrain, water crossings, and traffic safely. They need to be strong, surefooted, and level-headed.

for simple things such as haltering, leading, tying, and picking up his feet. Now also, there is this other mouth to feed—Mama's provision only goes so far, for so long. And let's not forget the extra costs for tack and stable gear, plus all the time and labor of grooming and mucking out (fig. 3.6).

By the time the horse reaches the age of two or three you can be sure there's been an investment of well over $1,500. The breeder either starts the horse himself, or sends it to a trainer for those all-important first few months under saddle (a young horse should be ridden four days a week at a minimum during the first three months of training).

Once initial training is completed, the horse is still young and only "green broke." A horse being brought along properly will not have his smooth saddle gaits established at such a young age. At least two more years of regular use is required to get a "finished" horse—though not necessarily one that is "safe and calm" on the trail. Often, horses don't "settle down" until they're at least seven years old.

Many people prefer geldings. Unfortunately, Mother Nature has no such bias. So a breeder may have three finished mares for sale on his place, and only one gelding. If you were him, what is the chance you would sell that one finished gelding for $1,500, or less?

Most reputable horse breeders and dealers, especially those providing "only" trail horses (who often require more training than some types of show horses), work for their love of horses rather than for money (fig. 3.7). Few can afford to make it their full-time occupation. While they certainly bond with their animals—and finding good homes for those that are sold is of utmost concern—they still must be compensated to be able to stay in business. If you hope to purchase a good horse from a reputable source, you would do well to take all this into consideration when planning your budget.

The flip side of this coin is that there are a number of less-than-reputable people who purchase "problem" horses at rock-bottom prices either at auction or by relieving distressed owners of their unruly animals, and resell them for little more than they originally paid. They have little money invested and only work with the horse a short while to make him just safe enough to show to potential buyers. The name of this game is "quick turnover," so the time-consuming, long-lasting training that a problem horse requires is never undertaken. The gullible buyer, looking for a cheap, pretty horse comes on the scene, and before you know it, she is at home, dealing with a "wiener," and taking chances with her life every time she mounts up. It is little wonder so many people give up horses altogether after this all-too-common experience.

By supporting the reputable horse seller, and paying a fair price for your horse, you help ensure that such dedicated people continue the all-important job of breeding, raising, and training safe, high-quality animals. This in turn means good horses on the market. Most importantly, you also greatly improve the odds that your horse purchase will have a happy ending. Now, how much is *that* worth?

CHAPTER 4

Conformation Considerations

Conformed to Perform

MOST GAITED HORSE OWNERS PURCHASE A HORSE of a particular breed and expect the animal to naturally perform the gait considered standard for that breed. It is assumed, for example, that a Tennessee Walking Horse will do a correct, natural flat walk and running walk; a Missouri Fox Trotting Horse will execute an easy fox trot; an Icelandic Horse will tolt, and so on (see p. 15 for a sidebar on signature gaits for various breeds).

This does not necessarily hold true. The smooth saddle gaits a horse performs naturally are not based on his registration (horses never learn how to read those papers), but rather are determined by the animal's conformation. Like all living creatures, function follows form.

Most pleasure riders aren't concerned if their gaited horse doesn't perform his breed's signature gaits—they are content when the horse is smooth to ride, whatever the gait. The only time it is essential for a horse to perform a particular saddle gait is when he is shown. People who plan to show need to be responsible about purchasing animals well conformed for their particular show ring gaits.

Unfortunately, far too often show horses are purchased for their bloodlines, beauty, personality, trainability, or color, only to have to be "'fixed" to properly perform the required movements. When this is the case, the signature gait is actually "artificial" or "man-made." Forcing a horse to use his body in a manner contrary to his natural conformation requires unwise training practices, and is detrimental to long-term soundness. So if you plan to show your gaited horse, be absolutely certain he is conformed to perform the required show ring gaits. Even if he demonstrated those gaits when you evaluated him for purchase, there is no guarantee he will continue to do so once you get him home.

Unfortunately, far too often show horses are purchased for their bloodlines, beauty, personality, trainability, or color, only to have to be "'fixed" to properly perform the required movements.

GAIT "BAIT AND SWITCH" TACTICS

Let me offer a common scenario: A rider purchases a Tennessee Walking Horse for show. She has the best of intentions: to train the horse using simple riding techniques and suitable tack, and ride him in humane show classes.

In the show ring, Tennessee Walking Horses are expected to demonstrate a deep head nod, high-lifting, animated forelegs, and a long overstride in the hind legs. But the conformation of this particular horse limits his ability to lift his forelegs very high or to produce overstride, and he demonstrates only a slight head nod.

When the rider first looked at the horse he moved "correctly," but she didn't know that heavy shoes and pads, and various other training devices were utilized to prepare the horse prior to presentation to a prospective buyer, then removed just before her arrival. (This shady practice is common in some show barns, regardless of breed.)

Unless the new owner is willing to resort to the same devices, this horse is simply not going to cut it in the show ring. What should she do with him? He certainly cost more than he would bring on the trail-horse market. But if he is resold to another show rider, it's possible he will be subjected to inhumane training practices again. So this rider must take a financial hit, keep the horse as a family pet, or sell him to someone else who will have to make these same hard choices. What often happens is the rider sends the horse to the training barn he came from for an occasional training "tune-up." In the end, the barn profits first from the sale of the horse, then from ongoing training services, while both horse and rider pay the price.

If this rider had understood how conformation affects horse gaits and overall movement, she would have known what qualities to look for in a show horse and been spared the financial and emotional expenses of this experience.

Conformation and Movement

FOREQUARTERS: SHOULDER AND ARM

The horse's shoulder (scapula) and arm (humerus) work together to determine the way he moves his forequarters. The length of the shoulder is measured from the front edge of the scapula just in front of the withers down to the point of shoulder (see fig. 4.2, Line 1). The arm is measured from the point of shoulder to the point of elbow (see fig. 4.2, Line 2). (You can mark these spots on a horse with a water-based marker, and then draw a line between them.)

STRIDE HEIGHT AND LENGTH

The angle of the arm in relation to the shoulder determines how high the front legs lift and how long the stride will be. (Note: This also applies to the angle of the hip and thigh—see p. 94.) If you open a protractor to various angles you will notice that a wide angle provides more area to accommodate the upward motion of the arm (or thigh) toward the shoulder (or hip), while a narrow angle limits how much space is available (figs. 4.1 A–C).

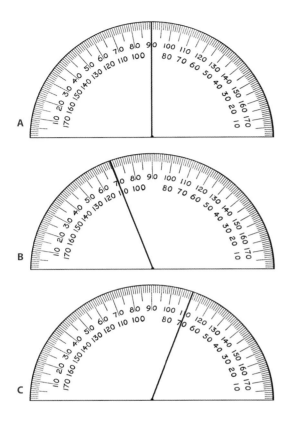

4.1 A–C A line has been drawn, dividing the protractor in A into two 90-degree angles. This is an average angle for the horse's forequarters (shoulder and arm) and hindquarters (hip and thigh), and produces an average amount of both stride length and stride height.

In B, the left side of the protractor shows a 70-degree angle, which is "closed" (acute). If the horse's forequarters (shoulder and arm) or hindquarters (hip and thigh) have this angle, it indicates a natural short stride height with a long stride length.

In C, the left side of the protractor illustrates a 110-degree angle, which is "open" (obtuse). When the horse's forequarters (shoulder and arm) or hindquarters (hip and thigh) have this angle, it indicates a high stride height with a short stride length.

- An average angle between the shoulder and arm is 90 degrees. A horse built this way has an *average stride length* and *moderate stride height* in his forequarters.
- A closed narrow (acute) angle between the shoulder and arm——anything less than 90 degrees——indicates less lift and longer stride. The more closed this angle, the more the horse will tend toward a *long stride length* with *minimal stride height*.
- An open (obtuse) angle between the shoulder and arm——anything over 90 degrees——gives the horse *greater ability for stride height* with *less stride length*. The more obtuse this angle, the higher lifting and short-strided the horse.

Visualizing the Horse's Stride Length

Extend an imaginary line down the line of the shoulder to the ground, and you'll see the horse's stride length. A horse with a deeply sloped shoulder has a longer stride than one with a steep, upright shoulder (fig. 4.2).

Where the horse's forelegs emerge from his body also affects stride length. A horse that is *camped under* with his forelegs set deeply beneath him has a shorter front stride than one with a more forward positioning of his forelegs. (See p. 102 for more information about foreleg positioning and how it affects the horse's motion and balance.)

Range of Motion

The length of the arm determines the forehand's range of motion. A horse with a long, upright

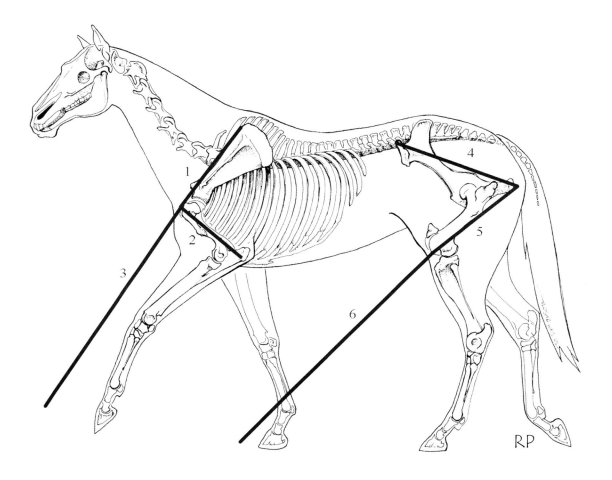

4.2 You can accurately predict how a horse will move in gait by considering his bone structure. Drawing lines from the top front edge of the scapula (shoulder) to the point of shoulder, and another from there to the point of elbow along the humerus (arm) reveal the underlying structure of the front end (see Lines 1 and 2). Continuing Line 1 from the point of shoulder to the ground offers a good indication of how long the horse's stride will be in front (see Line 3). Drawing lines from the point of hip to the point of buttock and another from there down to the stifle joint reveal how the hindquarters are built (see Lines 4 and 5). Continuing Line 5 to the ground indicates the length of stride behind (see Line 6).

How Forequarter and Hindquarter Angles Affect Gait

By understanding how the angles of the forequarters and hindquarters affect the horse's movement, it becomes possible to determine the gaits the horse will naturally perform based on that information. But keep in mind that other conformational factors play equally important roles in determining gait—these are discussed through the remainder of this chapter.

- **RUNNING WALK** A horse with an open angle between his shoulder and arm will take short-to-medium length, high-lifting strides with his forelegs (fig. 4.3). As he increases speed a moment of suspension will appear between one forefoot picking up and the other setting down. This gives the impression he is "trotting in front." When this horse also has a closed angle between his hip and thigh, he will have a long, low, sweeping hind stride, giving the appearance of "walking behind." A horse that appears to be "trotting in front and walking behind" is performing a running walk (see p. 11).

- **FOX TROT** A horse with a closed angle between his shoulder and arm will have minimal stride height and a long stride length in front, with little or no suspension between one foot picking up and the other setting down (fig. 4.4). He will, therefore, appear to be "walking in front." The open angle between his hip and thigh gives him a high stride height in back, with short stride length, and there will be a distinct period of suspension between one hind foot picking up and the other setting down. This gives the impression that he is "trotting behind." A horse that appears to be "walking in front and trotting behind" is performing a fox trot (see p. 6).

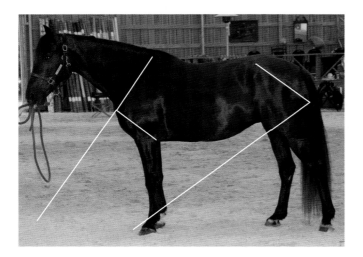

4.3 This Tennessee Walking Horse mare's steep shoulder and vertical arm combine for an open angle of 85 degrees in front, indicating she will have moderate stride height and stride length. There is a 70-degree (closed) angle between the hip and stifle, giving her a long, low stride behind. This, combined with a short back, permits the horse to stride deeply beneath herself and perform a running walk with considerable overstride. Horses built so that their body and legs form a box shape with long legs and a short back are most likely to have an overstride.

- **RACK** A horse with equal, or nearly equal, angles in the forequarters and hindquarters will have similar length and height of stride in his front and hind legs (fig. 4.5). Such horses perform a variation of the rack (see p. 12)—which particular variation is determined by whether the angles are closed, open, or average. When closed, the gait will be one with high (flashy) stride height and short-to-medium stride length. Open angles give the horse a long stride with minimal lift—such horses are called "daisy clippers" (fig. 4.6). Average angles result in moderate stride height and stride length.

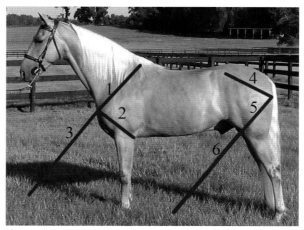

4.4 (Top) The lovely Missouri Fox Trotting stallion Prince Moon Beam has a 70-degree (closed) angle in front, giving him a long, low sweeping stride. The 90-degree angle between his hip and stifle give him moderate height of stride, with average length of stride. A longer, lower stride in front with a shorter, more lifting stride in back is the signature of a true fox-trot gait.

4.5 (Middle) The nearly equal and moderate angles in front (90 degrees) and behind (80 degrees) suggest this horse will rack with moderate stride height and length in the forehand, with a slightly less high and longer stride behind.

4.6 (Bottom) *Paso Fino* means "fine step", which is a short-strided, low-slung gait. The closed 70-degree angles of the fore- and hindquarters indicate this Paso Fino will perform the "daisy-clipping" gait for which the breed is known.

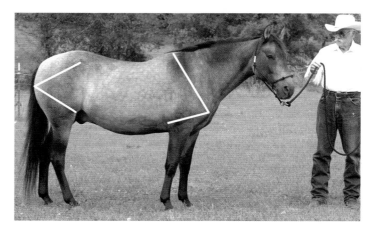

arm has a greater range of motion (also known as "scope")—and receives less concussion—than one with a short, horizontal arm. The arm should be at least 50 percent as long as the shoulder, with 60 percent being ideal.

HINDQUARTERS: HIP AND THIGH

The rule of thumb regarding wide and narrow angles in the forequarters holds equally true for the horse's hindquarters: A more *open* angle means greater lift of stride, while a more closed angle suggests a lower, "walking" type of stride.

The hip angle is measured from the point of hip to the point of buttock—the outermost point. The thigh runs from the point of buttock to the stifle joint, which is the top joint of the horse's hind leg. An indentation in the flesh indicates where the stifle joint is located. You may wish to use a water-based marker to mark these angles on the horse in order to see them clearly.

- A 90-degree angle between the hip and thigh is average. A horse built this way will have an average length of stride and moderate amount of lift in his hind legs.
- A closed narrow, (acute) angle between the hip and thigh—anything less than 90 degrees—indicates less lift and longer stride. The more closed this angle, the more the horse will tend toward a long stride with minimal lift.
- An open (obtuse) angle between the hip and thigh—anything over 90 degrees—gives the horse the ability to lift his legs high, and he will take short strides. The more open this angle, the more high-lifting and short-strided the horse.

Loin Coupling and Gait Orientation

How a horse is coupled (the length of the area where the back joins the croup) also gives you an indication about his innate gait orientation. Horses with *average-length* coupling easily learn to perform one or more of the square (intermediate) gaits; *long- or loosely-coupled* horses are laterally oriented; and *short- or tightly coupled* horses prefer the diagonal gaits.

Determine how the horse is coupled by running the flat front edge of the fingers of one hand firmly down the horse's spine and marking the last vertebra you can feel—where the last rib is attached. Still pressing firmly, continue to run your fingers rearward until you feel a "shelf." This is the lumbosacral (L-S) joint where the loins join into the back. The area between the last rib vertebra and the L-S joint is the length of the horse's coupling.

AVERAGE COUPLING

When the horse's coupling is about 3 inches long (on an average-sized horse), he is likely to have *intermediate (square) orientation*—that is, he is highly quadridextrous, and it is easy for him to move each leg independently (see p. 5). Such a horse may have inconsistent gaits and move all along the Gait Spectrum between pace and trot, or he may consistently move in an evenly timed four-beat gait at any speed. Don't be concerned if a horse like this tends to "slip gears" from one gait to another, as this indicates he can easily learn to perform smooth, evenly timed, four-beat gaits. A horse with a 3-inch loin measurement often possesses the innate capacity to perform several of the smooth saddle gaits—the ones at which he will excel are ultimately determined by how he is otherwise conformed (see sidebar, p. 92).

LOOSELY COUPLED

If the space between the last vertebra and the L-S joint is greater than 3 inches, the horse is called "loosely coupled" and likely to have *lateral orientation*. This horse is "pacey," with a tendency to move with a level or hollowed-out frame, which will take a heavy toll on his body. Teaching a loosely coupled horse to collect is a challenge because he naturally wants to carry too much

How a horse is coupled (the length of the area where the back joins the croup) also gives you an indication about his innate gait orientation.

of his weight on his forehand. However, by schooling him with the methods taught on p. 226, it is possible to condition such a horse to collect properly, "square up," and perform a rack, running walk, or both, which will help maintain soundness. After he has been taught to perform the rack or running walk (depending on his conformation) rather than pace or stepping pace, he will usually perform his square (intermediate) gaits with slightly lateral action.

CLOSE-COUPLED

When the horse's coupling is less than 3 inches, the horse is said to be "close-coupled" and will be *diagonally oriented*. Sometimes the hindquarters of close-coupled horses are so densely muscled it is impossible to feel the L-S joint. A close-coupled horse may sometimes slip into a hard, two-beat trot, or may perform a natural fox trot. If the angles of his fore- and hindquarters are not suited for the fox trot, he may perform a running walk, a rack, or be capable of both. A diagonally oriented horse that performs the rack or running walk usually does so with slightly diagonal orientation.

General Conformation Considerations

OVERALL BALANCE

One of the first things I look for when evaluating conformation is good overall balance. A well-balanced horse's body can be divided into thirds from point of chest to point of buttock, and his body will be as deep as his legs are long. A horse with good balance carries himself and his rider with ease and efficiency of motion (fig. 4.7).

HINDQUARTERS

A horse's hindquarters should be at least one-third the length of his body in order to efficiently handle the rearward shift of weight that transpires when he is correctly ridden. A too short croup will not be able to support that weight, and the horse will travel in a hollow, strung-out fashion with his weight being pulled forward by his forelegs. A horse thus built will tend to

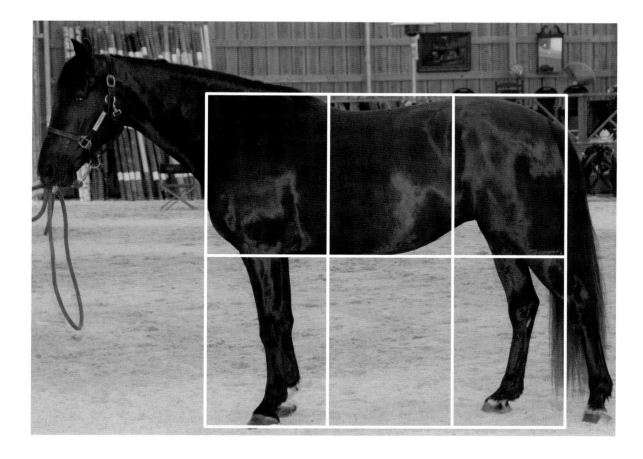

slip to a pace and stepping pace (see p. 16), and over time risks developing a swayed back as well as soundness issues.

The horse's croup—the line running from the highest point of the rump to the tail—should be level with his withers. A horse with a croup higher than his withers is a challenge to ride and train. His weight is carried forward over the forehand, causing him to be heavy in the bridle and hard to collect. Some young horses experience growth spurts and are rump-high until their front end grows to catch up. Therefore, until the horse is at least four years old it can be difficult to determine if this is a permanent conformational flaw. I especially discourage a heavy person from considering a rump-high horse as he will have poor weight-bearing capacity. Carrying too much weight over the forehand not only leads to rough gaits and early

4.7 This lovely Tennessee Walking Horse mare demonstrates the principles of good balance. Her torso can be equally divided into thirds, and her body is as deep as her legs are long.

breakdown, but may cause stumbling and falling, and a rump-high horse has an especially difficult time traveling downhill.

The horse's coupling should be smooth and well-muscled. Some horses have a "goose rump," where there is a raised bump at the top of the croup. This is primarily a cosmetic flaw, and rarely affects usefulness.

BACK

The horse's back from the rear of the withers to the point of hip should ideally be one-third the length of the horse's torso (see fig. 4.7, p. 97). A *longer back* has low weight-bearing capacity, is difficult to strengthen and develop, and weakens and becomes swayed (fig. 4.8). A *shorter back* has greater weight-bearing ability, but the horse may forge (his hind feet interfere with the action of his forefeet) and be less agile than a horse with a well-proportioned back.

4.8 This American Saddlebred has a long back and shallow hip that is horizontal to the ground, characteristics that increased his chances of becoming sway-backed.

As discussed earlier, it used to be *mistaken* "common knowledge" that a gaited horse needs to be ridden with a hollowed back (rather than the rounded-up back that I now recommend). For that reason, many gaited horses were bred to have a poorly conformed, weak back in order to "facilitate" their gaits. Many horses still suffer the consequences of those efforts in the form of a *swayed* back (a dipped appearance or downward curvature of the spine) and otherwise weak back conformation. For this reason, it is essential to carefully evaluate the horse's back to determine if it can remain functional and sound throughout the horse's lifetime.

The horse's back is not naturally constructed for bearing weight, but rather for transferring energy from the hindquarters to the forequarters. If this transmission of energy is interrupted because of poor back conformation, it causes the back to become weakened, which leads to a swayed back and other issues affecting soundness.

A *roached* back is an upward curve in the spine caused by spinal vertebrae that are raised above the horse's topline, creating a noticeable bump. This can interfere with the saddle, causing pain, and the horse may also be in pain because of impingement of the vertebrae. Roach-backed horses are stiffer and less agile than those with correct vertebral alignment. Because this condition interferes with the transfer of energy from the hindquarters, these horses are prone to develop a swayed back, which leads to other soundness issues.

The Back as It Affects Gait

If you plan to show your horse and need one that has a lot of overstride and a deep head nod, or if your breed standards call for a strong head shake, look for a horse with a *short back*. When there is less area under the horse's torso for his hind legs to cover, it is easy to achieve overstride. A short back transfers the energy from the hindquarters quickly through to the neck and head, which produces a strong head nod, or shake.

A very *long back* "absorbs" more of this forward energy before it reaches the neck, and therefore the horse will have less head nod or shake. A long-backed horse is less likely to have much, if any, overstride because of the length of stride needed to cover the ground under his long body.

HEAD AND NECK

The head and neck affect the animal's ability to give to his rider's hands, how much natural head nod is expressed, how easily he can maintain his balance under saddle, and how light he is on his forehand.

Head

As noted earlier, the head acts as a fulcrum to enable the horse to balance himself. Standards for the appearance of the horse's head vary widely from breed to breed.

In general, the head should be in proportion to the horse's overall body size and structure. The jaw and muzzle should not be excessively wide or narrow, as either condition makes it difficult to find an effective bit for the horse. The average-sized mouth should measure between $4\frac{1}{2}$ inches and $5\frac{1}{2}$ inches across. (You can determine the width of the horse's mouth by laying a piece of string across it at the bars, and then measuring the length of string required to go from one corner of the horse's mouth to the other.)

To ensure an unrestricted flow of air to the horse's lungs, the nostrils should be large and well-shaped. This is especially important for horses who participate in speed racking or other rigorous competitive events.

A horse with an upper jaw that extends further out than the lower jaw is said to have a *parrot mouth,* while one with a lower jaw that extends further out than the upper jaw has a *monkey mouth.* While these conditions are rare, they can affect the horse's ability to graze or chew food properly, which in turn affects thriftiness and the horse's overall condition.

Neck

The neck plays an important role in a horse's balance and maneuverability under saddle, and contributes to the head nodding or shaking characteristics of many of the smooth saddle gaits. A low-to-medium headset facilitates the running walk's signature deep head nod, which originates in the shoulders, while a high headset gives the horse a shallower "shaking" head motion that originates at the withers and is common to the fox trotting or racking horse.

The head should set into the neck at an angle, creating a long clean throatlatch that is neither overly thick, nor too thin (fig. 4.9). A thick throatlatch makes it difficult for the horse to flex at the poll and come onto the bridle, and a very thin throatlatch may interfere with breathing. There should be room enough for your fist to fit between the upper jowls and neck, and the poll should be arched or rounded rather than "hatchet shaped," otherwise the horse will lack sufficient ability to flex to the bridle.

A horse with a short-to-medium length neck (less than one-third the length of the horse's torso length) may be highly functional, assuming the neck is neither too thin nor too heavy (see below). An exceptionally long neck (more than one-third the length of the torso) may cause the horse to move with too much weight on the forehand. The ideal horse has a shapely neck with a smooth arch from the poll to the withers. This conformation is lovely to look at and indicates the horse is well-balanced and able to give softly to the bridle.

When the horse's neck is long and thin, he may be prone to overflexion and "false collection" (see p. 19). A horse with a short, thick, over-muscled neck is *bull-necked.* This causes him to go "heavy" on the forehand, and he will find it easy to stiffen through the neck and poll to resist the rider's rein aids. A *ewe neck* is a thin, underdeveloped neck with a concave dip on the top and a bulge on the bottom. Ewe-necked horses are often "stargazers" that tend to go hollow through the back, leading to unsoundness.

4.9 A Tennessee Walking Horse with a nicely set neck and neat throatlatch finds it easier to give softly to the bridle.

Other Conformational Considerations

A GOOD FOUNDATION

Good feet and legs are an important predictor of a long, sound riding career for the horse. No matter how willing and kind he may be, there's nothing rewarding about owning a relatively young horse that becomes unsound and expensive to maintain.

Check to see if there is swelling or scarring at any of the joints of the legs. Capped hocks, splints, ringbone or sidebone, bog spavin, and wind puffs are all signs of potential trouble. Many times these conditions are a result of poor conformation of the feet and legs.

FORELEGS: FRONT VIEW

Ideally, the horse's legs should emerge from the body in such a manner that when viewed from the front, a straight line drawn from the point of shoulder to the ground will bisect the forelegs (fig. 4.10 A).

4.10 A–C Ideally, a line drawn from the point of shoulder to the ground will bisect the front legs (A). Base-narrow (B) or base-wide (C) conformation can lead to unsoundness.

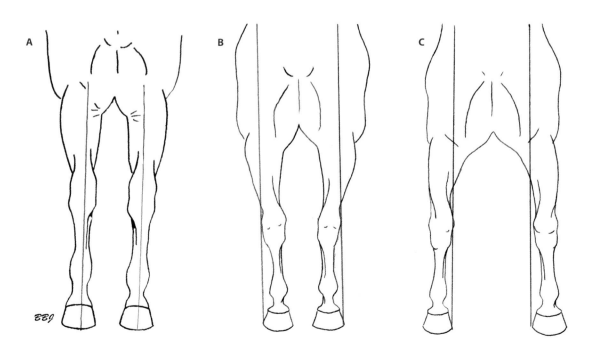

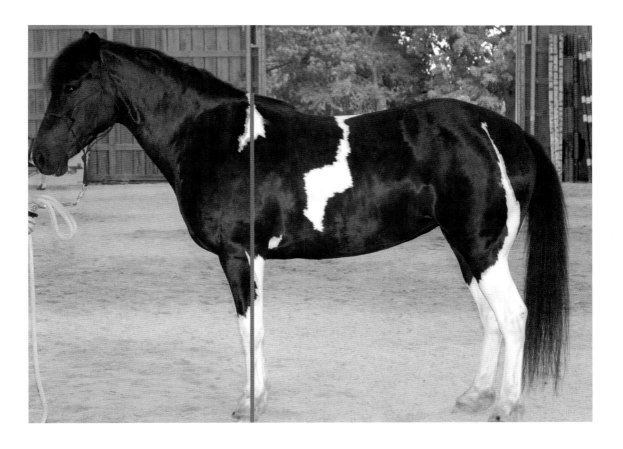

Some heavily muscled horses stand *base-narrow*—that is, with their feet closer together on the ground than where they spring from the chest (fig. 4.10 B). Such horses land on their feet unevenly, resulting in soundness problems, such as corns, sidebone, ringbone, or bruising of the heel. Horses with *base-wide* conformation also land unevenly on their feet, and suffer similar problems (fig. 4.10 C).

The leg should be straight from the shoulder to the ground. Knees that *bow out* ("bow-kneed"), or *bow in* ("knock-kneed"), place undue strain on lower legs, which can cause arthritis and other stress-related joint problems.

4.11 An imaginary line drawn from the front of the withers to the ground should bisect the horse's foreleg, ending at the heel as it does on this Spotted Saddle Horse.

FORELEGS: SIDE VIEW

Viewing the front of the standing horse from the side, you should be able to draw an imaginary line from the center of the scapula (high point of the withers) down through the center of the forelegs, ending at the heel of the front foot (fig. 4.11). A horse built this way will carry an appropriate percentage of weight on his forehand. As mentioned earlier in this chapter, length of stride in front will be hindered when the legs are set too far back *(camped under)* and the horse will be "front heavy." Forelegs set too far forward *(camped out)* place excessive stress on the knees, fetlocks, and feet, and are a cause of laminitis and navicular disease.

The horse's *pasterns* should have moderate length and angle. Upright pasterns cause disproportionate concussion to the foot and leg, while long, steeply angled pasterns exert excess stress on the pastern joint with every stride. Both of these conditions contribute to foreleg unsoundness.

On occasion, horses with an excessively steep angle to their pasterns *(coon-footed)* demonstrate a predisposition toward Degenerative

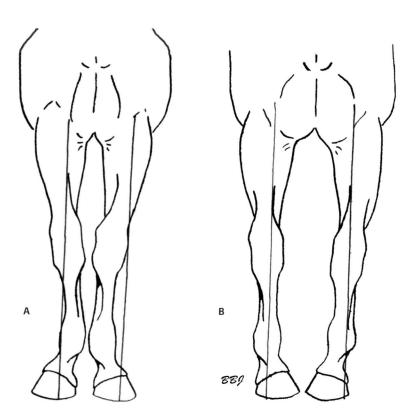

4.12 A & B A horse that toes out will tend to "paddle," or swing his legs outward with each stride (A). A horse that is toed-in will tend to "wing," or swing his legs inward with each stride.

Suspensory Ligament Desmitis (DSLD). This is especially to be suspected when the horse also has *wind puffs*, which are puffy swellings in the pasterns. Horses of Spanish origin are slightly more predisposed to this disease than the general gaited horse population.

FOREFEET

You like both feet to be directed straight forward—but this is seldom the case. A moderate degree of *toeing out* is acceptable, and may even be desirable for horses that have a great degree of overstride, as this condition helps avoid *forging*, which is when the toe of a hind foot interferes with the front foot.

Toeing out (fig. 4.12 A) results in a horse that "paddles"—that is, his forelegs swing outward, while a horse that *toes in* (fig. 4.12 B) "wings," or swings his forelegs inward with each stride. Either condition results in uneven weight distribution on the foot (fig. 4.13).

The forefeet should be identical in size and shape, without deep rings or ridges in the hoof wall. The coronary band (sometimes called the "coronet") is the ring of hairless hard tissue at the top of the foot, where the hoof originates. This should exhibit no injuries, scarring, lumps, or bumps because damage to the coronary band can negatively affect new hoof growth.

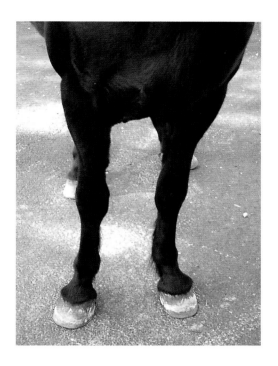

4.13 This horse is base-narrow, toes out, and has crooked bone from the point of chest to the ground. These kinds of conformational defects severely limit the useful life of the horse.

HIND LEG CONFORMATION

The horse's hind legs not only support the majority of his weight when he is being ridden with collection, and therefore need to be sturdy and correct in order to bear the majority of the horse and rider's weight, they are also the "power generators" that create impulsion (energy), for forward motion.

HIND LEGS: REAR VIEW

When viewing the horse from behind, plumb lines drawn from the buttocks to the ground should bisect the hind legs and feet (fig. 4.14 A). Deviations

4.14 A–C Plumb lines drawn from the buttocks to the ground should bisect the hind legs and feet (A). A horse that stands with his hocks close together and his toes pointed outward is said to be "cow-hocked" (B), and when the hocks bow outward and the toes point inward, he is "bandy-legged" (C).

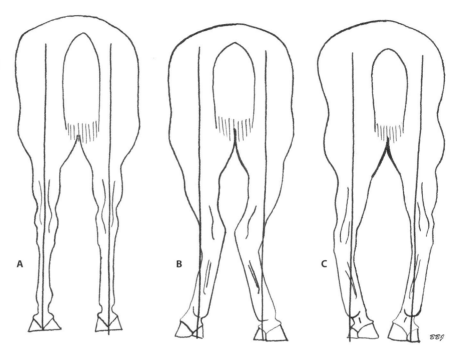

from this include horses that are *cow-hocked*—that is, they stand with their hocks close together and their toes pointed outward (fig. 4.14 B), also those that are *bandy-legged*, with hocks bowed outward and toes pointed inward (fig. 4.14 C). These deviations cause the horse to land unevenly on his feet, exerting excess stress on the joints, ligaments, and tendons. A bandy-legged horse, especially, should be avoided, as this condition makes the horse susceptible to stifle problems, and gaited horses, in general, are more prone to these issues.

Most horses are slightly cow-hocked, which is not problematic when they have large, well-formed hocks, and like toeing out, may prevent an especially long-strided horse from forging. When the condition is extreme, or the hocks are not large enough, this conformation predisposes the horse to *bone spavin,* a type of osteoarthritis.

The hind legs may also be *base-narrow* (too close together), or *base-wide* (too far apart). These conditions cause weight to be unevenly distributed on the feet and joints, leading to lameness.

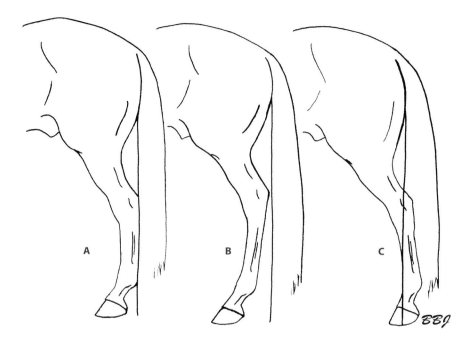

4.15 A–C "Ideal" hind-leg conformation, whereby an imaginary line drawn from the point of buttocks to the ground follows the cannon bone straight to the ground (A). Slightly "sickle-hocked" (B), is acceptable in some breeds of gaited horses, as it indicates long hind legs. However, the horse should not be extremely "under himself" (as shown in fig. 4.16 B, p. 108). When the horse is slightly sickle-hocked, he should have clean, strong bone to ensure adequate weight support and large, well-formed hocks to give them the ability to absorb shock. "Camped-out" (C) places excess strain on the hocks and stifles, and may cause the horse to be prone to unsoundness.

HIND LEGS: SIDE VIEW

It is widely taught that the horse's hind limbs should be "straight"—that is, when an imaginary line is dropped from the point of buttock to the ground, it should fall down the back of the horse until it reaches the cannon bone and parallel the line of the cannon bone to the ground, ending slightly behind the foot (fig. 4.15 A).

This rule of thumb isn't necessarily true with gaited horses, as many are slightly *sickle-hocked.* A sickle-hocked horse's hind cannons are angled inward under the body, rather than running straight up and down. It is acceptable for a horse to be slightly sickle-hocked, providing his hocks are large and well-formed so they can act as effective "shock absorbers" with each hind stride (fig. 4.15 B). An extremely sickle-hocked horse, or one with small or misshapen hocks, should be avoided.

A horse that is *camped-out* tends to travel with his legs dragging behind him, making it difficult for him to generate sufficient energy from the hindquarters and collect properly on the bridle (fig. 4.15 C).

4.16 A & B A little curve at the back of the gaskin (thigh) and short cannon bones causes a horse to be short- or "post-legged" (A). A post-legged horse has choppy gaits and his legs suffer from the effects of excess concussion. The condition prevents the horse from being able to carry his weight efficiently, and predisposes him to conditions such as arthritis and locking stifles. In contrast, a deep curve to the back of the gaskin and very long cannon bones cause a horse to be unacceptably sickle-hocked (B).

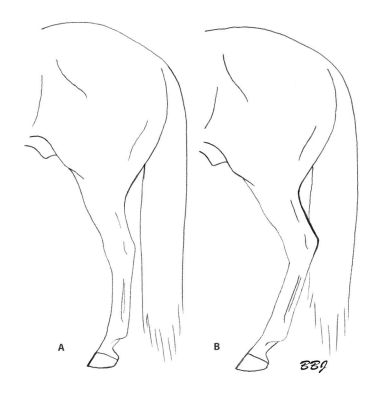

There is a curve at the back of the thigh *(gaskin)*, which contributes to the length of the hind leg. When the gaskin is too straight, and the cannons bones short, the horse is "post-legged" (fig. 4.16 A). This is a serious conformational fault in any breed of gaited horse. It prevents the horse from being able to get his hind legs underneath him for collection, predisposes him to arthritis, and contributes to an *upward fixated patella,* or "locking stifle." I advise readers to avoid purchasing a gaited horse with this conformational flaw.

A horse with too much curve at the back of the gaskin and too-long cannon bones will have excessively long hind legs, causing him to be unacceptably sickle-hocked (fig. 4.16 B).

CHAPTER 5

Bits and Bitting

Tacking Up for Success

MANY UNEDUCATED RIDERS WHO PURCHASE A NEW horse make the mistake of using whatever tack the seller used, not realizing only a small percentage of owners really understand what works best for their horse. Or, they just throw on the same bridle and saddle they used on their former mount. They assume—incorrectly—there is little difference from one horse to another. Though nothing could be further from the truth, there are enough similarities among gaited horses to be able to make some correct assumptions about the kind of tack most appropriate for your animal, *but only if you understand the dynamics of his motion* (see Evaluating Saddle Dynamics, p. 127).

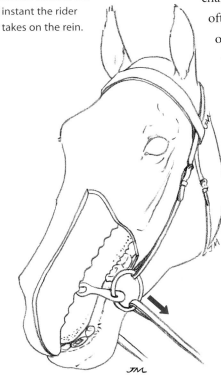

5.1 A snaffle bit works directly from the rider's hand and rein to the horse's mouth. It takes finesse to correctly work a horse in a snaffle bit, as the mouthpiece makes contact the instant the rider takes on the rein.

A horse can only perform well when he is fitted with suitable tack. Many problems I encounter when working with clients are rooted in their inappropriate choices in this department. And, because good tack is expensive to purchase, some riders are reluctant to make necessary changes. Unfortunately, any short-term savings achieved this way are often outweighed by long-term losses when the horse goes unsound or develops dangerous pain-related behavioral issues. Because of this, I have devoted a great deal of this book to helping you determine the kind of tack best for you and your horse. Should you fail to make progress in your training, you would do well to come back to this material in order to reassess your horse's equipment, as it is commonly the root cause of otherwise "mystifying" problems.

I discuss bits in this chapter, and deal with saddles next, in chapter 6 (see p. 123).

Bits

Though we're discussing gaited horses, it should be noted that any good bit can be used on any kind of horse, gaited or otherwise. Some breeds of gaited horses have a sad history of abuse, including the use of harsh bits. It seems only fitting that they benefit first from the increased understanding horsemen are beginning to have regarding the mechanics of bitting.

5.2 Simple "O"-ring snaffle bit. Some common snaffle bits have "D"-rings, or straight cheeks, and there are also three-piece mouthpieces—the so-called "dog bone" or French-mouth snaffles. The action in the horse's mouth with any jointed snaffle is similar, and the rider should always check for the potential of pinching at the center joint(s).

5.3 The Imus Training Transition Bit™ has a rounded or "barrel-shaped" mouthpiece to allow plenty of room for the horse's tongue. The mouthpiece has a center joint, covered by a copper roller to prevent the joint from pinching the horse's tongue. The mouthpiece is designed to extend slightly beyond the corners of the horse's lips to prevent chafing—this also allows it to fit a wider variety of horses.

SNAFFLE BITS

A snaffle bit is one that allows *direct* communication from the rider's hand to the horse's tongue, bars, and cheeks—as opposed to a curb bit, which works more *indirectly* (fig. 5.1, and see p. 113 for more on curbs). A snaffle is the best bit for a very young horse for several reasons. First, he may become confused by rein cues coming from the poll, chin, and mouth, which is the case when using a curb bit. Second, when I start riding a young horse I pull his head directly around turns using a "leading" rein. Most curb bits cannot be used this way. Last but not least, a young horse may suddenly stumble or trip, as he is not yet used to balancing a rider. The leverage on even a well-designed curb bit can have disastrous effects on a tender "baby-skin" tongue if the rider should, by mistake, instinctively pull back hard on the reins. Many horses bear tongue scars that prove this point.

The snaffle works directly off the rider's hands. There are no shanks, no leverage, no action at the poll or on the chin groove (fig. 5.2). The rider takes on the rein and the mouthpiece engages. The rider needs to have a fairly secure seat and soft, yielding hands, and give very clear, direct signals to the young horse using the reins to "lead" him in the right direction. There's little chance of damaging the horse's tongue and bars (assuming the mouthpiece isn't too thin, or twisted—see p. 112), as there is no leverage between the mouthpiece and a curb strap or chain, as there is with a curb bit.

A good snaffle bit has a fairly thick mouthpiece that prevents cutting into the tender membranes. I prefer a "barrel-shaped" mouthpiece with a slight upward curve. It may be jointed or have a center pivot, but cannot be solid. It can fit close to the side of the horse's lips or, if designed like my Imus Training Transition Bit™, it may extend as much as $^1/_2$ inch beyond them (fig. 5.3).

When using a jointed snaffle bit, you should determine there is no way for it to pinch the horse's tongue. Do this by laying the bit across the underside of your forearm, and twist it back and forth to see if the joint grabs skin at the center, pinching it (figs. 5.4 A & B). If it does, either replace the bit or wrap the center joint with "bit tape," a product that can be purchased online and in most tack shops. (Note: Snaffle cheek pieces should also have smooth joints to avoid pinching or chafing the corners of the horse's lips.)

Some people use a snaffle bit with a twisted wire mouthpiece, claiming it "sensitizes" the mouth. If you consider a horse with an abraded, tender, sore tongue and bars to be sensitized, then I guess that's a true statement. I prefer to maintain my horse's comfort and peace-of-mind, and work at developing straightforward communication.

While there are exceptions to this rule, most riders have neither the time nor skill required to train a horse to gait in correct form using a snaffle bit only. Therefore, it is generally advisable to move the horse into a well-designed curb bit once he is pretty well green-broke. By this, I mean he can balance a rider over all kinds of terrain, is sure of his footing, and responds quickly and easily to all basic riding cues, such as turn, halt, stop, and rein-back.

5.4 A & B Here I demonstrate how just laying this jointed snaffle bit on my arm—without any pressure taken on it—causes it to pinch (A). After removing the bit, this is the bruise that resulted (B). Imagine how a horse's delicate tongue responds to this type of discomfort.

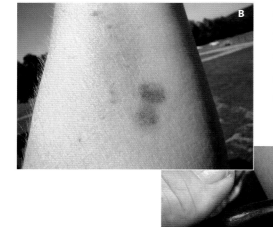

CURB BITS

Rather than working directly from the rider's hand to the horse's mouth as a snaffle does, a curb bit exerts pressure at the poll, chin groove, mouth, bars, and lips (fig. 5.5). How much pressure is created depends on the length and design of the upper and lower shanks, because shanks create leveraged pressure on the horse's tongue. This means that the pressure the rider puts on the rein is multiplied by the time the chin strap and mouthpiece are engaged. This is why a poorly designed curb bit—especially one with very long shanks—can cause the horse a lot of discomfort.

After a horse is four years old, when the tongue has become less "baby-like" and is not so susceptible to inadvertent damage, a curb bit can be safely introduced (fig. 5.6). It offers the rider the opportunity for logical and consecutive communication not available with a snaffle. When you use a well-designed curb bit your horse is mentally and physically prepared for your request in a logical 1-2-3—"Lower, Tuck, Take"—manner.

Lower

Because of the purchase (see p. 115), slight pressure is exerted at the poll when you pull on the reins. This notifies the horse of an impending request, while encouraging him to lower his head. You can see how this works by placing light downward pressure at the back and top of someone's head. Note how it requires very little pressure to cause her to lower her head. This head-lowering serves to a) relax the horse, and b) prepare the animal physically for the next step of the request.

Tuck

After the poll pressure, the action of the curb strap (or chain) comes into play. It should be attached on the top ring of the bit—beneath the headstall—and adjusted so there's approximately 3 inches between the chin groove and the curb strap when the reins are at

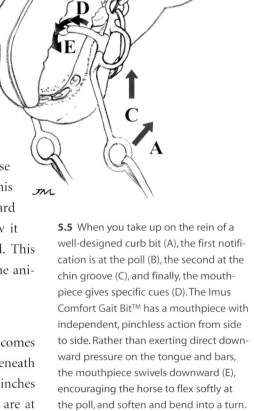

5.5 When you take up on the rein of a well-designed curb bit (A), the first notification is at the poll (B), the second at the chin groove (C), and finally, the mouthpiece gives specific cues (D). The Imus Comfort Gait Bit™ has a mouthpiece with independent, pinchless action from side to side. Rather than exerting direct downward pressure on the tongue and bars, the mouthpiece swivels downward (E), encouraging the horse to flex softly at the poll, and soften and bend into a turn.

rest. To measure, place three fingers sideways between the curb strap and chin groove. With this proper adjustment, there will be a beat of time between the horse being notified at the poll to lower his head, and when the curb strap contacts the chin groove.

If you look straight ahead, lower your head, and tuck your chin, you'll notice this action stretches and relaxes your upper neck and spine. It is the human physical equivalent of a horse "stretching to meet the bit," which is what is happening when the horse first lowers his head, then flexes at the poll to tuck his chin. You now have the very early stages of collection before you've even engaged the mouthpiece. (I say "early stages" because true collection involves the entire horse's body, and not just his neck and head.)

Take

Finally, the mouthpiece takes hold and communicates your specific request, whether it is to halt, turn, rein back, half-halt, or perform some other movement.

"Lower, Tuck, and Take" is why the mechanics of a good curb bit can be advantageous as you school your older horse. Of course, the problem is that many bits on the market are not designed to permit this kind of logical, sequential communication.

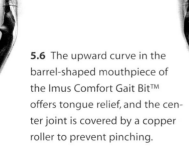

5.6 The upward curve in the barrel-shaped mouthpiece of the Imus Comfort Gait Bit™ offers tongue relief, and the center joint is covered by a copper roller to prevent pinching.

I'm often asked if it's necessary to use a curb strap or chain with a curb bit. My answer is an emphatic "Yes." Without the curb strap, the mouthpiece merely gets pulled around in the horse's mouth. You lose the important request for the horse to "Tuck" and will most likely teach him to stargaze, as opposed to engaging properly and collecting his forward energy on the bit.

UNDERSTANDING EFFECTIVE CURB BIT DESIGN

Let's consider what constitutes a good, effective, and pain-free curb bit. It is not necessarily true that any bit with long shanks is very severe. The entire design is what determines severity.

Upper Purchase and Lower Shank

When considering a curb bit, an important feature is the relationship of the *purchase* (upper shank) to the lower shank. This relationship determines the timing and severity of contact at the poll, chin groove, and mouth.

The purchase should be approximately half the length of the lower shank. When the purchase is *too short* there's no early communication at the poll encouraging the horse to lower his head, and the horse is simply grabbed in the chin and mouth at approximately the same time. This can cause a high-headed position with little engagement through the body, promoting "false collection" (see p. 19).

On the other hand, when the purchase is *too long* there's an exaggerated request at the poll, and all of the actions take hold at one time. You are likely to get overflexing with this kind of bit—rather than holdng his head vertical to the ground, the horse will be "behind the vertical," with his nose tucked toward his chest.

A 2 1/2-inch purchase gives an acceptable amount of pressure at the poll. Given the ideal two-to-one proportion of purchase to shank, this means the lower shank is approximately 5 inches long. Combine this with a 1/2-inch thick mouthpiece, and the curb bit has a total shank length of 8 inches.

Many people mistakenly assume this length shank to be an extremely severe bit because the shank's leverage increases the amount of pressure exerted when the rein is pulled—the longer the shanks, the greater the pressure. However, the design elements I just outlined cause the pressure to be effectively distributed, rather than concentrated primarily on the tongue and bars. Also, a long shank has to be pulled back farther than a bit with a short shank before pressure is applied, which gives the horse more time to respond. A properly designed long-shanked bit is an effective and forgiving tool for communication between horse and rider, as well as an excellent mechanical aid to help the horse perform his smooth saddle gaits in good form.

5.7 This curb bit combines a solid mouthpiece with loose cheeks. This is always a bad idea, as it gives the rider the incorrect impression that it can be effectively used for direct reining or one-rein stops. In truth, when the rider tries to direct rein, the whole bit is pulled out of position, causing discomfort and confusion for the horse.

Mouthpiece

The mouthpiece of a good curb bit should be smooth and reasonably thick, with a jointed center pivot so the rider can work the horse with one or two reins. The center joint needs to be pinch-free, meaning it is covered with a roller, and there can be little or no "play" in the center of the mouthpiece. A thin mouthpiece has a cutting action on the soft tissues of the horse's tongue and bars, and as in the case of the snaffle, this is especially true with a twisted wire mouthpiece.

Bit Misconceptions

Once broken down, it's easy to comprehend the mechanical action of various types of bits. However, there are a several common misconceptions that I would like to eliminate. Here are 10 bit "myths" to lay to rest:

MYTH 1: There are no harsh bits, only harsh hands.
Truth: Certainly, there are bits with a harsh effect regardless of how tactful the rider may be. This is especially true of long-shanked bits with short purchases (see p. 115).

MYTH 2: All bits can be severe in the wrong hands.
Truth: A well-designed curb bit can be very forgiving, even in insensitive hands.

MYTH 3: Bits with "broken" (jointed) mouthpieces are snaffle bits.
Truth: Not all bits with broken mouthpieces are snaffle bits. Any bit that has shanks to which the reins attach is a curb bit, whether the mouthpiece is solid or jointed. Snaffle bits have "O"- or "D"-rings, or full cheekpieces, attached to both sides of the mouthpiece, and the reins work directly from the rider's hand to these.

MYTH 4: Snaffle bits are inherently milder than curb bits.
Truth: A snaffle bit works directly from the rider's seat and hands to the horse's mouth. Therefore, when the rider has anything less than perfect balance and timing, the horse is likely to experience a continuous "snatching" on his sensitive mouth. For this reason, some curb (shanked) bits are more humane than snaffle (non-shanked) bits.

MYTH 5: All long-shanked bits are inhumane, unforgiving, and severe.
Truth: A bit with the proper ratio of purchase (upper shank to lower shank) and a well designed mouthpiece is an effective, humane communication device, even when in less tactful hands (see more about curb bits on p. 113).

Like the snaffle, I prefer a jointed mouthpiece that has a barrel shape to each side offering plenty of tongue relief, since a horse has a thick tongue. When a mouthpiece has a center joint and is barrel-shaped rather than pressing directly onto the tongue, each side can pivot forward and down on the tongue and bars. This action encourages the horse to drop his head and bend into turns when the rider takes on one rein. As horses instinctively resist *direct* pressure, this type of *indirect* pressure is effective at eliciting a relaxed response. A horse that is soft and yielding is responsive to his rider

MYTH 6: A horse that is difficult to stop requires a more severe bit.

Truth: A horse that is difficult to stop doesn't need a harsher bit; he needs to be retrained to give to lighter and lighter rein pressure. Increasing the severity of the bit only increases the horse's ability to resist his rider's aids, ultimately exacerbating the problem.

MYTH 7: Bits with solid mouthpieces can be used for direct reining.

Truth: Bits with a one-piece, solid mouthpiece—such as a grazing bit—should never be used for direct reining, lateral work, or one-rein stops. At best, the horse is just yanked around by his mouth. At worst, he devel-

ops a strong insensitivity to his rider's rein. A loose-cheeked curb bit with a solid mouthpiece—such as a port bit with hinged cheek-pieces—is even worse than one that is solid at the cheeks because it gives the rider the illusion that he can work effectively off one rein, but the solid mouthpiece makes that impossible, and confuses the horse (fig. 5.7).

MYTH 8: The Tom Thumb bit is very mild.

Truth: So called "Tom Thumb" bits—or any other bit that combines a broken mouthpiece without a copper roller with shanks—can be extraordinarily severe (see p. 120 for further discussion).

MYTH 9: The "Wonder" bit is an effective tool for gaited horses, and creates a good "headset."

Truth: Some trainers claim they use a "Wonder" bit (otherwise known as the gag or elevator bit) to help a horse "find" his correct headset. Unfortunately, these bits also work on the pain-avoidance principle (see p. 118).

MYTH 10: Bitless bridles and hackamores are more humane than metal bits.

Truth: The idea of riding without a bit might seem ideal, but a hackamore and other bitless bridles are often very painful for the horse because they exert pressure on the tender cartilage of the head (see p. 121 for more).

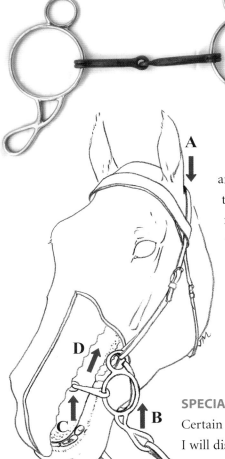

5.8 The Wonder bit—also called a "gag" or "elevator" bit—creates an exaggerated "headset": When the cheek pieces rotate in response to the rein, an excess amount of pressure is exerted at the poll. The mouthpiece slides upward on the loose cheek rings and presses at the very top of the horse's tongue. The horse tucks his chin as tightly as possible toward his chest to avoid all this pressure.

5.9 A gag bit places extreme stress at the poll (A) and chin strap (B). This encourages the horse to quickly flex at the poll and tuck his chin, creating "false collection" (see p. 19). To further encourage an exaggerated, tucked headset, the mouthpiece collapses across the tongue and bars (C) while rotating up high against the horse's palate (D).

and less prone to resistance. When the mouthpiece lies straight across the mouth, the tongue is "trapped," and it's impossible for the animal to swallow. I get a kick out of how impressed some people are when a horse exhibits a foamy mouth. Excessive drooling is a result of the tongue being trapped by a straight-mouthed bit. While you want the horse to have a moist mouth, it's not necessary for an animal to slobber all the way down the rail or trail!

In addition to these features, a curb mouthpiece designed to extend wider than the horse's lips allows a bit to fit a variety of horses, and avoids pinching the corners of the mouth.

SPECIALIZED BITS AND BRIDLES

Certain curb bits are used to produce a specific action, or headset, and here I will discuss the ones most commonly used with gaited horses.

Gag (Elevator) Bits

A gag bit—such as the "Wonder" bit—is utilized to achieve a "tucked-in" headset. Because a gag bit's shanks rotate downward when the rider takes on the rein, there's exaggerated pressure at the poll (fig. 5.8). When the mouthpiece engages it suddenly pulls hard and collapses across the tongue and bars. At the same time, the mouthpiece rotates up high on the tongue, presses hard at the corners of the horse's mouth, and the center joint raises to hit the very back of the horse's palate. This action is why it is called a "gag" bit (fig. 5.9).

To avoid the pain of this contact, the horse overflexes and tucks his neck in, giving the horse's head and neck a "collected" appearance. When he fails to respond in this manner as soon as the rider takes on the reins, he receives a sudden and severe gag action once the bit is fully engaged. The time between the rider taking up the reins and the mouthpiece engaging is only about one second, so most horses learn to quickly respond to the initial rein pressure by overflexing—though many become "stargazers" in an attempt to avoid this unpleasant contact.

Besides the immediate pain inflicted, there are other negative long-term effects of using such a bit. True collection originates through the haunches, loins and back, allowing the horse to move in a way that is healthy and well-balanced. Encouraging "false collection" like this with the bit, results in a hollow back, and hock and stifle issues, which are highly detrimental to the horse's long-term soundness.

Walking Horse Bit

Tennessee Walking Horses are often trained for a high headset with an elevated neck and the nose tucked toward the chest. Traditional Walking Horse bits have a very short purchase and long shanks, which fosters this appearance (fig. 5.10). Because of the short purchase there is no initial notification at the horse's poll when the rider takes on the reins, so the horse does not know to lower his head and neck in preparation for contact at the chin groove and mouth. The mouthpiece and curb chain take hold while his head is still "up in the air," and there is severe pressure on his tongue and bars because of the leverage created by the long shanks. He quickly tucks his chin in an effort to avoid this painful contact, which results in a horse with a high, tucked-in headset, and once again we have the problem of "false collection."

Double-Twisted Wire Walking Horse Bit

A trainer who wants to develop more head nod in a Tennessee Walking Horse—something highly desired in the show ring—may resort to the long-shanked, double-twisted wire bit (fig. 5.11). All horses have some degree of head nod when performing a running walk. This bit takes advantage of that. The double-twisted mouthpiece abrades the horse's tongue and bars. Every

5.10 This common Walking Horse bit has a very short purchase and long shanks. It gives no notification at the poll before taking at the chin strap and mouth so the horse is encouraged to maintain a high headset with an exaggerated amount of flexion at the poll. The port is not high enough to be effective, and the loose cheeks will pinch unless bit guards are used. (Unfortunately, bit guards eliminate effective communication with the corners of the horse's sensitive lips, so the rider's goal should be to use a bit that does not pinch or chafe, and therefore doesn't need them.) The solid mouthpiece combined with loose cheeks makes this an ineffective bit for any kind of direct rein (see p. 117).

5.11 The double-twisted wire Walking Horse bit creates a false head nod and is extremely harsh. The twisted mouthpieces cause the horse's tongue and bars to become sore. Every time the horse's head comes down in a natural nod, for balance, the mouthpiece collapses severely over the tender tongue and bars, and the center joints rise to hit the horse's palate, causing him to quickly snatch his head upward, away from the discomfort. The center joints are offset and hit the roof of the mouth in different places so the horse cannot learn to place his head in any one position to avoid the pain.

time the horse's head comes down in its natural nod, the mouthpiece collapses across the sored tongue and bars, while the two center joints rise to hit the palate, over and over again. The horse quickly raises his head higher to avoid this painful contact. This gives the *impression* of a greater head nod.

However, it should be noted that this head-nodding appearance is deceptive. The artificial head nod produced by this style of bit causes the horse to snap his head *upward* with each stride. The *true* head nod of a running-walk horse is produced as the horse uses his neck and head for balance with each stride.

Because the rear-stride length of a running walk is exceptionally long, the head nod is usually deeper than with another type of gait. This natural head nod originates in the upper shoulders, and the head nods deeply *downward* with each stride.

Tom Thumb Bit

Many bits that combine shanks with broken mouthpieces without a copper roller, such as the Tom Thumb bit, are extraordinarily severe. The slightest take on the reins causes the mouthpiece to collapse across the horse's tongue and bars, the joint in the middle to rise to hit the upper palate, and the curb chain to tighten up, placing the horse's entire lower jaw in a vice-like grip (fig. 5.12).

This type of bit, like many others, works off the principle of "pain avoidance." Many riders confuse a fast, obedient response with willing cooperation. There's a vast difference between the two. Although horses seemingly "work well" out of these rollerless, jointed curbs (all bits with shanks are curb bits, regardless of the style of the mouthpiece), it is simply because they are responding quickly to the pain in order to have as little contact with the bit as possible.

Colt-Training Bit

While I don't believe in starting young horses in a curb bit, some trainers do—and one of the "bits of choice" is particularly severe. This is a so-called "colt-training" bit with a thin, jointed mouthpiece and an equal length of purchase and shank (fig. 5.13). As discussed before, many people assume that short shanks and jointed mouthpieces are inherently mild, which is *not* the case. This kind of bit actually takes a strong hold on the horse's poll, chin groove, and mouth all at once, and the thin mouthpiece cuts deeply into the young horse's delicate tongue and bars. Again, the rider attains compliance through the horse's avoidance of pain.

Hackamores and Bitless Bridles

Hackamores and many bitless bridles also work off the principle of pain avoidance by causing the cartilage that runs down each side of the horse's head to become sore and tender. To understand how much pain pressure from these devices can cause, take your index finger and push hard on the cartilage at the side of your nose and hold it there for five seconds. Repeat this a dozen times over the next hour. Wait an hour or so, and do this again. It is remarkable how sore that area becomes when regular pressure is applied! The cartilage on the horse's face is equally sensitive, and the pressure of a hackamore or bitless bridle against that soft tissue creates swelling and tenderness that the horse avoids by responding quickly to a rider's cues. These tack items may seem effective, but are not necessarily humane.

There are several bitless bridle designs, and some of these will not cause pain. Even so, it has been my experience that a good bit does more to help a horse remain collected when he is gaiting.

5.12 A Tom Thumb bit exerts pressure at several locations—some of it very painful—including: pressure at the poll (A) but not very much before the bit takes a strong hold at the chin groove (B), creating leverage. Again, with little advance warning, the rollerless jointed mouthpiece collapses across the tongue and bars (C & E)—often pinching the tongue—before the jointed center rises to poke the horse's palate (D).

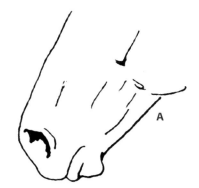

Proper Bit Adjustment

I'm often asked if there should be one or two wrinkles at the corners of the horse's mouth when the bridle is properly adjusted. There is no correct answer to this question, as the way a bit is adjusted depends on the conformation of the horse's mouth. Some horses have a shallow mouth and lips, and deeper-set bars (fig. 5.14 A). By the time the mouthpiece of the bit is properly adjusted on the bars, there may be a wrinkle or two at the corners of the lips. Other horses have a very deep mouth and lips, with bars set more forward (fig. 5.14 B). These horses may have minimum contact at the corners of the lips when the bit is properly adjusted. For this reason, the old "two wrinkles at the corners" adage should be thrown out of the window.

When adjusting the bit, make sure it is contacting the corners of the lips and not just hanging loose, or you risk it banging around and hitting teeth. Fit it to the corners of the lips, over the bars. Run your index and middle finger along each side of the mouthpiece and work the reins to make sure the bit isn't going to hit any teeth when used. Then touch the horse's tongue to make sure he can't get his tongue over the bit. If everything checks out, you can ride on. However, you may want to adjust the bit up or down, depending on how the horse responds to your cues.

5.13 This type of bit is often marketed for training young horses, and people have the misconception that the short shanks make it a mild choice. The equal length of the purchase to the lower shank causes bits such as this to take hold of the horse's mouth suddenly. Combining a jointed mouthpiece without a copper roller with shanks—of any length—often causes a bit to be severe.

5.14 A & B When adjusting the bit on a horse with a shallow mouth (A), there may be a wrinkle or two at the corners of the lips. If you deliberately adjust the bit so there are two wrinkles on a horse with a deep mouth (B), the bit is probably set far too high.

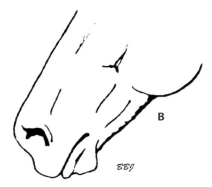

CHAPTER 6

Saddle Fit and Dynamics

The Rider's Seat Position

HOW YOU SIT AND RIDE THE GAITED HORSE HAS A strong impact on how well—or even if—he can perform a smooth saddle gait. While good position on a trotting horse is important, the truth is that no matter how you are seated, when you ask this horse to speed up from the walk, he is going to transition to a trot or canter. Nothing is that automatic with our multi-geared gaited horses! I include information about gaited-horse equitation in this chapter because the saddle you choose largely determines your ability to maintain a correct seat, and many saddles on the market today do not encourage a naturally balanced bareback riding position, which is the ideal seat for riding a gaited horse.

Traditionally, gaited-horse riders have been taught to sit back toward the loins to encourage the gaits. This helped (according to the theories of the day) to free up the horse's shoulders and lighten his front end, and thus encourage the gait. For this reason, photos of gaited horses often show people riding in very poor form: buttocks pushed against the cantle, shoulders slouched, toes pointed straight down, and hands either placed too far forward, or tucked up under their chest. (I call this the "turtle position.") When riding this way, the rider's weight is situated too far back, interfering with the wave-like action of the gaited horse's back muscles that I discuss on p. 128.

In contrast, there are riding instructors who insist the "correct" form of the seat is when a rider's ears, spine, hip, and heels are in perfect alignment, whether riding English or Western. While this might make sense for people who need their feet directly beneath them for posting the trot or standing in the stirrups over a jump, in my opinion—and experience—it is not the best profile for riding a gaited horse. This rigid position throws the rider's weight and center of gravity forward, which is only required when the rider needs to compensate for being seated behind the horse's true center of gravity. The majority of saddles on the market are designed to place the rider in the "correct" seat, with stirrup placement that virtually forces the rider's leg into an unnatural position directly beneath her.

BAREBACK SEAT

I have asked students who enjoy riding bareback to demonstrate various types of equitation without a saddle in order to better understand which riding position is best for riding gaited horses. Believe me, when a saddle is no longer there to help a rider balance, you can be sure she is seated in the ideal riding position—otherwise, she'll fall off!

Consequently, it is apparent to me the best possible seat position is identical to the one taken by naturally talented bareback riders who position themselves immediately behind the withers, over the horse's true center of gravity (figs. 6.1 A & B). Their legs tend to drift slightly forward and their upper body may—or may not—lean slightly back. What I've observed is that the upper body position largely depends on the individual's center of gravity.

A person with a long waist tends to position her upper body slightly behind her seat, while one with a short waist and upper body rides more vertically.

SADDLE POSITION

The majority of saddles on the market are designed to be placed so the front edge of the saddle-tree bars rest—or press—in the groove just behind either side of the withers at the top edge of the horse's scapula (where horses often develop white hairs). This positioning places riders 3 to 4 inches further back than they would sit when riding bareback. It forces the bulk of their weight onto the horse's back just in front of the lumbosacral area of the spine—the weakest point of the horse's back. Weight placed here significantly interferes with the rolling, back-to-front motion of the gaited-horse's topline (see sidebar, p. 132), causing the horse to flatten out and stiffen up when the motion meets the resistance of the rider's weight on the rear portion of the saddle-tree bars.

When a rider is positioned more forward, in the natural bareback riding position, her weight does not interfere with the natural action of the

6.1 A & B This rider naturally assumes the most secure seat when riding bareback: immediately behind the withers, with her feet slightly forward (A). Her horse appears comfortable and unconcerned. I ask the rider to move 3 inches further back—where saddles normally seat a rider—and to assume the "correct" equitation position with her ears, spine, and heels in alignment (B). The horse immediately stiffens and becomes alert and the rider has trouble balancing in this position without the aid of a saddle.

topline, nor does it press into the most vulnerable point on the back. Positioned over the horse's true center of gravity, the rider feels a good deal more "with" her horse's motion, more secure, and able to respond promptly to the horse's actions. She also won't experience the feeling of a "camel walk" (see p. 222) so severely—she is over the "hinge" part of the horse's topline where there is the least amount of motion, as opposed to closer to where the action of the hind legs transfers up through to the loins and back.

When a saddle enables riders to position their leg in this more natural position, it relieves stress on hips, knees, and ankles, thus promoting rider relaxation. As horses tend to "mirror" their riders, this leads to a more relaxed and responsive mount.

For all of these reasons, I highly recommend a riding seat identical to a bareback rider's—that is, seated immediately behind the withers and shoulders, with the legs slightly forward, the feet level, and the upper body assuming a natural position based on the rider's individual structure.

How a Saddle Can "Make or Break" the Horse

I personally understand how choosing the right saddle for a horse is both a financial and emotional investment—not only are good quality saddles expensive, but a conscientious rider is dismayed when she discovers her saddle has caused pain to her horse.

When I acquired my first gaited horse, Fancy, like most new gaited horse owners, I had a number of issues to resolve. Fancy performed a hard, very uncomfortable pace. On the trail, she was unpredictable and spooky, and generally became worse as the ride went on, and more unmanageable as the riding season progressed. She was "buddy sour" and had a tendency to rush, especially when headed for home. My background, though informal, had been in dressage, and I was continually thwarted in my attempt to get her to work off the haunches in a soft, properly collected form. As a result, she was stiff and unresponsive to my seat, leg, and rein cues—it was like trying to ride an out-of-control freight train!

Though I had four young children at home and could ill afford to spend more money on horse tack, I was convinced that many of Fancy's problems were due to poorly fitting tack. It was just a gut feeling, but one I couldn't shake. So I read up on the subject and bought a so-called "gaited-horse" saddle, expecting great results. To my consternation, my purchase produced no improvement.

As it happened, a local tack store owner was carrying a new style of saddle that boasted flexible tree bars, which purported to offer a horse greater liberty of motion through the topline. This concept made immediate sense to me. Fortunately, I was able to trade my new gaited-horse saddle for the one with the flexible tree bars. The change in Fancy was immediate and remarkable. Within ten minutes of my mounting, she relaxed and lowered her head—both firsts. I was able to obtain a nice flat walk with good energy. After only a couple of rides in her new saddle, she became less dependent on her buddies, and more responsive to me. Her spooky behavior disappeared and her saddle gaits became smoother. Best of all, I discovered a horse who *loved to go!*

This was my first hint that fitting a saddle on a gaited horse is not as straightforward as fitting other horses. My curiosity was aroused: Was this experience a fluke? As I began working with a number of gaited horses, it became apparent that many behavioral problems originated with discomfort experienced from improper *saddle dynamics* as well as poor saddle fit. These are two separate but interrelated issues.

As I began working with a number of gaited horses, it became apparent that many behavioral problems originated with discomfort experienced from improper saddle dynamics as well as poor saddle fit.

Saddle Dynamics

Let's first consider saddle dynamics (see also p. 138). A saddle is the interface between two flexible bodies—the rider's and the horse's. It's a fairly easy matter to create saddles that are comfortable for the rider as that's long been the primary consideration when designing them. Until relatively recently, the horse's comfort received less attention. This has changed over the past decade, and especially so for gaited horses. Many people taking up gaited riding are mature and just getting into (or back into) horses, and are hungry for information. They possess great empathy for their animals, are not deeply steeped in traditional dogma, and are determined to do things right. All this bodes well for the horse!

UNIQUE ACTION OF THE GAITED HORSE'S BACK

As I worked with a larger number of gaited horses, another aspect of choosing an appropriate saddle became evident. I observed that, unlike a trotting horse whose back muscle moves up and down, the back muscle *(longissimus dorsi)* of a gaited horse has a side-to-side, rolling, hind-to-fore, wavelike action when the horse is moving in gait. This makes sense when you recall that every fast saddle gait is identical, or similar, to the walk. When you watch any horse *walking* across a field this hind-to-fore action is very obvious and is ultimately expressed as a head bob or nod in front. (It's less evident with a saddle on.)

Because of this unique action along the topline, even when a saddle appears to fit the horse standing still (and you might also obtain a nice, even sweat pattern after a ride), it is very possible the saddle is seriously hindering this rolling, hind-to-fore action, and causing pressure sensitivity or soreness to develop on the rear portion of the horse's back, under the tree bars. A horse in pain often develops behavioral issues. He sees gremlins behind every waving leaf, and develops a dependency on his buddies to protect him. He may become "cinchy" when being saddled, reluctant to leave the barn, and anxious to return.

Also, a horse is a prey animal. Humans are natural predators. A predator on the horse's back normally causes the animal to instinctively revert to the "fight or flight" mode. Given these circumstances, it is little short of a miracle that man has succeeded in training horses to be ridden at all. However, when a domesticated horse experiences pain in the back under the weight of a natural predator, it is normal for him to revert to strong instinctual behavior. Depending on the individual horse's innate predisposition, he may develop the habit of rushing and bolting (flight), or else try to rear, buck, whirl, or scrape the frightening offender off his back (fight).

Rather than systematically analyzing the situation to see what the horse's behavior is trying to communicate, all too frequently, the rider assumes—or is advised by an "old-time" horseman—that it constitutes misbehavior. So, instead of discovering the root of the problem and resolving it, she disciplines (punishes) the horse in various ways. When the problem escalates and the rider gets hurt (all too common), then the rider becomes fearful. It can become a fast downhill slide from there.

Some kinds of horses simply tune out pain and become stoic. These animals have learned that any effort to communicate their discomfort to their rider results in discipline, so they somehow train themselves to ignore and work through it. There have been times when I've evaluated an animal for saddle fit, and the horse has flinched hard the first time I pressed on a spot that appeared to be compromised. Typically, the next time I press on that point—or perhaps the one on the opposite side—there is no longer any discernible pain reaction. The horse literally "blanks out" his expression and appears to look to some point in the far distance. Though I'm amazed at such animals' ability to cope with pain, I'm also aware that at some point there can be potentially serious consequences if a problem isn't pinpointed and dealt with in an appropriate manner. Figuratively closing our eyes to this kind of problem certainly does *not* make it go away!

Saddle Fit

Saddle fit, especially for Western-style saddles, can be tricky because many gaited horses have an "A-" or "rafter"-shaped topline with spines situated above the level of the barrel and ribs springing out at a lower point, as opposed to the more commonly seen "O-" or "barrel"-shaped stock horses. (This is often true of Thoroughbred horses, as well.)

Fitting "A"-shaped horses with saddles built for "O"-shaped horses creates pressure soreness along a thin strip on the back where the lower edges of the saddle-tree bars rest. This can be a challenge to identify. It is common practice to check for pressure points just behind the withers, at the rearward part of the back, and directly on each side of the spine, but soreness resulting from an "A" versus an "O" topline is located 3 to 4 inches below the spine. It also is not evident unless the horse is evaluated with a rider mounted

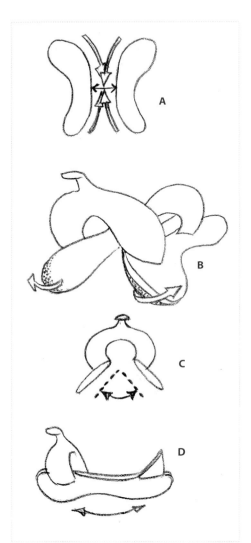

6.2 A–D The term "twist" can be confusing, as it refers to two different things related to the configuration of the tree bars. In this drawing, the twist is the narrowest part of the saddle's seat between the rider's thighs (where all the arrows point in A). When the tree bars are situated close together at this point, the seat has a "narrow twist." When the tree bars are positioned wider apart, the seat has a "broad twist." A "narrow twist" can give the rider a "closer feel" for the horse. Most saddle trees have various degrees of "flare" at the front and rear edges of the tree bars (B). Tree bars are angled to fit different toplines—narrow, medium, or wide (C). The "rocker" of the saddle bars is the amount of "dip" at the center of the saddle (D).

because the muscles are not compromised at a superficial level, but deeper within the tissues at the depth where the rider's weight comes to rest. It is difficult or impossible to duplicate that amount of pressure by merely pressing along the likely pressure points of the horse with your bare hands (see also Evaluating Saddle Dynamics and Fit, p. 138).

SADDLE-TREE TERMS

Most saddles of any style are built on a *saddle tree,* a wooden or fiberglass "skeleton," over which leather and padding is installed. Essentially, a saddle tree consists of four parts: the *pommel,* the *cantle,* and two tree *"bars."* The saddle tree bars are long, flat pieces of wood, fiberglass, metal, or a flexible composite material. These lie along each side of the horse's spine and help to evenly distribute the rider's weight along his topline. Tree bars have varying angles to suit different-shaped horses: a steep downward angle for a steep-sided or "A"-shaped horse; an average angle for a less steep, but not a barrel-shaped horse; and a wide angle for a wide, "O"-shaped barrel.

The *rocker* of the bars describes the amount of "dip" at the center of the tree bars, from top to bottom. Some saddle bars are nearly straight from front to back, while others are made for horses with hollow backs. Many so-called "gaited-horse saddles" fall into the latter category. If the horse isn't already hollow-backed, he needs to hollow his back to avoid contact with

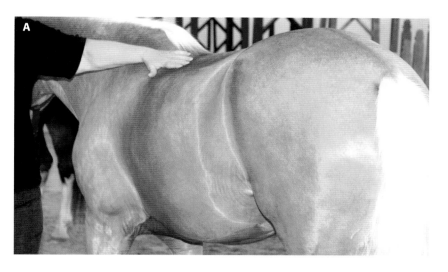

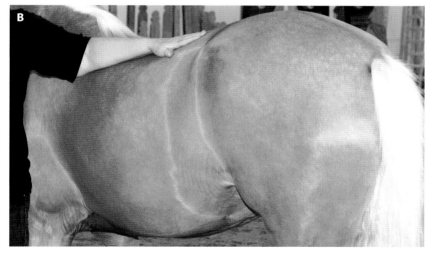

6.3 A & B These photos illustrate how the twist relates to the way tree bars conform to the shape of the horse's back. The front portion of the horse's back, just behind the withers, drops off sharply, while the back is flatter toward the loins. The twist in the bottom, flat part of the tree bars allows them to accommodate this varying degree of incline. My hand in A shows the degree of incline at the front of this horse's topline and in B shows the degree of incline where the back edge of the saddle bars sit. Tree bars are twisted from front to back in order to follow these contours.

the saddle's rocker and over time, this will cause him to *become* hollow-backed. The *twist* of the saddle bars describes the width of the tree bars between the rider's legs as well as the angle of the tree bars on the bottom flat portion, from front to back. Toward the withers, this is quite a steep angle, as there is a sharp drop-off at each side, but the angle becomes flatter as it goes across the back, and is flattest toward the back edge of the bars (figs. 6.2 A–D and 6.3 A & B).

Trees (and saddles) come in innumerable configurations. A problem when choosing a saddle is the lack of common specifications regarding the angle of the twist and of the tree bars. One manufacturer will have a tree with "semi-Quarter-Horse bars" that measure very closely to another company's "full-Quarter-Horse bars." A rider whose horse has been successfully fit with one of these saddles may mistakenly assume that any other saddle with a similarly labeled tree will also be a good fit. That may not be the case, and it could be many months before the horse exhibits obvious signs of distress. If the rider assumes the saddle has been working well up to that point, she may not recognize the problem that actually underlies her horse's issues.

Special Challenges when Fitting a Saddle to a Gaited Horse

As mentioned, most saddles are built on rigid trees made of wood, fiberglass, metal, or a composite material. Some saddles position the rider's weight toward the loins, where the energy from the haunches is transmitted through to the back. All these saddles interfere with the natural hind-to-fore action of a gaited horse's topline. When ridden in a saddle that interferes with this motion, the gaited horse is unable to softly round up through the topline and collect on the bridle. When he's unable to transfer the energy generated from his loins through to his back muscles, his response is to stiffen up through the topline, hollow out, and pace or step pace.

Because gaited horses couldn't be properly collected and ridden in gait with most common types of saddles, it became traditional training dogma that gaited horses "have to" go in an inverted, hollow frame in order to achieve their gaits. This is inherently wrong, and results in poor horsemanship, which in turn causes problematic horses. What a gaited horse *requires* in order to perform his intermediate saddle gaits in good, functionally sound form is a much greater degree of liberty along his topline.

I discuss saddle fit and dynamics at length because your success at correctly fitting your horse with an appropriate saddle determines how successful you are at training your horse for smooth, functionally correct saddle gaits.

WESTERN SADDLES

The majority of pleasure riders in the United States ride in a Western saddle with a horn, high pommel and cantle, wide fenders, and large leather-covered stirrups, giving the rider a sense of stability and security (fig. 6.4). While it is possible to fit a gaited horse in a Western saddle built on a rigid wooden or fiberglass tree, in my experience it can hinder the natural hind-to-fore action of his back (see p. 128). Ridden in Western gear, the gaited horse generally does better with a saddle with *flexible* tree bars: The slight "give" in the hard, rubber-like material affords him more liberty of motion (fig. 6.5). Immediately after these types of trees were introduced, people who participated in roping and other Western performance events believed they would not stand up to hard competitive use. This has not proven to be the case, and many top competitors now swear by saddles built on flexible trees.

Be aware that some Western saddles being marketed specifically for gaited horses are actually not a good choice. Because gaited horses have unfortunately been ridden in a high-headed, hollow-backed frame that leads to a swayed back, these saddles have been purposely designed with

6.4 Western saddles have a horn, high cantle, wide fenders, and stirrups with wide, deep treads. These features offer the rider security in the saddle.

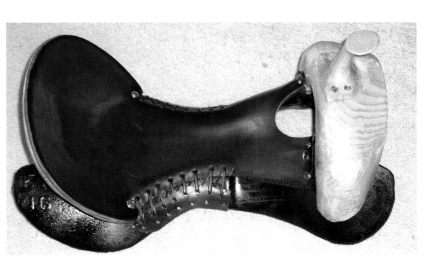

6.5 This Western saddle tree has flexible tree bars made of a material similar to hard rubber tires. The leather ground seat (the part of the saddle that supports the rider's seat bones and allows her to sit in the center of the saddle) "gives" with the slight motion of the tree bars beneath it. Some saddles built with flexible tree bars have rigid, fiberglass, or metal ground seats that limit or eliminate the flexibility of the tree bars.

enough rocker in the tree bars to work on gaited horses with inverted toplines. So, when you ride a "not-hollow" horse in this type of saddle, the horse will be forced to drop his back to avoid contact with the middle of the tree bars—and this eventually causes the horse to become sway-backed.

ENGLISH SADDLES

English saddles of various styles are used in the gaited horse show ring and for certain competitive events. Lighter in weight than Western saddles, they are also built on a wood or fiberglass tree, often reinforced with metal springs for a slight amount of "give." While Western saddles usually have a fleece lining on the underside, English saddles have stuffed leather panels. Leather straps, called *stirrup leathers,* secure metal stirrups, and the horse's torso is protected from these straps by sturdy leather flaps on the saddle.

Some English saddles have stirrups that can be adjusted forward or backward, making it easy for the rider to achieve a natural leg and foot position. Pommel and cantle height on English saddles varies widely. Like Western saddles, many of these place the rider's weight too far behind the horse's center of gravity where it interferes with the transmission of energy from the haunches to the back.

The stuffed panels on the bars of English saddles are often rounded in shape. When a rider is mounted these panels dig deeply into the rear part of the horse's back, often creating substantial pressure soreness (see Evaluating Saddle Dynamics and Fit for more on this—p. 138). You may even be able to see the panels pressing into the horse's flesh, creating a slight bulge around them. English saddle panels are ideally contoured to fit over and around the back, as opposed to "pushing" into it.

Gaited horses are usually ridden in a *cutback saddle*—otherwise known as a *saddle seat* saddle—in the show ring. This saddle is extremely light-weight, and there is a 3- to 4-inch cutout at the front of the pommel to

6.6 This cutback (saddle-seat) saddle has a contoured "cutout" that sometimes permits the saddle to be positioned more forward over the withers. This is the seat position most desirable for riding gaited horses.

accommodate the withers. It has an exceptionally flat seat and often has contoured bottom panels (fig. 6.6).

Though it is customary for saddle-seat riders to deliberately sit behind the horse's center of gravity (to "lighten" the horse's forehand) this is not the ideal riding position. Some cutback saddles can be placed forward over the withers, giving the rider a more balanced position. Riding in a good cutback saddle feels much like riding bareback.

AUSTRALIAN SADDLES

An Australian saddle is somewhat like a cross between an English and a Western saddle. They have "poleys," which are curved leather-covered knee pads on each side of the pommel, for rider security. While some also have a horn, most do not. The underside panels, known as "surge panels," need

6.7 There is a nearly endless variety of saddle models and configurations. Some very old saddles (like several pictured here) do not fit today's larger, wider-built horses.

to be cared for—and some restuffed—on a regular basis. The fenders are narrower than Western saddle fenders, with a 2- or 3-inch-wide leather strap at the bottom, to which metal stirrups with a large tread are attached. Australian saddles seat the rider forward over the horse's withers and shoulders, giving similar benefits to that of a "bareback" riding position (see p. 124).

Because of the optimum seat position of the rider, Australian saddles can be a good choice for riding gaited horses, but consider purchasing a saddle that is contoured on the underside to accommodate the shape of the horse's topline, or one that has a fleece lining. Surge panels are much thicker and rounder than their English-saddle counterparts, and if not restuffed regularly, they can become hard as rocks, causing severe pressure points on the horse's back.

TROOPER SADDLES

Trooper saddles originally were used by the English cavalry and became popular with the cavalry and mounted police in Canada and the United States. Many pleasure riders use them and they are especially popular with riders who enjoy the sport of field trials, where mounted hunters compete their retrievers, pointers, or flushing dogs against one another. A trooper

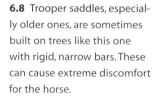

6.8 Trooper saddles, especially older ones, are sometimes built on trees like this one with rigid, narrow bars. These can cause extreme discomfort for the horse.

saddle is less bulky and lighter than a Western saddle, but heavier than an English saddle. It is built on a rigid tree, with very narrow "ski-like" bars that frequently press down hard at the back edge, causing pressure on the horse's back (fig. 6.8). The effects are a hardening and deterioration of the muscle there. I've evaluated hundreds of trooper saddles on gaited horses, and rarely found one that was appropriate. If you already own this style of saddle, carefully evaluate it to be absolutely *sure* it isn't causing problems for your horse.

TREELESS SADDLES

Over the past 20 years, *treeless* saddles of both English and Western styles, have appeared on the market. Going treeless helps eliminate any soreness caused by a rigid saddle tree, but many riders are too heavy or unbalanced to use one. When a rider is of light or moderate weight, enjoys good balance, and uses a weight distribution pad under the saddle, then a treeless saddle can be a good choice for a gaited horse.

FLEXIBLE PANEL SADDLES

Manufacturers of saddles with "flexible panels" claim they are "one-size-fits-all." They are built with flexible panels situated on either side of the horse's spine and are attached to a solid tree upon which the rider sits. How the lower panels are attached to the upper tree is of prime consideration: Many are attached with two "ball-bearing" joints on the front and back of each panel. Though the panels do indeed flex to accommodate the shape and movement of the horse, there is a tremendous amount of pressure concentrated just under these joints, causing them to dig in and create soreness and muscle deterioration.

Determining whether a flexible panel saddle will work on your horse must be based on his movement and behavior when being ridden, as it will probably *fit* perfectly, but may cause discomfort when the horse is moving—and it may not be evident for many weeks (or months) until the pain has become severe enough to cause obvious problems. I would not purchase such a saddle unless the seller offered a liberal return policy.

Evaluating Saddle Dynamics and Fit

PRIMARY CONSIDERATIONS

When evaluating a saddle you own, or one you plan to purchase, consider the following:

- Is the underside material of a Western or trooper saddle thick, soft, and forgiving enough to prevent the tree bars from pressing hard into the horse's back?
- Are the panels of an English or Australian saddle contoured, rather than rounded? Do the contours fit the shape of your horse's back? (This doesn't need to be a perfect fit, but only a close one, as contouring enables the panels to "mold" to the shape of the back over time.)
- Will the back edge of the saddle tree interfere with the transmission of energy from the loins to the horse's back once a rider is mounted?
- Does the pommel area pinch or restrict shoulder motion?
- Does the gullet sit too low and rub the horse's withers?
- Is the saddle built on a tree specifically made for the shape of your horse's topline—that is, wide, standard, or narrow (see p. 130)?
- Will you be able to place the saddle far enough forward on your horse's back, as if you were riding bareback and seated just behind his withers? This is the best position for riding a gaited horse. (Saddles must be built for this; you cannot successfully take a saddle made to sit behind the withers and just "prop" it forward.)

Point of Hip Test

To determine if the saddle you are evaluating (and this evaluation is appropriate for *all* saddle styles) is comfortable for your horse when he is *being ridden,* saddle up as usual.

Before you mount, stand next to the horse's side, in front of the hip. Make sure you're out of kicking range, because this can be painful, and some horses may kick out. Take your hand, and press firmly in a circular motion all around the horse's point of hip. Some soreness may have transferred to

this area. When this is the case, your horse will definitely show he is sore by flinching, pinning his ears, or kicking.

Under Gullet

While mounted and standing still, have someone from the ground slip the flat of her hand between the front edge of your saddle and the front edge of the horse's scapula (fig. 6.9). If the gullet is too narrow, your helper will be unable to insert her hand. When she can, it may feel tight. This is because the horse's shoulder rotates slightly outward at the top when at rest. Ask the horse to move forward a few steps, so she can judge how tight the saddle really is at the front edge of the saddle bars. If her hand is pinched, then you

6.9 You can check for saddle pressure points by placing the flat of your hand under the saddle at various points, with a rider mounted. To accurately check for pinching at the front edge of the tree bars, you need to have the horse take a few steps with your hand in place.

have a too-narrow gullet that is creating pressure sensitivity and restricting your horse's motion.

Under Rear of Saddle

Next, have your assistant place the flat of her hand under the panels or tree bars just under your seat bones, and press firmly. Observe the horse to see if he flinches, swings his head, steps away quickly, or pins his ears. Any of these reactions can be an indication of a pressure point. (As already mentioned, you don't usually get this reaction without a rider in the saddle because bruising from saddle soreness can be deep within the tissues.) If there is a negative but mild reaction, have your assistant step away while you casually ride away and back again before you repeat the procedure. (If the test is repeated immediately, the horse may become stoic and not react to this soreness—see p. 129.)

On the other hand, even if you have not ridden in the saddle for a while and the horse is currently not sore he often flinches out of habit when pressure is applied to that spot. I've had clients who were stumped because they hadn't ridden in weeks or months, but their horse still demonstrated an extremely strong reaction when they did this evaluation.

Under the Middle of Saddle

While still mounted, ask your assistant to place her hand under the middle of the saddle to make sure there is no gap—called *"bridging"*—where the tree bars don't contact the horse's back but instead rest on four narrow points of the horse: One on each side just behind the pommel and at the rear edges of the saddle panels or tree bars. You can only get your hand inserted there if there *is* a gap. When this is the case, you need to use a *bridging pad* to help distribute your weight more evenly along your horse's topline (see p. 141).

TESTING FOR FREEDOM OF MOTION

Even when your horse shows no evidence of soreness from the preceding tests, you need to make absolutely certain the saddle isn't restricting his movement. Ask the horse to walk with good impulsion from his hindquarters, then to increase his speed gradually while maintaining a soft, relaxed frame. The speed gain must be accompanied by willingness from the horse to maintain contact with the rider's hand and soft flexion at the poll. Do not allow him to suddenly go faster, or to "jump up" into the faster gait. If the horse persistently jumps from a slow walk right up to a stiff, high-headed gait, he is likely avoiding contact with the saddle tree by hollowing through the back.

When the horse has no "second gear," but raises his head, hollows his back, and goes immediately to a very fast gait, it is a good indication that he is *unable* to round up through the back because of restriction from the saddle. As the motion of the gait rolls up through the loins to the back edge of the panels or tree bars, it runs into an uncomfortable obstacle: the rider's weight settled over a concentrated area at the weakest point of the back just before the lumbosacral joint. When this is the case, the horse naturally stiffens up to avoid the saddle contacting his back.

CORRECTIVE PADDING

There are many kinds of corrective padding that can help in your effort to achieve proper weight distribution. The secret to padding well is to *pad away from the pressure*. When the saddle creates pressure near the lumbosacral joint, for example, you redistribute the rider's weight over a larger area by leveling the saddle using *saddle shims* or *wedge cushions* under the *front* of the saddle.

Saddle Shims

Saddle shims are cushions—usually made of felt or foam rubber—that fit into pockets sewn into a saddle pad. Shims of varying thickness are inserted into these pockets so that the rider's weight is evenly balanced on the horse's back. Shims are especially useful for a horse that is asymmetrical, sway-backed, or whose body is rapidly changing due to maturity, conditioning, or both. They help to balance the saddle and rider properly from back to front, as well as from side to side—but remember, shims are never an appropriate compensation for using a poorly fitted saddle.

> When the horse has no "second gear," but raises his head, hollows his back, and goes immediately to a very fast gait, it is a good indication that he is unable to round up through the back because of restriction from the saddle.

Wedge Cushions (Riser Pads)

You can use a *wedge cushion* or *reverse wedge cushion* (also known as *"riser pads"*) to adjust the saddle to sit level on the horse's back for even weight distribution. A wedge cushion is a cushion that is thicker in the front than in the back, with a cutout for the withers. It is used on a high-backed ("rump-high") horse, and placed beneath the pommel to lift the front of the saddle to be level with the back of it. A reverse wedge cushion does just the opposite: It is used for a "low-backed" horse whose croup is lower than his withers. It is thicker at the back and thinner at the front, and raises the back of the saddle to sit evenly with the front.

TREE CONFIGURATION

Though the pads mentioned above can help with asymmetry, bridging, and leveling the saddle, no type or amount of padding will compensate for a truly ill-fitting saddle. When the saddle tree and underpinnings (stuffed panels, fleece, and cushioning under the tree) don't conform closely to the shape of your horse, there is really little to be done but to begin the search for a new saddle. Trying to add padding for a too tight or incorrect fit, such as when the angle or twist of the tree bars is wrong, is akin to pulling on thick socks because your shoes are too small—it just makes the problem worse. The panels or tree bars of the saddle *must* closely conform to the shape of your horse's topline in order to avoid creating pressure points and restricting motion.

ACHIEVING "FIT FORGIVENESS"

Because each horse's back is unique, it is impossible to build a standardized saddle tree that *perfectly* suits a large number of horses; a saddle may be a "close fit," but not "fit like a glove." If the fit of a saddle is at least a close one, some "fit forgiveness" can be achieved by using the right pad.

For this purpose, I greatly appreciate the SupraCor® line of saddle pads made of medical-grade material originally used to help prevent sores from developing on bedridden patients. It was later installed in wheelchairs as well as in seats for airline pilots who suffer from "pressure fatigue" during long flights. The inventor, a horseman, eventually brought it to the equestrian market.

This tough, lightweight, extremely resilient padding lasts for many years—even under hard use—and does a superb job of preventing pressure sores by filling in any slight gaps that exist between the angles of the tree and the angles of the horse's back. The honeycomb design has light perforations that allow moisture to wick away from the back. Sweat evaporation is the primary way a horse maintains a healthy core body temperature when exercising; when this process is interrupted, the horse may suffer heat stroke or exhaustion. The SupraCor® material also offers some liberty of motion through the back that is helpful if you are riding in a saddle with a rigid tree.

PADS NOT RECOMMENDED

There are a couple of types of pads I do not like to use. In theory, a "gel pad"—a sealed plastic pad filled with a thick jelly-like material—is the perfect weight-distributing system. The problem is that gel pads are heavy and do not allow moisture to wick away from the horse's back.

Pads made of open-cell foam, commonly called "memory foam," also interfere with moisture wicking. Another drawback is that they compress wherever there is pressure and heat, so wherever there is a pressure point between the saddle and the horse's warm body, the foam collapses, failing to provide adequate protective cushioning.

Devising a Suitable "Saddle System"

As you can see, fitting a horse with appropriate riding gear is more complex than simply throwing a saddle on his back and strapping it on. To meet the unique needs of each individual horse the rider must give thoughtful consideration to every aspect of saddle and accessory design and purpose.

For example, in my own Imus 4-Beat™ Saddle System, I use flexible tree bars and install SupraCor® padding as an integral and permanent part of the saddle—between the bars and the fleece. In effect, this is the equivalent of an equine "sports shoe" as the system offers flexibility to accommodate action; a superior grade of cushioning to prevent pressure soreness and allow the saddle to fit a wider variety of horses; and includes a dense fleece that is akin to a heavy sports sock. The tree is configured to place the rider directly over the horse's center of gravity, enhancing balance and the horse and rider's ability to move "together."

Although I've instituted all these features in my system, I am quick to point out to clients that *they* are still responsible to help it work for their horse. It may be necessary to add a bridge pad if the horse is sway-backed from improper saddle dynamics or improper training. Shims may be required to ensure *even* weight distribution. The horse may need a breast collar to keep a saddle from slipping forward and back, or a crupper to prevent it from rolling from side to side. The rider needs to remain stable on the horse to bring out his best performance in every circumstance.

The thought, time, and expense taken to ensure good saddle fit and dynamics pays off in the form of a willing, pain-free horse that is able to perform his smooth saddle gaits in good form, and who will remain sound into his old age.

CHAPTER 7

Basic Training

First Lessons

YIELDING TO PRESSURE

Horses have a natural instinct to resist pressure—that is, if you pull on them, they pull back; if you push on them, they push back. Anyone who has ever worked with a young unhandled horse can attest to this! The first important lesson I teach the young horse is to *yield* ("give") to pressure, whether it is to *move his entire body toward me* when I pull on a lead rope, or *move away from me* when I place pressure on any part of his body (see Moving Away from Pressure, p. 146). This initial work eventually results in a soft, willing horse that is a pleasure to work around and ride.

Begin by teaching the foal to lead with a halter and lead rope, and then to tie. Start by placing a well-fitted foal halter on the foal, and attach a large, soft cotton lead rope to it. Cut the lead rope so that about 3 inches lies on the ground when the foal is standing upright. You may need to tie a knot at the end of the rope to prevent it from fraying and tangling in his legs. Make certain there are no objects on the ground or in the stall area that could tangle in the lead rope, and watch the foal closely. Let the foal carry the lead rope for an hour or two each day (never leave a haltered foal unattended); every time he steps on it, he will be unable to fight the pressure of his own weight on the rope. Within a couple of days he will have effectively taught himself to yield to pressure on the lead rope, making your next lesson easy.

Once the foal learns to stop whenever he steps on the rope, place a regular length lead rope on him and give light, intermittent pulls. If he resists, step to his side and pull firmly in that direction. This action unbalances him so he will step toward you to maintain his balance. When he does, give up all pressure immediately, and pet and praise him profusely. Repeat this several times.

After he routinely yields to the pressure of the lead rope, begin leading him alongside his dam. Foals can be a real challenge to train to lead, but calm confidence and persistence pay off after several training sessions.

Next, I teach him to tie. Tie a bungee cord or small bicycle inner tube to a strong post and tie the foal to that so if he decides to pull back hard he doesn't risk damaging his neck by hitting the end of an unyielding rope. Leave about 3 feet between his head and the post so if he pulls back he won't generate enough velocity to harm himself. It is helpful to teach this lesson when you're feeding grain to the mare and foal because she will be more interested in her grain than in the foal's antics, and he will equate being tied with receiving a treat.

Moving Away from Pressure

Once the horse leads and stands tied—and all mine are able to do this by the time they are two or three weeks old—teach him to *move away* from pressure by pressing at the *hip* until he steps away. Again, release all pressure immediately. It is the *release of pressure* that is your best training tool, so timing it so that the release comes at the moment of compliance is imperative. Repeat this training at the *shoulder* and at the *chest,* where you teach the horse to back up. Use the command, "Back," when you get to this point, as verbal commands will come in handy at later stages in your training.

By the time the horse is a four to six weeks of age, you will have already gained control over every part of his body and impressed upon him that you are the "alpha" of his herd.

TEACHING COMPOSURE AND PATIENCE

You can't start teaching a horse how to maintain composure too soon. If you happen to have a calm horse from which to pony another, this is an excellent way to habituate a young horse to the everyday world. However, I do not recommend "ponying" a young horse unless you are already experienced, so I do not go into instructional details in this book.

Some people ride their mares out on the trail with the foals coming along at liberty. I've never been comfortable with this practice. If the foal should wander too far off (and they do get curious and confident after journeying forth a time or two) the mare gets too distracted to pay attention to her rider, and should the foal get himself into trouble, you're really going to have a handful trying to control the mare and help the foal.

I generally just get out my walking boots and go for a stroll, young horse in hand. This teaches him to learn about new sights and sounds, to leave his dam and herdmates without too much fuss, and to cross water and obstacles. It also builds a bond of trust between human and animal. (And the human gets some exercise, too!) The first time or two out, I usually go with a friend who brings along the dam or an older, placid-natured pasturemate, just to keep things calm and give the young horse some confidence. Later on, it's useful to bring the young horse out alone, as it helps prevent him from becoming herdbound.

A friend of mine who has trained more horses than I can count once told me the most important lesson she teaches is that of patience—and her horses are always patient. She does this by tying them outdoors to a livestock trailer located near the road in front of her house. She gives them hay, and

> **You can't start teaching a horse how to maintain composure too soon.**

lets them stand. If they start to fuss, she simply ignores it. After an appropriate length of time (depending on the horse's age, and assuming he's being quiet and well-behaved) she walks them onto the trailer for some grain, then takes them back to the pasture or barn. Keep in mind that "patience" is relative—the younger the horse, the shorter the lesson. A three-month-old foal should not be expected to stand tied alone for more than 15 minutes, while a yearling should be fine standing for an hour.

This very simple lesson ensures that the horse understands that being away from the barn is not the end of the world. He learns that strange vehicles whizzing by are not going to gobble him up, and he becomes comfortable being tied to, and walked on and off, the trailer. Many riders would get much more pleasure out of riding if they took the time to teach this lesson as early on as possible in the horse's development, though it can be taught to a horse of any age.

Early Ground Training

ROUND-PEN WORK

When the horse is two years old, I begin round-pen training. The primary purpose of round-penning is to establish the human/horse hierarchy and develop communication. The pen's limited space prevents the horse from being able to resist or ignore the handler's requests, though the pen should be at least 50 feet in diameter, and 60 feet is better. It is useful for teaching the horse to learn voice commands like "Walk"; "Pick-it-up"; "Whoa"; "Easy"; and "Turn around"; as well as to move away from the "pressure" created as you "push," "slow," or "stop" with your body language (see p. 149). Your ability to control the horse's actions this way establishes you as a higher-ranking member of his "herd," and develops respect and obedience.

Schooling in a round pen muscles up the young horse just a bit, while its gentle arc creates lateral suppleness. This latter is especially important for gaited horses. In a few months, you can teach the horse to work nicely off his haunches by encouraging fast turns toward the outside of the pen, performing a type of rollback at liberty.

Round-penning should not be overdone for the first several months, as delicate joints can be overstressed and damaged, especially the knees and stifles. At the beginning, working five to seven minutes to each side is sufficient. After a month, you can work 10 to 12 minutes in each direction.

Body Language Cues

The cue to push a horse *forward* is for you to move slightly toward him, "pushing" him forward with your body parallel to his hip or hind end. To *slow down,* move toward his shoulder. To *halt* him completely, move in toward the chest with your whip pointed at the space in front of the chest, and stop. To give these cues most effectively, carry your lunge whip in the hand toward the rear end of the horse. When *pushing forward* direct the whip toward the horse's hip. Direct it toward the horse's shoulder and chest when cuing him to *move out of your space, slow down, stop,* or *turn.* You are essentially setting up a body language "barrier," with the lunge whip as an extension of your arm.

Do not permit your horse to walk in toward you at the end of a session, but hold him to the outside of the circle, and walk toward him. After you've established all the basic rules, teach him to come toward you by turning your body away from him and looking over your shoulder to invite him into your space. It's been my experience that horses greatly enjoy this type of bonding.

First Round Pen Lesson

To start, bring the horse into the pen, take off the lead and let him explore the space for a few moments. Using a lunge whip (some trainers use a 12-foot length of rope but I feel I have more control with the whip), push him to the outside of the ring, safely away from the "kick zone." Always maintaining a safe distance out of kicking range, follow him at the walk with your shoulders parallel to the horse's hip. When he is going to the left, hold your whip in your right hand—and vice versa.

As you walk, push the horse forward to the left with your body language and an occasional flick of the whip behind his hind end if need be. At the same time, say the "Walk" command. If he resists, do not hit him with the whip directly. You want to avoid engendering fear. Instead, become more aggressive with your body language by stepping behind the line of his hip and toward him, while flicking the whip more vigorously and speaking slightly louder.

If the horse tries to turn in toward you, use the whip toward his shoulder to push him back to the pen's perimeter. Be patient, and remember this is all strange to him. *You* know from the outset what is expected, but he does not. From the horse's point of view, it makes no sense whatsoever!

Initially, the horse is likely to get confused and excited, and rush around the pen. Just continue to insist that he move forward and use a calm voice. Once he's moving forward without attempting to turn in toward you, reposition yourself more in front of his hip and point the whip toward his shoulder as you verbally request "Easy." (I do not use the word "Slow" because it sounds too much like "Whoa," and "Whoa" should *always* mean nothing other than "*Stop Right Now!*") When you ask him to go "Easy," he may stop altogether. If so, push him forward again.

If he abruptly changes direction, step vigorously toward his chest and use your whip in front of him to turn him back, and then work him in that direction for another minute or so. It might seem sensible to just work him in the direction he chooses, but since your primary purpose is to establish respect and obedience, the direction of travel must always be *your* decision.

Depending on the horse, and your experience and natural communication skills, it takes at least two sessions to teach the horse how to properly round pen in both directions. It's important to be generous in your praise, as horses do enjoy a sense of accomplishment when they have mastered a new skill.

Pace and Trot—or Not?

Many gaited horses tend to "switch gears" from one gait to another when being worked at liberty and there are different views regarding whether they should be permitted to trot or pace. I don't mind if a horse breaks into an undesirable gait because I can easily retrain him to his most suitable saddle gait after saddle work has begun. When the horse is "pacey," I try to teach him to canter to help break up that habit-forming, two-beat lateral gait:

Cantering requires one set of diagonals to work in synchrony and one set to work in opposition. Some extremely pacey horses simply will not canter, but instead pick up a faster and faster pace.

Under no circumstances should the work become rushed, chaotic and confusing. Your manner should remain unruffled, your cues consistent, and your voice calm. You want your horse to think and to learn—neither are possible if he's been made anxious or fearful.

LINE-DRIVING

My next step in training the young horse is to teach him to line-drive, also called "ground-driving" or "long-lining." Two lightweight lines at least 18 feet long are used as long reins attached to a simple snaffle bridle. This

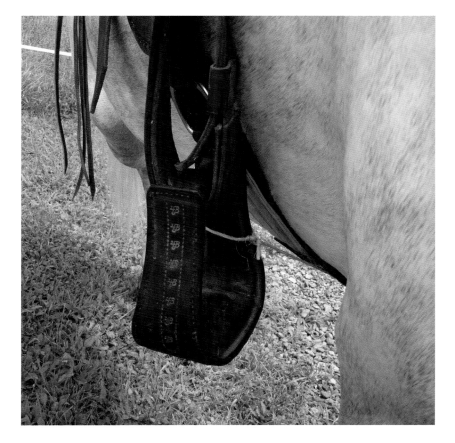

7.1 When long-lining or line-driving your horse with a saddle, tie the stirrups together with a rope or piece of twine under the horse, and run the long lines from the bit through the stirrups to your hands.

accustoms him, first, to respond to you even when you are not in his direct range of vision, and second, to working from a bit: performing turns, halts, and rein-backs. Depending on the horse's maturity, I generally start this work at about two-and-a-half years of age.

Tactfully Introducing Tack

Preparation begins before you actually start line-driving. I start by placing a saddle pad, and then a saddle, on the back of my two-year-olds, just to accustom them to the feeling. I also get them used to carrying a bit for 10 to 15 minutes. (A little fruit roll-up—dried, flattened fruit that can be purchased in the candy department of most grocery stores—can be wrapped around the middle of the snaffle mouthpiece to make even a nervous horse eager to get his "bit treat.") Then I ask my young horses to bring their head around to each side, teaching them to yield to direct pressure on each rein. After they're familiar with round-penning, I'll occasionally round-pen them when they are fully tacked up. This is all a slow progression to working under saddle.

When I'm ready to ground-drive, I tack up with a snaffle bit—minus the reins—and the saddle and work in the familiar round pen. Though you may choose to use a surcingle and run your two long lines or long reins to the bit, I prefer to use stirrups to accustom the horse to the feel of working while wearing a saddle. In order to keep the stirrups still, I run a piece of rope or twine through one stirrup, under the horse's belly, through the other stirrup, then tie it off firmly (fig. 7.1).

Next, snap a lightweight lunge line to each side of the bit. It is best if the lines are different colors so you aren't confused about which one controls which side of the horse. Run each lunge line back through the stirrup, bringing the outside line around the horse's hind end to your hand. When you start driving the horse to the left, the outside rein is in your right hand, the inside rein in your left (fig. 7.2).

Forward, Halt, and Rein Back

Forward

Move out to where you would stand when round-penning, and begin to push the horse at a walk around the pen. After he has relaxed, slowly position yourself behind him—at a safe distance—and "drive" him around the pen. This is one reason why I believe that voice cues are an integral part of round-pen training—they can be used to help when you begin working the horse from a vantage point where he can no longer see you. I always use a "chuck" noise when asking the horse to begin walking in the round pen, as this easily communicates my desire once I ground-drive him, as well as when I start saddle training.

It is usually a very easy transition from round-penning to ground-driving at a nice calm walk. Once the horse is moving well in one direction, use the reins to turn him in the other. For the first two sessions or so, concentrate on teaching the horse to turn, halt, and *stand quietly*.

7.2 Long-lining helps teach the horse basic cues in preparation for work under saddle, and strengthens your bond with him. Working outdoors accustoms the horse to stimuli he will be exposed to when he's ridden.

Halt

Because of the way you will work the horse when it is time for gait training, it is crucial that the *halt* and *rein-back* be taught correctly. Some Western disciplines encourage riders to teach their horses to halt on a loose rein. This is counterproductive to training gaited horses, so here I explain a traditional dressage approach.

To ask for a *halt,* drive the horse forward, and then check his forward energy by taking up on the reins, and using the (by-now-familiar) command, "Whoa." This can confuse the horse at first, so you might need to repeat the request several times, using increased pressure on the reins each time until he comes to a halt. As always, repeat the routine in both directions.

Rein-Back

Once the horse understands the halt command, it's time to train for the *rein-back.* Ask for a halt and after the horse stops, increase the pressure on the reins while giving the command to "Back." The first few times you do this, it helps to have an assistant stand at the horse's chest giving light nudges with her hand to encourage him to move backward. (Remember, you've long taught him to quickly move away from pressure on his body.) When he leans back, even slightly, take all pressure off the reins and give him an "Atta-boy!" Drive him forward and repeat several times until he's finally given you one step backward. Then ask him to "Whoa."

This move can usually be taught in one training session. Once achieved, stop for the day, and repeat the lesson the next day, asking for another step or two backward.

Training Routine

My usual training routine is to work two days, and give one day off. When I teach a horse a new lesson, once he's comprehended the basics of what I'm asking, I give him a day's rest before resuming. I find that most of the time the horse comes back after a day off with more energy and enthusiasm for the training session than if I push him to immediately repeat his performance. In addition, on occasion when I sense a horse getting confused and frustrated, I lay off the lesson and let him have a day of "R & R." This is contradictory to the old adage, "Always quit on a positive note." In the real world, it is not always possible. Sometimes it's wiser to admit that the stars aren't aligned quite right for progress on a particular day, give up the fight, go back and repeat an easier schooling routine, and let the horse settle back into a more positive frame of mind. While lots of one-on-one work is important, sometimes it's best to give the horse time to just be a horse!

Once your ground-driving lessons are well established, you can enjoy ground-driving the horse around the farm, trails, and even roads to accustom him to traffic.

CARRIAGE DRIVING

I've never mastered the art of driving with a cart. (The harness is confusing to me.) Learning to drive my horses is on my "To-Do List." However, I am a strong believer in having a horse trained to drive before beginning work under saddle, whenever possible. I'm fortunate to know a local person who excels at this discipline and teaches each of my horses to pull a cart after he's been taught to line-drive.

Driving the young horse helps muscle him up in preparation for carrying a rider's weight. He becomes accustomed to traffic and learns to tolerate the straps, shafts, and harness around his body, to say nothing of a rattling cart "chasing" him from behind. I believe driving also helps teach him to focus and extends his normally short attention span. Besides, a horse that both rides and drives is more valuable, should you ever decide to sell.

If you don't know how to carriage drive and you don't have a reputable trainer nearby that can do it for you, it's certainly possible to eliminate this stage of training without harm done. After all, you've already put in a lot of worthwhile preparation, all of which is about to pay big dividends as you start training your gaited horse to work under saddle.

Sometimes it's wiser to give up the fight, go back and repeat an easier schooling routine, and let the horse settle back into a more positive frame of mind.

Early Saddle Training

END OF SECOND YEAR

I don't believe horses should be ridden regularly, or for any extended length of time, until their third year. However, we often do mount and ride horses *late in their second year,* on a limited basis. The person doing this work should be lightweight, well balanced, and experienced. Thirty minutes is the maximum length of time a horse this young should be ridden, and he should not be faced with steep hills or challenging terrain. Generally, I work the horse lightly for a few months, and then let him go on hiatus until the following spring.

The reason for starting basic work under saddle at such a young age is that two-year-olds are often less set in their ways than three- or four-year-olds. They are more compliant and adapt quickly to their new role as a saddle horse. They look to their rider for confidence, whereas an unridden three-year-old may exhibit more independent thought and action. A three-year-old with these early, short training lessons is likely to maintain a more positive pattern of training.

First Mounting

Once again, I recommend starting this training in the round pen. Saddle and bridle the horse, and spend a few moments quietly round-penning to get his attention. When the horse is calm and focused on you, ask him to halt. With an assistant at the horse's head holding the bridle, slowly raise your weight up in the stirrup, while keeping as low a profile (head and upper body down) as possible. Repeat this once or twice until the horse accepts it calmly.

Next, stay up in the stirrup, and lay your weight across the saddle. Pet his neck and speak calmly. Most horses accept this without fuss, but some need to move their feet around to maintain their balance. With your helper controlling the head, it's okay to let the horse shift his weight or take a step or two. Rest calmly on his back while continuing to reassure him.

Moving Out

Now comes the moment many of us anticipate for years: mounting up and actually sit-
ting on the horse. Again, keep a low profile
when mounting, continue to pet and talk to
the horse, and mount slowly and easily.
Once up, just sit for a moment or two and
let him get accustomed to this new feeling.
Your assistant is still standing at the front of
your horse.

To get the horse to move, take a long,
low *leading rein* and pull him to one side
while pushing him with the opposite leg—
another instance where the "yield-to-pres-
sure" training pays off (fig. 7.3). Be sure to
"give" with your opposite hand and rein forward—*not* upward—so your horse doesn't
receive conflicting signals. Just as you pulled to the side to teach a foal to
lead, this side pressure forces him to take a step to rebalance. Be sure to
relieve all pressure as soon as he has complied and taken a step.

Turn him in this manner, first in one direction, then the other. Your
assistant should remain nearby, but no longer control the reins. Be sure the
turns you ask for aren't too tight. You could seriously unbalance your horse,
resulting in a "train wreck," should he panic. It is important that this first
ride be as positive as possible.

After the horse has moved around a bit, use your seat and leg—and a
"chucking" noise—to ask him to take a few steps. He will probably be quite
uncertain, so carefully judge just how much pressure you need to use.
Usually, this is not a difficult stage to move into, but there is the occasional
horse that becomes so nervous it's unwise to pressure him and force him
into forward action. Instead, have your assistant lead the horse with you on
top. Though he's being led, stiffen your seat and take lightly on the reins to
cue for a stop, and push with your seat and legs to cue for forward motion—

7.3 Use a long, low leading rein, as this rider is doing here, to encourage your horse to take his first steps under saddle.

in other words, ask him to focus on you, rather than on your assistant. Ideally, this lesson ends with you riding the horse around the round pen two or three times in each direction, cueing for stops and turns from the saddle. If you manage this much success, it's time to slowly dismount and reward your horse for a job well done!

Following this session, put increasingly more time into riding the horse, primarily in the round pen, then on short, easy trail rides with a calm horse and experienced rider as companions, if you so desire. The horse should be ridden a minimum of 30 minutes and a maximum of 45 minutes over easy terrain, four days a week, for two months or so. Riding less than this just prolongs the training experience, while riding more is too stressful for a young animal. After two months of work as a "long" two-year-old, I recommend a layoff until the horse is three.

THREE-YEAR-OLD

At three years of age, all under-saddle work should be limited to an hour or so. During this year the horse should be ridden in a simple snaffle bit only (see p. 111).

When you return to training, repeat the round-pen lesson a time or two just to reacquaint the horse with being ridden. Then, you can ride in an arena, paddock, or out on the trails. As before, the first several trail experiences should be with a companion.

You should not expect to develop a finished horse, or accomplish much gait work, during the horse's third year. You're still laying groundwork. The slower your progress, the more deeply ingrained the results will become. The training you accomplished during the latter part of your horse's second year focused on teaching your horse to carry weight, to turn, to halt, and to stand. This first full season of riding teaches your horse how to balance your weight over a variety of footing and terrain; respond automatically to your seat, leg, and rein aids; become accustomed to everyday stimuli; and allows you to condition him for more vigorous work in the future.

Young horses can become overly dependent on their buddies, especially out on the trail. I recommend that you make it a habit to switch up your

Rules for Going Solo

When you sense the horse has gained sufficient experience and confidence, it's advisable to go for short solo trail rides, as this prevents the horse from becoming "buddy sour." When on such rides, make it a practice to dismount and let your horse graze—essentially to rest and enjoy the experience.

When riding solo always let someone know where you are going and when to expect you back. Wear a safety helmet and carry a cell phone on your person. If you should take a fall and be too hurt to walk home, the cell phone stashed in your saddle bag won't do you a lick of good!

riding pattern as much as possible: Ride in the front, middle, and rear of the pack. Ride out ahead of the group for a ways, then fall back and ride a bit behind. Take a different route home than other riders. Ride around trees. Practice leg cues, and keep the horse's attention on you during most of the ride. You want him to depend on you for protection and direction, rather than on the other horses.

Half-Halts to Develop Saddle Gaits

While working on developing your horse's *fast* saddle gaits isn't advisable during the third year because it is too strenuous for the horse's young joints, by the end of his third year you can train him to transition from a dog walk, to a working walk, to a flat walk (see p. 3).

Since the working walk and flat walk require light to moderate collection, you need to teach your horse the *half-halt*. Half-halts are the heart of teaching your horse how to carry himself properly, at gait and otherwise, and are the center of much of your ongoing schooling. They generate forward energy that is "caught" on the bridle so that the horse is encouraged to shorten his frame by lifting his back, and shift his weight rearward over his haunches. This, in turn, lightens up the front end, changing a gait's timing.

Begin by asking for a correct *halt,* then finesse this to a half-halt. Start by asking the horse to move forward energetically at a working walk with very light contact on the bridle. Then, request a halt by deepening your seat and taking back on your reins—remember, push down with your seat, *then* take back on the reins. What you're doing is "collecting" the forward energy "on" the bridle: Your seat and legs generate forward energy and the bridle acts like a wall against which this generated energy is gathered and stopped. When the horse's energy is brought up against the bridle and he begins to slow down, continue squeezing with your thighs, take a slight amount more on the reins (how much rein you need to take differs from horse to horse), and ask him to stop energetically. Pretend it's a mini sliding stop.

The horse may raise his head and gape his mouth the first time or two he's asked to perform a halt in this manner, but he should quietly flex to the bridle and halt within a short time. If he fails to do so, you may be taking up too much rein while pushing too hard with your seat and legs. Experiment with lightening-up your cues to find out what works best (figs. 7.4 A & B).

As with line-driving (see p. 151), once you have a feel for the halt, try some backing-up. To do a proper rein-back, start with the halt, but rather than pushing your horse immediately forward, continue to push with your seat and legs, and take back on the reins until the horse moves a step back. Then ask for forward action and maintain appropriate contact on the bit. All of this helps tremendously to get your horse "gathered up" and moving off his haunches.

Once you've mastered a correct halt and rein-back, it's time to practice the half-halt. This is the *most important* exercise for helping to rebalance and correct the horse's position, and for establishing a correctly executed saddle gait once your horse is ready.

Start exactly as though you are going to ask the horse to halt. The instant you feel the horse hesitate, *maintain rein contact* and push the horse forward into an even more active walk. You've now rebalanced the horse over his haunches, rounded-up the back, and lifted his belly. When you move from a working walk with light rein contact to a flat walk with slightly more contact on the bridle—the beginning stages of true gait work—you do so by using half-halts as you ask for slightly increased speed.

Half-halts are also essential for teaching a horse to balance a rider properly on a *downhill incline.* Each time your young horse comes to such a hill, give a strong half-halt as you reach the incline. Within a very short period of time, your horse will begin to automatically shift his weight rearward as he starts down—a very handy habit to make your hill riding more safe and comfortable (fig. 7.5).

LESS CAN BE MORE

It's good to teach young horses new skills and develop those they already possess. However, sometimes more schooling on a young horse, is actually less. I've seen riders

Choosing Rding Partners

When you're riding your young horse on the trail, be selective regarding riding partners. You need to choose people to ride with that understand your horse is young and won't hamper your training "progress" by riding too fast, or on terrain your horse is not yet prepared to handle. One woman I rode with insisted her mare always had to be at the front of the line (she was unwilling to train her to be ridden elsewhere). Eventually my horse refused to go first, regardless of the company. At that point, I chose another partner in order to work out a problem that should never have developed in the first place.

carry schooling to extremes, making for a frustrated animal. One fellow who used to ride with my group of friends could never just relax and enjoy a ride—and neither could his horses. Every moment of every ride was like a formal schooling session whereby he continually picked at the horse to "Do this," or "Do that." He not only did this to his youngsters but continued to overtrain even his seasoned mounts.

Eventually, his horses tuned him out altogether, which made him feel justified in even *more* training. There were occasions when the rest of our riding group was relaxing around the fire, our horses cooled-out, brushed, and chewing hay contentedly, and he was still out in some field, trying to "fine-tune" his poor, hard-working, weary mount.

Aim to strike a balance between keeping your horse focused and learning, and just moving along, enjoying the scenery and conversation with your fellow horsemen. If riding becomes all work and no play, neither horse nor rider will continue to take pleasure in the experience.

7.4 A & B This rider is performing an incorrect halt, remaining passive and just pulling back on the reins (A). The result is a stiff, unresponsive horse. When the rider uses her seat and legs to generate impulsion, she can then "catch" that energy on the bridle for a correct halt (B). The horse's response is to soften and give to the bridle.

7.5 It is imperative that a gaited horse learn how to balance his weight over his haunches when traveling downhill. This is accomplished through half-halts.

Early Gait Training

Toward the *end of the horse's third year,* you can begin to ask your horse to speed up his walk into a soft saddle gait, though limit this work to just several minutes in an hour's session.

With the exception of the fox trot, *all* of the acceptable saddle gaits are based on the same footfall pattern as the walk, though individual horses may perform them slightly more on the lateral or diagonal end of the Gait Spectrum (see p. 3). Therefore, to begin to develop your horse's best saddle gaits, all you need do is use halts and half-halts to ensure the horse is moving well off the haunches in an active, four-beat working walk, keep him on the bridle, and ask for more speed until he hits a nice flat walk.

TECHNIQUES FOR OBTAINING A FLAT WALK

The young horse will often "fall out of form" and slip from the walk to an undesirable gait, rather than transition right up into a flat walk. He needs your help to maintain collection while "working the walk" (see p. 164).

Halts

When your horse's head stops nodding and you feel you've lost the sense of a rolling action through his topline, you need to help him get his weight balanced back over his haunches and his energy collected on the bridle. You can do this by asking for a correct halt, and then *immediately* ask him to move energetically forward while maintaining contact on the bridle. When my horse moves off, I give back *half* the contact I took when I asked for the halt. This works for most horses, but you need to experiment to discover how much contact is "just right" for yours—you'll know you've managed it successfully when your horse moves off energetically, in good form, while maintaining a well-timed saddle gait.

Half-Halts

After you've mastered recollecting your horse using the halt, you can obtain similar results by employing the half-halt (see p. 159)—but only once you've learned to *anticipate* when your horse is just about to fall out of form. Learning to do this is very important, as your horse is cued to maintain correct timing and form *before* he's actually fallen out.

Each time you sense your horse's timing beginning to change, almost imperceptibly push with your legs and seat, and check him in the bridle. You may need to do this frequently at first—as often as every sixth or seventh stride—but within a short time your horse will understand what you expect of him and maintain his form and timing even as you push for greater speed.

THE FLAT WALK

You'll know your horse has hit a flat walk when you see his head nodding perceptibly in time with each hind stride, and there's a smooth, gently rolling sensation from the saddle. You will hear evenly timed, four-beat footfalls and will be traveling faster than the average horse can walk.

Continue to work in a flat walk for several minutes of every training session, though for no more than three or four minutes at a time. The goal is to ride the horse right to the edge of his ability to maintain correct timing and form, and hold him to that point. This is called "working the walk," and is the heart of *all* good gait training.

Purpose of the Flat Walk

The flat walk conditions the horse's body for the faster saddle gaits and establishes "neurological memory" for maintaining a *well-timed,* four-beat gait. By "well-timed" I mean timing that is *not* exceptionally lateral. For example, it is still acceptable and in good form when the four-beat timing is uneven and *diagonally* oriented, as it is in a fox walk or fox trot (see p. 6).

However, you need to keep the very *laterally* oriented horse's walk as evenly timed as possible, as these gaits are destructive to the horse's body (see p. 16). The footfall pattern of the step pace is uneven, with two feet landing at nearly the same time, and there's an extra beat of time before the opposite feet land: 1-2—3-4. To maintain correct timing, walk your horse only as fast as he can go in good form without suddenly "shifting gears" to a pace or step pace.

As you work the walk and your horse gains the ability to increase speed, he will eventually easily and seamlessly "shift up" into the smooth saddle gait he is designed to perform, whether the fox trot, rack, or running walk.

ADJUSTMENTS IN CONTACT

If your horse persistently lifts his head and breaks to another gait—such as the pace, step pace, or an ordinary two-beat trot—check him back with half-halts until he realizes what you're asking. You need the appropriate amount of contact on the bridle to help him achieve your goal: to ride your horse as fast as he can go while maintaining correct four-beat timing and collected form, and then to keep working him right "on the edge." Over time, he will achieve faster and faster speeds before reaching his limit.

If your horse seems to get stiffer and stiffer, rather than softening-up and "giving," you may be maintaining too much pressure on the bridle. Give him a little more rein, and try again. To use the driving analogy again, this work is akin to learning how to drive a car with a standard transmission, when you need to balance between engaging the clutch and pressing on the accelerator.

THE IMPORTANCE OF CONDITIONING

As I discussed on p. 5, the gaited horse is *quadridextrous*—that is, he can move all four legs independently of each other. A horse that is quadridextrous needs to condition the muscles equally on both sides of his body. This takes time and dedicated effort. The degree of quadridexterity varies from animal to animal: Some take up and easily maintain an evenly timed, four-beat gait, so conditioning seems effortless. Others want to break to the pace or trot at relatively low speeds, so require more time and patience.

Liken this to a person learning to play drums: Some extremely musical, ambidextrous people are able to learn complex rhythms in a relatively short period of time; however, others need to start with simple rhythms performed slowly and work at increasing their speed and arrangement complexity over time.

The Most Common Gait-Training Error

The most common mistake gaited horse owners and trainers make when attempting to develop their horse's saddle gaits is to ask *for too much speed, too soon.* This causes the horse to stiffen up and resort to the pace or step pace. As with humans, horses become physically conditioned and neurologically "wired," or habituated, to repetitive tasks. The more the task is repeated, the stronger the conditioning and patterning.

This is why when we begin to drive a car we have to think carefully and pay close attention to everything around us, yet can drive nearly on automatic pilot after a year or two of practice. If we—or our horse—learn to perform a task incorrectly, the incorrect "wiring" that develops needs to be "unwired" before new and better patterns can be established. This is why it is better *never* to permit the horse to perform extremely lateral gaits when under saddle but to allow him plenty of time to learn how to gait properly before asking for higher speeds.

While it might not be obvious, a correctly performed smooth saddle gait is the most strenuous gait for a horse to execute. It requires tremendous coordination to move each leg independently, and the *longissmus dorsi* (back muscle—see p. 128) works much harder than when the horse merely trots, paces, or canters—or when he's permitted to stiffen up and go with a hollow back while performing his intermediate (square) gaits. As with any new physical undertaking, be sure to condition the horse for the speed and length of time you are asking him to work.

FOUR-YEAR-OLD

At *four years,* introduce the curb bit, which enables a horse to more easily round up and work off his haunches (see p. 113). Gradually condition him until he can handle up to ten minutes of gaiting, while "stretching the envelope"—incrementally increase collection and speed. Break up this work with lots of transitions between the working walk, flat walk, and the fox trot, rack, or running walk.

Progress very much depends on the individual horse's abilities, as well as on the rider's patience and riding skills. As time goes on—as long as you *do not* permit the horse to break to pace or trot, or go high-headed and hollow at the fox trot, rack, or running walk—he will develop his ability to gait at faster speeds while maintaining good form. It is especially important to maintain your focus on these goals while the horse is still young, as he is developing habits that will serve you well for many years to come.

Horses are still not physically mature at this stage of development. Allowing them to go too fast in a high-headed, hollow-backed frame places excess stress on their tender young joints. Because of this, many gaited horses that are trained in the "traditional" manner eventually develop hock and stifle issues.

Diagonal Equals Downhill and Pace Equals Uphill

When you have a horse that is strongly diagonally "wired" toward a regular two-beat trot (see p. 5), you can help "square him up" by asking for more speed on a *downhill* incline. Be sure to get his hind end under him first to avoid a nasty fall (see p. 159). Once he has his legs well underneath him, push him on, and give him a little more rein.

When you have a "pacey" horse, work him at speed on an *uphill* slope. In either scenario, I encourage you to take full advantage of hill work, if you can.

CANTERING

One of the most common questions I receive from gaited-horse owners is whether it is all right to canter. The answer is, "That depends."

The Laterally Oriented Horse

The individual who rides a *laterally oriented* horse may do well to encourage the horse to canter. It teaches him how to break up that addictive, lazy habit of pacing or step pacing because the canter requires the horse to use one set of diagonal legs in synchrony, and the other set of diagonal legs in opposition to one another. This is a far cry from using both sets of lateral legs together (which the horse in question favors) and goes a long way toward "rewiring" his neurological memory.

Cantering also teaches the basics of collection—working off the haunches and rounding-up through the back—which helps to strengthen the horse overall. And, the stronger and better conditioned the horse, the less likely he is to pace.

A primary challenge when trying to teach laterally oriented horses to canter is their tendency to *cross-canter*—that is, take up opposite leads with the front and back legs. There is a strong possibility that a cross-cantering horse will trip himself up, which may result in a very nasty somersault-type tumble for both horse and rider. Therefore, when you ask for the canter and feel as though you're being violently pushed out of the saddle with each stride, immediately bring the horse to a halt or walk, and start again. If the cross-cantering persists, then give up teaching the canter until the basics of collection are better established.

One of the easiest methods for teaching a "pacey" horse to canter is to ask for the gait on an uphill grade or incline (see also p. 226). This gets the horse's weight over his haunches and lightens up the front end, making the strike-off for a canter lead much easier. If you have a riding friend with a horse that canters, so much the better. Often, when a lead horse starts to canter, the horse following comes up into the gait as well.

If you live or ride in a flat, hill-free area, teach your horse to balance his weight more on his hind end while rounding up through his back with a strong half-halt prior to cueing for the canter (see p. 159). This means you're "collecting energy" through his body, which can then be utilized for a correct canter departure.

The Diagonally Oriented Horse

It's another story altogether when your horse is more on the "trotty" end of the Gait Spectrum (see p. 3). Such horses find cantering all too easy, especially when compared with the hard work of performing a four-beat gait in good form. Gaiting requires a lot of motion—front-to-back—through the horse's back, while trotting only requires the horse to jump from one set of diagonal legs to the other, demanding much less coordination and effort.

Often—when a diagonally oriented horse has already been permitted to canter—as the rider cues for more speed, the horse attempts to jump into a canter rather than transition up into a smooth saddle gait. The rider often then checks the horse back to walk and again asks him to transition into his smooth saddle gait, but the horse instead jumps into the *opposite* canter lead. The result is that the horse soon learns he can just "shuffle" on his forelegs while jumping from side to side on his hind legs and not do all the

---

Effective Canter Cues

A canter (on the right lead in this example) is correctly performed as follows: The horse sets down the left hind leg, followed by the right hind and left fore, then the right foreleg. The true "leading" leg is actually the right hind leg, and the "leading" foreleg is the one on the same side. The leading hind leg sets deeper under the horse than the non-leading leg, and the leading foreleg strides out further than its counterpart.

You initiate a canter by asking for a strong half-halt, with a bit more take on the outside rein (the side opposite the leading leg) to slightly tilt the horse's head to the outside. This simple action helps to lighten the horse's weight over the front leading shoulder, making a cross-canter less likely. Hold your outside leg behind the girth and your inside leg straight and steady at the girth. Once your horse shifts his weight to the rear, use your outside leg to vigorously push him forward. When he starts to spring forward as a result of these cues, lean forward in the saddle and release some—though not all—tension on the reins. With a little practice, this method should encourage a correct canter from even a very laterally oriented horse.

strenuous work required by a correctly executed saddle gait. There's little the hapless rider can do to correct this situation.

I call this mishmash gait the "cant-a-lope," and once a horse has developed the habit, it is difficult to correct. For this reason, I recommend that a diagonally oriented horse never be allowed to canter until his smooth saddle gaits have been very well established, often not until late into his *fifth year*—if then. If you do decide you'd like to canter your trotting horse, always cue for the canter from the halt or walk, and never from a smooth gait (this is true for *every* gaited horse). Establish very clear and different cues for canter and for the smooth gaits. I recommend including verbal cues such as "Canter!" and "Walk on!" Be very consistent with your cues, and do not practicing cantering over his smooth saddle gaits, or you may have to go back to square one to redevelop them.

SHOULD THE GAITED HORSE TROT?

The Laterally Oriented Horse

Some people want to train, or allow, their gaited horse to trot (though personally, I can see no good reason for *ever* trotting a gaited horse!) Most laterally oriented horses become confused and refuse to trot at first, and it is better to work the walk until the gait is established than to push the issue. However, once his smooth saddle gaits have been established for a season or two, you may attempt to ask for a trot again. Do so by pushing him very quickly over ground poles set about 10 feet apart. Stand in your stirrups and give the command "Trot!" Reward him when he complies.

Another technique for developing a trot is to ride with a trotting horse and have both horses cued for trot at the same time. This is most effective when traveling uphill. Horses often pick up the footfall cadence of other horses and "fall into step" with them. This is one reason why it can be detrimental to ride too often with trotting horses when you're training for smooth saddle gaits. (Another reason is that a trotting horse cannot keep up with the smooth gaits of a gaited horse without forcing his rider to post or endure much jarring in the saddle.)

Some laterally oriented horses will simply never learn to trot, while others can eventually pick up this extra gait.

The Diagonally Oriented Horse

What is true of a laterally oriented horse does not apply to the diagonally oriented horse. Still, do not allow trotting horses to actually trot until their smooth saddle gaits have been well confirmed. Again, this is because you are in the process of building muscle condition and neurological memory for the intermediate (square) gaits. To allow the trot during this process can confuse the horse and therefore be counterproductive.

All of this may appear rather complicated in print, but when you're on your horse and have gained a feel for his movement, you'll find this early schooling fun and rewarding. It will pay off not only in smooth saddle gaits and long-term soundness, but in the inevitable bond that forms between a horse and an active, conscientious rider.

CHAPTER 8

Advanced Schooling

The Importance of "Supple" and "Soft"

A YOUNG, UNSCHOOLED HORSE IS NATURALLY STIFF under saddle. A stiff horse finds it easy to resist his rider's aids, while a supple horse has been so conditioned to "giving" himself to the rider's cues that resistance becomes nearly impossible. For this reason, it's important to condition him to become—and remain—*supple* and *soft*.

In this chapter I offer a few exercises for this purpose. Practice them at least a couple times a week. The more complex routines described later in this chapter may be ignored if you don't enjoy this type of work, although I do recommend you read the exercises through because you might just find yourself playing around with them while out on the trail. The more you experience the sort of change brought about by this type of work, the more likely you will begin to enjoy your horse!

Flexion

The secret to developing a supple horse is *flexion*. There is *lateral* and *vertical* flexion. *Lateral flexion* is stretching and compressing the muscles along each side of the horse; *vertical flexion* is contracting and expanding muscles from back to front.

The ability to attain good vertical flexion is paramount to teaching a horse to collect properly, and the key to obtaining it is to develop good lateral flexion, first! Although it's not reasonable to repeat all the flexion exercises I've included here every day, practicing a few of them each time you ride pays dividends in the form of a focused, willing horse that responds promptly and quietly to your riding cues. The following exercises are not only fun to practice but also help ensure a soft, willing, and dependable riding partner.

Perfecting Riding Cues

Your cues should be strong and exaggerated when you begin these exercises. However, as schooling progresses, lighten your aids. Ideally, they will eventually become so subtle that only you and your horse are aware of them; it will appear to others that you are communicating "psychically." By now, become so attuned to one another that this might be partially the truth!

Exercise 1
LATERAL NECK BENDING

This is a lateral flexion exercise that can begin when your horse is *three years old.* It helps supple the muscles along both sides of his neck, making it easy for him to respond to your rein aids. Standing to one side of your horse, ask him to bend his neck as far around to his side as he can, while keeping his feet planted. Repeat this two or three times, and then move to the opposite side (figs. 8.1 A & B). I find offering a treat as a reward can be very helpful, but I do not do so when the horse is wearing a bit.

Next, put on the horse's saddle and bridle, mount up, and move one hand from its normal position on the rein about a foot down toward the horse's head, while leaving the opposite rein slack. Using a give-and-take action on the rein, ask the horse to bend his nose back to your stirrup, and reward him with a neck rub and verbal approval when he complies. Repeat two or three times to each side, making sure his feet stay planted. Do this exercise at least three to five times a week—and prior to every ride (fig. 8.2).

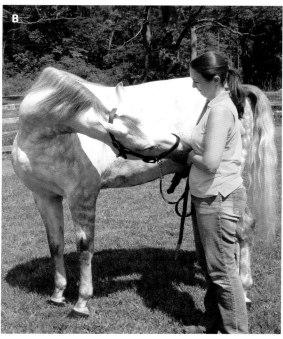

Exercise 2
LATERAL BODY BENDING

Horses naturally tend to move with a *crooked* frame. The best way to teach a horse to work with a *straight* body is to teach him to bend softly to each side. In order to attain proper collection the horse must be able to move straight—that is, the hind feet follow the same tracks as the front feet, rather than tracking to the outside of the horse's body. To accomplish straightness, the horse needs to be kept "between the rider's seat and hands." Your seat and legs create energy from the horse's hind end that is carried through the horse's body and "caught" on the bridle (fig. 8.3 and see discussion of half-halt on p. 159). A horse thus ridden is like a "coiled spring," always ready for his rider's next request.

A crooked horse is poorly connected to his rider's aids and lacks impulsion from behind. Any energy that is generated "leaks out," so the horse becomes front heavy, poorly balanced, and unresponsive. Crooked horses are often stiff-muscled, causing them to become slab-sided and their mus-

8.1 A & B Teach your horse to bend laterally by asking him to bend his neck to each side while keeping his feet still (A). Once the horse understands your request, ask for an increasing amount of lateral bend, until the horse's nose can touch the rear-most portion of his barrel (B).

8.2 Repeat the lateral neck bending exercise from the saddle to increase the horse's softness and sensitivity to the rein.

cles to develop asymmetrically. When regularly ridden this way a number of problems with saddle dynamics develop (see p. 127), as well as a tendency to pace. (Remember: The pace and step pace are detrimental to the horse—see p. 16.)

You teach a horse to bend in both directions to help develop his muscles evenly on both sides, and so he learns to "give" willingly and softly to your cues. While these lessons won't pay off overnight, a few weeks' work will bring great improvement. You may begin to teach these next lateral exercises when the horse is about *three-and-a-half years old*.

Part One: Circles

Riding in circles (and I don't mean getting lost on the trail!) helps develop your riding skills and improves your horse's flexibility and responsiveness to your riding aids. To start, the circle should have a circumference of 60 feet; once you've mastered the exercise, you may gradually decrease the circumference to 50, and then 40 feet in order to help your horse become even more flexible and responsive. Place a training cone in the center of your circle, and four more cones just to the outside of its perimeter (33 feet from the center cone) to help maintain a true circle pattern.

To circle to the *right,* start riding at an active working walk with light collection.

- **Seat:** Sit in the center of your saddle; do not lean forward or in toward the center of the circle. Deepen and "push" a little with your seat in time to your horse's strides to maintain impulsion.
- **Hands:** Take contact with the right (inside the bend) rein and, holding it just above your knee, pull your horse's head slightly toward the right while keeping a light, even pressure with your left (outside the bend) rein, giving just enough outside rein to allow the horse to give his head

to the right. On a 60-foot circle you should be able to see the outside corner of your horse's right eye (when you've mastered a 40-foot circle, you see the entire inside eye). Allow the outside rein to lightly touch the side of your horse's neck, but do not bring the rein *over* his neck or withers.

- **Legs:** Press your right inside leg firmly on the horse's side *at* the girth, and your left outside leg into the horse's barrel slightly *behind* the girth. Your inside leg acts like a "pole" for your horse to bend around, and your outside leg helps prevent the horse's hindquarters from drifting to the outside of the circle. If your horse loses impulsion, you may tap him with your outside leg to cue him forward.

Reverse these riding aids to circle to the left: Take on the left rein, release slightly with the right; push with the left leg *at* the girth; push with the right leg *behind* the girth.

Use your seat, leg, and rein to encourage the horse to keep his body, neck, and head on the same smooth arc. If he tries to drop his nose *inside* the arc of the circle, use your inside rein to lift his head and your outside rein to bring it back into line. If he tips his head *outside* the arc, use your inside rein to bring it back into place. As mentioned earlier, you should just be able to see the outside corner of his inside eye. If you see more than this on a 60-foot circle, then he is cheating his way through the cones—that is, he is avoiding the effort of working his neck and torso muscles along their entire length, and just "rubbernecking" around the cones while remaining stiff through the body (fig. 8.3).

Part Two: Figure Eights

Your horse should be able to easily perform 40-foot circles to both the left and the right before beginning figure eights. Start by setting out two training cones 60 feet apart. Ride the horse in a 30-foot circle around one cone, then when you are at the center point between the two cones, reverse your aids to ride a 30-foot circle around the second cone.

While you don't need to possess high-level dressage skills to achieve results, it is important to maintain appropriate rein and leg contact.

8.3 It's important to maintain light contact on the outside rein to avoid "rubbernecking" and maintain the bend through the horse's body. The rider's outside leg is positioned slightly behind the girth to keep the horse's haunches from "swinging wide."

Otherwise, your horse will either drop a shoulder to the inside of your circles to avoid working his lateral muscles, or just rubberneck around the turns, with his haunches swinging out wide, like a semi trailer. If you allow this, it defeats the purpose—getting a nice soft lateral bend through your horse's body (figs. 8.4 A–C).

Part Three: Spiraling In and Out

This exercise maximizes your horse's lateral bending abilities and is not difficult to master once your horse is working well on circles and figure eights, which is when you should start this schooling. To spiral from the outside of the circle inward, position your horse on the outside of a 60-foot circle (you may again use cones to help you visualize the circle). Ask for a walk and, using the same aids that you use for your circles and figure eights (see pp. 174 and 175), ride your horse in an ever-decreasing-sized circle (spiral), until he is in the center, turning on his haunches. Next, work the spiral pattern in reverse, from inside to outside. Allow your horse to relax in a fast, straight, vigorous but uncollected walk before repeating the exercise in the opposite direction (fig. 8.5).

Part Four: Serpentines

After you've mastered figure eights, later in the horse's third year, try working him in serpentine patterns—again maintaining a smooth arc through the body. I set 10-foot-long jump poles or square landscape poles on the ground at 10-foot intervals, and work my serpentines back and forth through the gaps between the poles. The goal is to continue to develop lateral softness through the horse's body. This exercise also teaches the horse not to be fearful of working with poles on the ground.

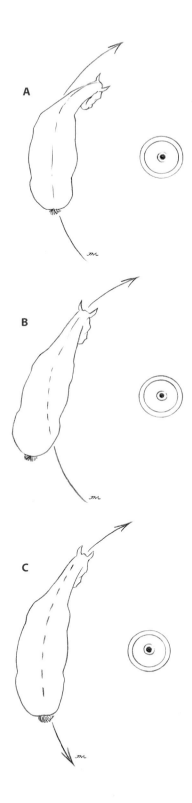

8.4 A–C The horse in A is rubbernecking around a cone and avoiding the physical challenge of softly bending his entire body. When permitted, the horse will swing his haunches wide, as shown in B, rather than remain softly on the circle. Properly executed, the horse stretches and contracts the muscles along both sides of his body, as in C. The rider's inside leg (used at the girth) and outside leg (just behind the girth) help keep the shoulders and haunches from falling out of place on the bend. The inside rein is active, and the outside rein is supportive.

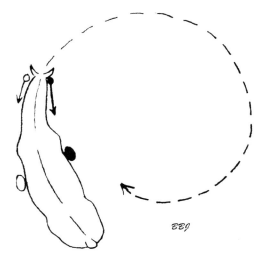

8.5 Teaching your horse to spiral in and out on a circle maximizes lateral softness. Use the same aids as when working on the circle: inside leg at the girth (black) and outside leg just behind it (white).

Exercise 3
HEAD LOWERING AND NECK STRETCHING

This is a four-part exercise, started when your horse is *three years old,* and it is practiced first from the ground with the horse wearing a halter, and then from the saddle with the horse in a bridle. The goal is to encourage your horse to stretch his neck and lower his head in preparation for "softening up" on the bridle. You may choose to eliminate this exercise, or decide to practice it only from the saddle or only from the ground. Any work you do in this area has some benefit!

Part One

Stand at the horse's left shoulder with a treat in hand. Hold it low, near the point of shoulder and ask the horse to lower his head down as far as he can comfortably get a bite. Repeat this stretching exercise to the front and center of the horse's chest, then move to the other side and repeat at the right shoulder.

Part Two

Use the treat incentive to ask your horse to stretch his head and neck to the side—first to the elbow, then the lower barrel. Increase the stretch until you ask the horse to reach all the way back to his stifle. Now, repeat these side-bending exercises, only this time ask him to reach up higher on his body—to the center of his shoulder blade, mid-barrel, and hip. Be sure to repeat each sequence on both sides.

Part Three

Next, standing at the horse's side, position the treat under the horse's barrel between his front legs right behind the knees. Again, move the treat so the horse has to stretch his neck down and tuck his chin in to gain a bite of reward (fig. 8.6). Any time he moves his feet, quietly put him back in position and ask again. Once you can ask the horse to stretch his neck and lower his head you've done a good job preparing him to connect with the bridle.

Part Four

Once he's mastered this, mount up and lower your hands to withers height at each side. With light intermittent tugs, first on one side and then the other, encourage your horse to lower his head and stretch his neck down. As he does so, give him slightly more rein to encourage more stretching and lowering.

When his head is quite low, reward him by letting his mouth just "meet" the bit. Then, very slowly and with light hands, bring your hands up to pommel height and shorten the reins while giving short rhythmic tugs on each rein, encouraging him to yield to the bit and flex at the poll.

Once the horse has mastered this at a standstill, repeat it while walking. This is not true collection, but an exercise in preparation for that important development. (If you've practiced half-halts on the trail, you've probably achieved some collection already, in any case.) This exercise increases the horse's softness in the bridle and your communication through the reins.

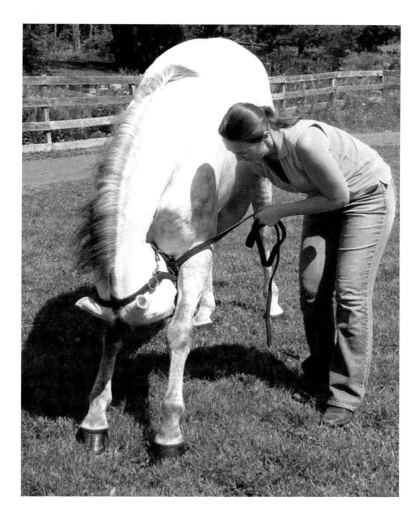

8.6 Use a treat to encourage your horse to stretch and lower his head and neck.

Developing the Ability for Collection

I call the next exercise "Conscious Collection" because it helps the rider be very aware of his relationship to the horse when the horse is brought up to and ridden in a light, collected frame. While this frame can be developed using the simple half-halt techniques described earlier (see p. 159), devoting time exclusively to developing roundness and collection helps the rider focus more closely on the job at hand.

Exercise 4
CONSCIOUS COLLECTION

Begin this work only when your horse is responding well to all parts of the three exercises discussed previously. Start with the neck-stretching and head-lowering exercises on a large circle or straight line. Use your seat and legs to push the horse vigorously forward while shortening the reins to encourage him to bring his head up to the bit and flex at the poll.

At a vigorous walk, perform several half-halts, taking up slightly more rein with each one. Be careful not to "pump" the reins with your arms as this negates the energy generated from the haunches with each stride. Instead, give only a slight amount with your elbows and hands in time to the action of the horse's head. I tell my riding students to imagine they have a 3-inch-long bungee cord tied to their elbow and their waist (see p. 193). This gives you just enough latitude to be soft, but not so much as to defeat the purpose of maintaining the horse in good form.

As you "catch and hold" the energy generated from the haunches to your bridle, you will begin to feel the horse round-up through the back and become lighter on the bit. Once you achieve this and maintain it for several strides, lengthen the reins and allow the horse to stretch out.

Repeat this process two or three times, lengthening the time you ask your horse to maintain collection each time you ride. At first, just a minute or two is all that should be expected. Within a month, the young horse might hold a good frame for eight-to-ten minutes at a time. Start at a dog

As you "catch and hold" the energy generated from the haunches to your bridle, you will begin to feel the horse round-up through the back and become lighter on the bit.

walk and increase speed and collection to a working walk, and then proceed to practice collection at a flat walk. During the horse's third year you should not yet attempt this exercise at a running walk or rack, as working in collected form in these saddle gaits takes months of conditioning and practice. Be sure to mix up this position with lots of easy, slow walking (not collected) because the horse may start to become tense if not permitted to relax and stretch out intermittently.

Exercise 5
WORKING OVER POLES

By the *end of his third year* you can begin to work your horse over poles. This is useful because it helps prevent extremely lateral timing at the working and flat walk—if your horse tends to be pacey, working him over poles helps "square" him up. This exercise also teaches him to look where he is going and to lift his legs high enough to clear obstacles without stumbling.

Again, use poles at least 10 feet long and heavy enough so your horse can't easily knock them around. Landscape timbers work well, and are easy to acquire at any building supply or landscaping retailer. I space the poles out approximately one-and-a-half times the length of the horse's body, from chest to point of buttock—on average, this is about a 10-foot distance. Usually, this length accommodates your horse's stride but if you find him tripping often, or if he has to shorten stride as he approaches the poles, experiment to discover the distance that works best (fig. 8.7).

Each time you approach the lineup of poles, give a strong half-halt. Your horse will look down to see where to place his feet, which causes his back to round and his neck to flex—actions that are beneficial. A word of caution: If your horse tends to be "trotty," limit this pole schooling to a working walk, as riding fast over ground poles encourages diagonal gaits.

Exercise 6
ROLLBACK

At a working walk, cue the horse to perform a 180-degree spin (turn) toward the wall or rail. This turn brings the horse so close to the obstacle that to avoid running into it he is forced to "roll" his weight rearward and pivot over his inside hind leg.

The rollback is an excellent exercise to help increase your horse's balance, strength, and agility, and sets his body in an excellent frame for correctly performing his smooth saddle gaits. Like all schooling exercises, it should be performed in both directions.

For a rollback to the left, position your horse 6 or 7 feet away from a wall or rail on your left—leave just enough room so that he is forced, when executing the turn, to shift his weight rearward and roll over his hindquar-

Neck Reining

Most of the exercises suggested in this chapter must be performed using a *direct* rein, (though you can neck rein your horse through a rollback). While a horse doesn't need to be taught to neck rein *(indirect* rein), it is a handy skill for him to have, especially when you ride out on the trail. The neck rein is actually a combination of seat and leg aids, as well as "guiding" the horse with a rein along his neck. To teach the neck rein to the right:

- Hold one rein in each hand, focus on an object on the right you want to turn toward, and begin walking.
- Pull your horse's nose toward the object with your right rein with a *leading* rein (see p. 157) while giving enough with the left rein to permit the horse's nose to turn to the right.
- Move your left hand forward, and lay the rein across your horse's neck halfway between the withers and poll. Do not *pull* on the rein; just lay it across his neck.

- Use your left leg slightly behind the girth to "push" your horse to the right while keeping your right leg passive at the girth.
- When the horse begins the turn, release pressure on the right rein and continue guiding him using only left rein and your leg and seat aids. If he becomes confused, take up your right rein again.
- Practice neck reining to the other side by "mirroring" these aids.

I like to practice neck reining on the trail where I use it to negotiate around practical objects—horses learn faster if the exercise makes *sense* to them. This training becomes an unconscious practice, until one day I just find myself holding the reins in one hand and expecting my horse to neck rein in whatever direction I want him to go!

ters through the turn. Ask for an active walk and when you approach the end of the rail, cue strongly for a halt (see p. 159). When your horse has stopped, *immediately* use your right leg at the girth to "push" the horse toward the wall while taking on your left rein (which should be lowered to just above your knee) to ask for a turn in that direction. Be sure to release enough of your right rein to permit the turn. (You may choose to neck rein through the turn—see sidebar, p. 182.)

Immediately after the turn your horse will be in excellent collected form, with a great deal of energy coming from his hindquarters and a "lightened" front end. This is an ideal time to ask for more speed, in gait. You do so by maintaining contact on the reins and *vigorously* pushing the horse forward with your seat and legs as soon as he has made the turn. Do not allow him to lose form or momentum.

Exercise 7
TEACHING TRANSITIONS

Developing the horse's ability to perform clean transitions from one gait to another, in good form, and from specific cues, is our next step. This begins in the horse's *fourth year*. It requires a lot of physical development and strength from the horse and attentive riding from the rider to teach a horse to respond in this manner. You cue for the speed you want by lengthening and shortening stride.

First, teach the horse to *extend* his stride on demand while maintaining collection, without breaking the four-beat pattern of footfalls (fig. 8.8 A). This causes the horse to smoothly transition up into a nicely collected, smooth saddle gait. To smoothly transition down to a slower gait, teach him to *shorten* his stride while still moving with engagement and forward energy. (Again, this collected work can be overdone, so give the horse regular

8.7 Working over poles helps even-up the timing of the horse's gait, makes him more surefooted, and helps him engage his haunches.

8.8 A & B Lengthening the horse's stride while maintaining contact on the bridle is an important element of training for your horse's best natural gait (A). To slow the gait, maintain contact and increase collection by giving less with your seat and hands (B). This shortens the horse's stride, but does not sacrifice good form.

breaks, allowing him to stretch out at a relaxing dog walk with minimal contact on the bridle.) These exercises can be practiced on the trails as well as in a more structured environment.

Part One: Upward Transitions

Move out at an active walk and ask the horse to collect. Perform a half-halt or two to get the horse "coiled for action." Now energetically press the horse forward with your seat and legs while using an easy give-and-take action on the reins, in time with the motion of the head and neck. Your shoulders should have some roll. Don't "pump" the reins, but allow them to actively follow the action of the horse's head and neck. You don't want to hinder this action because doing so creates tension throughout the horse's body, making it impossible for him to stay softly collected and relaxed.

If the horse breaks into the trot, or pace, or if he maintains the correct pattern of footfalls but stiffens up and loses his collected frame, try a half-halt to see if you can recollect and correct him. If that doesn't work, bring him back down to walk and repeat the exercise. If you practice diligently you'll suddenly feel as though you are effortlessly moving across the ground at a speed that is definitely faster than a normal walk. When you achieve this, allow the horse to remain at this gait and speed for a couple of minutes, just so he develops some neural and muscle memory from the experience.

Depending on your horse's natural gait inclinations, this early gait will likely be a flat walk or slow fox trot. At this point in training, developing speed is not on the agenda—your goal is to teach him to respond to your cues for collecting and extending stride. Speed is built from this foundation.

Part Two: Downward Transitions

To *shorten* stride and slow his speed, stop rolling your shoulders and notice-ably stiffen your arms and hands so you're not "giving" as much on the reins (fig. 8.8 B). At the same time, make your seat and legs less active, though not entirely passive. In other words, you still use your seat and legs to maintain forward energy and collection while shortening stride. The horse should maintain both the four-beat footfall rhythm and collection as his speed decreases.

This exercise not only teaches the horse to maintain collection while increasing and decreasing speed, but flexes and stretches the ring of muscles all along his topline and bottom line, and strengthens muscles of the shoulders, chest, and hindquarters. In short, it is excellent overall conditioning for both mind and body!

Benefits of Lateral Exercise for the Gaited Horse

Lateral work pays off when you're out riding and your horse gets a bit off balance and falls out of gait. It helps develop vertical flexion, the ability to contract and expand muscles from back to front, and thus the ability to collect. You can use your horse's well-developed skills to rebalance him, which changes the timing of the gait and "squares" him back up when needed.

This is how it works: Say the horse goes off balance and becomes front heavy. He then reverts to the trot, pace, or stepping pace. You do a strong half-halt or two, and his soft, responsive body immediately flexes and rounds up. His weight shifts rearward so his front end lightens up, and the front feet pick up faster because of a faster *breakover*. (Breakover is the point where the foot begins to lift off the ground. This is discussed more at length on p. 237.) Consequently, his strides even out, and his gait "squares" up again.

The smooth-gaited horse that hasn't had the benefit of this schooling, on the other hand, easily falls into an inflexible, front-heavy way of going. He reverts to the trot, pace, or stepping pace, and the rider's attempts to "square" him up by "pushing" him onto the bridle are not only ineffective, but counterproductive. The horse is too inflexible through the body to be able to round up and come onto his aids, so he becomes more rigid and "roots" at the bit instead, which causes him to become even more front heavy and hollow-backed.

A 10- or 15-minute advanced schooling session every other day prevents these problems, improves the bond of communication between horse and rider, and contributes to a longer, healthier riding career for the horse.

Collected Riding and "Self-Carriage"

I've had a number of people ask if it's always necessary to ride a gaited horse "on the bridle," or with contact on the bit. For the first few years of training, emphasis is placed on teaching the horse how to carry himself properly. This is why most of our schooling exercises require collection on the bridle, and the young gaited horse benefits from being ridden regularly this way.

Though it's good to ride your gaited horse in good form, it's also important to frequently allow him to stretch out his muscles and just relax. So when schooling your horse, vary the degree of collection you expect, and mix it up with slow uncollected riding.

A horse that is being asked for an extremely fast saddle gait cannot be expected to be collected while performing it—he needs to flatten right out and *fly*, and can hardly do so when he is being "contained" by the bridle. Occasional fast gaiting like this is fun and appropriate, but should not be overdone because of the stress it places on the horse.

Mix up this kind of riding with slow-to-medium speed gaiting, performed with collection.

As schooling progresses the horse's body becomes conditioned, and habituated, to traveling in good form. By the time he is *six or seven years old* he starts to develop "self carriage." This is when the rider collects the horse on the bridle and he automatically maintains good form even on a slack rein, with only an occasional half-halt or check on the bridle as a reminder of what is expected. You'll know you have done a great job of schooling when your horse can perform medium-speed saddle gaits in self-carriage!

Exercise 8

SHOULDER-FORE AND SHOULDER-IN

When performing the shoulder-fore and shoulder-in, your horse travels with his shoulders moved away from the rail to the left or right (depending on your direction of travel) while his hindquarters remain parallel to the rail (fig. 8.9). This requires the hind feet travel in a straight line while the forefeet move laterally to the left or right. This is called *three-tracking* because the outside foreleg and inside hind leg travel on the same (middle) track while the inside foreleg and outside hind leg travel on separate tracks. The shoulder-fore and shoulder-in are remarkably effective exercises to supple a horse, and for that reason are excellent for horses on the pacey end of the Gait Spectrum (see p. 3), as these lateral gaits create inflexibility.

Part One: Shoulder-Fore

It is not possible to teach a horse a true shoulder-in until he has mastered the much simpler *shoulder-fore,* a similar exercise that requires only half as much lateral bend.

For a shoulder-fore to the right, place your left leg on your horse's barrel just ahead of the girth using it to "push" his forequarters "off track" to the right while holding his haunches straight with steady pressure from your right (inside) leg just behind the girth. Use your left rein along his neck to steady the horse and help prevent him from dropping his inside shoulder, and your right rein to tip the horse's nose slightly in to the right.

The idea is to get the horse's body subtly "bending" to the right around your inside leg. Your body position and weight helps the horse balance correctly so place slightly more weight on your right seat bone and keep your shoulders pointed in the direction you want the horse's forequarters to take. To start, walk him in a straight line with his body bent for only three or four steps. Work the horse in both directions ("mirroring" the riding aids just described), but don't overdo it or ask for too much of a bend initially because this exercise is quite strenuous.

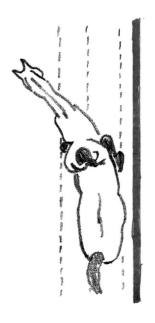

8.9 In the shoulder-in the horse travels on three tracks with his shoulders moved away from the rail to the inside of the arena while his hindquarters remain parallel to the rail.

8.10 In the haunches-in the horse travels on three tracks with his haunches moved away from the rail to the inside of the arena while the forehand remains on the rail.

Part Two: Shoulder-In

After he's become accustomed to the shoulder-fore and performs it easily, you can advance to the *shoulder-in,* progressively requesting additional bend through his body using stronger aids. Make sure he doesn't cheat you by dropping an inside shoulder to avoid the work of bending—a person from the ground or a mirror in the arena can help you determine if this is the case. Use the wall or fence initially to help prevent the horse from swinging his haunches out and avoiding the hard work of bending. Later, with practice, you can perform this move while going on down the trail or through the center of an arena.

Exercise 9

HAUNCHES-FORE AND HAUNCHES-IN

Haunches-in causes your horse to three-track with a lateral bend to the inside. The horse's outside hind leg follows the track of his inside foreleg, while the inside hind leg and outside foreleg track separately (fig. 8.10).

The haunches-in is preceded by the *haunches-fore,* a similar exercise requiring less lateral bend. To perform it to the right, hold your right leg firmly—without pushing—against the barrel at the girth. Place your left leg behind the girth and "push" the haunches in, while steadying his forequarters with light steady pressure on each rein. Again, only practice a slight bend for a few steps to start, and increase the length of travel and amount of lateral bend over many training sessions.

Additional Schooling Resources

There are several other advanced schooling exercises you might want to learn and practice, but because they do not relate specifically to the gaited horse they are outside the direct scope of this book. Nevertheless, this work can be fun and highly rewarding. For that reason I recommend reading and viewing some of the excellent books and DVDs available for different disciplines (see p. 240 for where you can purchase these resources).

CHAPTER 9

Solving Common Problems

Be Prepared for Challenges

UNFORTUNATELY, THERE ARE MANY PEOPLE WHO start riding gaited horses under the impression they do not need any specialized knowledge and can just saddle up and ride off into the sunset. It doesn't help that some general horse trainers and clinicians also promote the concept that there's no difference between training, fitting, and riding a gaited horse and other horses. They don't understand that gaited horses have unique physiological needs that must be accommodated.

Typically, gaited horses present more challenges and problems than non-gaited horses. There are many reasons for this:

• People don't understand or possess the right equitation skills to bring out the best in their gaited horse.

- Old-school gaited training techniques still prevail in many parts of the world, resulting in horses that rush, are uncooperative, and move in a "ventroflexed" frame (see p. 16).(see p. 16)
- As I discussed earlier in the book, saddles that don't allow the animal freedom of motion through the topline can cause negative issues with gait, behavior, and soundness (see p. 127).
- Horses subjected to farriers who "trim and shoe for gait" rather than follow the natural angle of the foot are prone to arthritis, navicular, and a plethora of other structural problems (see p. 234).

When you take all these factors into account, it is easy to understand why gaited horses as a whole are a rather troubled lot!

I don't want to discourage anyone from becoming, or remaining involved with gaited horses. Addressing common problems is not usually difficult once a person understands where they originate, and riding a smooth-gaited horse is worth the effort of obtaining the additional education and training required to do so properly.

The following list comprises some of the common problems people have with gaited horses, along with the page on which you can read related discussion.

RIDER ISSUES

BEHAVIORAL PROBLEMS

PHYSICAL ISSUES

GAIT ISSUES

RIDER ISSUES

Gaited Equitation Skills

SEAT

Earlier in the book I discussed the unique action of the gaited horse's back (see p. 128), and why it is important for the rider to accommodate that action by riding with a seat position identical to that taken by a person riding bareback (see p. 124).

A bareback rider instinctively seats herself immediately behind the horse's withers, with her legs hanging relaxed and positioned just slightly in front of her seat in what is sometimes disparagingly called a "chair seat." Now, I'm not talking about putting your feet "up on the dashboard," but neither are they directly under your seat. Your feet should be level, or the heels pointed slightly down—under no circumstances should you bear a lot of weight in the stirrups or in your heels.

When riding a gaited horse you should ride somewhat "on your pockets." That is, you don't want to ride with your crotch pushed into the seat, or leaning or hunching too far forward. Rather, stand up in your stirrups, tuck your pelvis, straighten your lower back, roll your shoulders back, and sit back down in the saddle, relaxed. Keep your seat bones and shoulders pointed straight forward or turned slightly in the direction of travel. Remember you're on a 1,000-plus-pound animal that can feel the impact of a gnat— how your weight is distributed is going to have a tremendous impact on his forward energy, gait, and general attitude.

9.1 This rider is in a position similar to one commonly assumed by bareback riders. It is evident from her posture and her Tennessee Walking Horse's excellent form and forward energy that she is using an active seat and legs. Note that she is seated somewhat "on her pockets," her foot falls slightly ahead of her seat, her knee is bent and relaxed, and her upper body is almost imperceptibly behind the vertical. Both horse and rider appear calm and comfortable.

One thing to avoid: Do not keep "booting" your horse with your foot. This is a common riding error committed by riders who are trying to urge their horse to move forward with greater energy. This repetitious tapping or kicking on the barrel is annoying to the horse and eventually causes him to "tune you out" and ignore your leg aids altogether. Another undesirable habit is to rely too much on the use of spurs. An animal continually prodded forward with a sharp jab to his side may or may not be induced to pick up speed, but he will almost certainly become rigid through his body and develop increased resistance to his rider's aids. (In fact, unless you are very confident of your seat and balance in the saddle, I do not recommend the use of spurs for the everyday, non-professional rider.)

Instead of booting, poking, or prodding your horse, use your seat and legs to "press" the horse forward, keeping time with the cadence of his gait by pressing with your seat and legs as each hind foot picks up (fig. 9.1). Maintain his forward impulsion by reinforcing these aids with a riding crop, humane spur, or the ends of your reins, if need be.

HANDS AND ARMS

Hand and arm position is also an important consideration. The rider should ride with some contact on the reins—at least until the horse has achieved enough training and experience to be able to balance himself without contact on the bridle. This is called achieving "self-carriage," (see sidebar, p. 186). Your shoulders should be loose and slightly rolling, and your elbows at your waist. Imagine 3-inch bungee cords at your elbows, allowing you some latitude for following the action of your horse's head, but not permitting you to throw your elbows—and upper body weight—far forward. When you ride with your elbows way out in front of your body you actually place far too much of your own weight forward, causing the horse to become front heavy and out of balance (figs. 9.2 A & B).

Your hand position should be just above the saddle pommel. Riding with too high hands causes the horse to go high-headed, and flat or hollow-

9.2 A & B In A, the rider's hands are too for forward and high, which throws her upper body weight onto the horse's forehand. This causes him to go in a stiff, front-heavy fashion, resulting in a stepping pace. After only a day of practice, the rider's poor hand and upper body position have improved, as seen in B. The direct result of this is that her horse is executing a flat walk with perfect timing and beautiful form.

backed, while carrying your hands too low causes too much of your weight to be thrown forward.

A horse's frame "mirrors" that of his rider. If you slouch and are hollow-backed, this is reflected in your horse's way of going. Pay attention to your body position whenever you ride and make it a habit to routinely correct poor riding posture. Assuming the right seat and hand position soon becomes second nature (figs. 9.3 A & B).

Conscious Attention and Communication

Many problems I encounter in clinics or lessons are caused by inattentive riding. The rider simply mounts up and allows her horse to carry her about in any way he chooses, and does nothing to help the horse carry her weight in an efficient manner. Horses are not really designed to carry weight; rather, they are built for forward motion. The weight of a rider on his back is a serious detriment to the horse's ability to generate forward motion and, left to his own devices, the hapless animal has no innate sense about how to help himself do so in a manner that does not stress his body (let alone one that allows his rider to ride in comfort).

9.3 A & B A horse's posture mirrors his rider's seat, hands, and energy level. In A, the horse is strung out and front heavy as his rider hunches too far forward. In B, there is some improvement in her equitation, and that is reflected in her horse moving out in better form.

On top of this, the inattentive rider pays little mind to any cues that the horse might be trying to convey a message to her: His reaction to pain goes unnoticed, as does a fearful response or one that indicates the horse feels tired or overwhelmed.

You owe it to your horse to learn and practice "horse language" and to be able to assist him in the job of carrying you on his back. Reading books such as this one is a start, but in my opinion, every rider should take at least one series of riding lessons from a qualified, competent instructor. You should also spend *time* with your horse, learning his habits, studying his responses to various situations—and just hanging out with him so you can get to know one another.

It's fine to pay attention to the scenery and the conversation of friends when you're riding, but don't do so at the expense of "listening" to your horse. One ear should be keenly tuned in to him at all times.

BEHAVIORAL PROBLEMS

THE IMPORTANCE OF TACK ASSESSMENT

Any time a horse exhibits undesirable behaviors, be sure to carefully examine your tack to be sure it's not causing discomfort. I cannot stress this enough—about 80 percent of the horses I work with have tack issues as the root of their problems. Once these have been resolved, the horse's behavior improves quickly, with just a little work on the part of the rider. If the tack isn't fixed, then neither is the behavior—at least, not for long.

Problem: Rushing and Barging

One of the most common problems presented to me is the horse that possesses little or no "whoa" and way too much "go!" A *rushing* horse is one that never relaxes but is always moving in "third gear," even when you want him to relax and move out more slowly. A barging horse is one over which you feel you have little or no control: He does what he wants, when he wants, and where he wants, paying little attention to your riding aids—or to your safety. He often insists on being the lead horse on the trail, and pushes too frequently into other horses' personal space, placing you at risk. When you head back toward home or to the trailhead, his misbehavior escalates. When he loses site of a pasturemate or horse he's befriended on the trail, he may take to bucking and rearing in his determination to be reunited with them. Note: If your horse is under three years of age, wait until he is at least four before addressing this problem.

SAFETY FIRST

The first order of business is to be safe whenever working with an out-of-control horse or one that has no "lower gears." I suggest working in an arena, round pen, safe pasture (never one with a barbed-wire fence or lots of rocks or woodchuck holes), or corral for the first lesson or two.

Start by making sure your horse has a well-fitted saddle-and-pad system that offers plenty of flexibility through the back. Assuming your horse is over three years of age (if not, wait until he is to address this kind of problem) I recommend you use the Imus Comfort Bit™ (see p. 114). You will not get the same results with a snaffle or hackamore. The design of my bit assures your horse's comfort, as well as your control. It allows you to do the lateral flexion exercises I outline here and in chapter 8 (see p. 171) to best effect in a short period of time, as well as encourages your horse to drop his head and bend softly in response to your rein aids. These are all imperative lessons for the rushing or barging horse to learn.

WHY GAITED HORSES RUSH AND BARGE

The reason many gaited horses have a habit of rushing or barging is because they have actually been trained to do so. Traditionally, it was taught that the only way to establish a good, fast gait was to ask the horse to move out at speed with as high a headset as possible. This gave the horse a higher center of gravity, which made it easy for him to be thrown off balance by the rider shifting her weight back and forth in the saddle while also see-sawing on the reins.

The reason many gaited horses have a habit of rushing or barging is because they have actually been trained to do so.

Indeed, this riding technique can encourage the young animal to move all four legs out of synchrony, resulting in a fast, smooth gait. To some trainers' way of thinking, an added benefit of this method is that they can start gait work with horses as young as 18 months, and it's not uncommon for two-year-olds to be run through auctions gaiting at very fast speeds. At many gaited-horse auctions, the faster the young animal gaits (rushes), the higher the bidding is likely to go.

I'm ashamed to admit that I bought into this technique early on, before I had the chance to work with enough horses to realize how faulty it is. There are some serious pitfalls to this method of gait training. First, it requires the horse to move in a stiff, head-up, hollow-backed frame. Second, to stop such an animal generally requires harsh bitting, which creates a resistant attitude. Last but not least, the horse is never taught to think his way through a situation, but simply responds to the rider's weight and aids by stiffening up and rushing forward.

Pain

The gaited horse may express pain in a number of ways, and when the saddle or bit create pain, the "fight-or-flight" instinct kicks in and the horse tries to "run away" from it. While it certainly won't help to run away from pain caused by tack that is firmly strapped in place, the horse is acting instinctively.

As time goes on, this "rushing" becomes firmly ingrained. A person riding such a horse usually resorts to stronger bits in an effort to achieve some measure of control. The problem with this thinking is that when a rider uses a harsh bit, the horse naturally stiffens against it to try to avoid the bit action that causes the pain. When the horse stiffens and resists, the rider pulls back harder on the reins, causing the horse more pain and giving him something firm to resist against. And, so on and so forth. This is usually why a *rushing* horse develops into a *barging* horse.

Trying to gain control of a rushing horse through harsher bits and stronger pulling is an exercise in futility. It creates an ongoing circle of frustration for both horse and rider, and only creates more difficult problems down the road.

9.4 A & B Every horse should be taught the one-rein stop for use in an emergency. To the right: Shorten the right rein and plant your hand on the saddle pommel or horn while holding the left (outside) hand on the horse's neck just in front of the withers (A). Use your right (inside) leg strongly to push the haunches to the outside. Look down at the ground on your right, and maintain this position until the horse comes to a stop, at which point you immediately release all pressure. Repeat this exercise many times, increasing speed over time, until your horse instantly disengages his hindquarters when you give the cue as with this Tennessee Walking Horse—note his cocked inside leg (B).

A

B

Another common element is that a painful horse feels "compromised" and unable to care for himself, so instinctively reacts by "looking for the herd" for safety and security, which can be virtually any other horse within close proximity.

The solution to this syndrome is simple, though at first it may seem counterintuitive: Use a milder, more tactful bit, and let go of the reins. When I first suggest this to my clients, the inevitable response is, "You gotta be kidding! If I go to a mild bit and don't hang onto the reins real tight, this horse is gonna kill me!"

Let me assure you: I haven't lost a student yet. In fact, I've found that without exception, when the rider eliminates pain and gives the horse nothing to resist against, the animal inevitably softens up and learns to listen and respond appropriately to aids in a remarkably short period of time. These magnificent creatures are incredibly forgiving, and most of them want to please. We only need offer them the chance to do so.

Solution: One-Rein Stop

The first lesson to teach either a rushing or barging horse (from here on I'll refer to this simply as "rushing") is the *one-rein stop*. The goal is to teach the horse to automatically disengage his hindquarters—his "drive train"—when he begins to rush. Now, I've seen people try to perform this tactic on an out-of-control horse when the horse has never been trained for it. This is a serious mistake and can lead to disaster. Although the one-rein stop is an extremely useful technique, it must be practiced over and over in order to be safe and effective.

Start by mounting up in a safe place. Place your *right hand* low on the rein, and bend your horse to the right by planting your hand on the saddle pommel (figs. 9.4 A & B). Some people bring this hand back to their thigh, but this may be easily overdone in an emergency and unbalance the rider. Place your left hand with a completely loose rein on the horse's neck just in front of the withers. While looking down at the ground on your right, use your inside (right) leg to push the haunches off track (the line he is on).

Once you've done this, energy generated from the haunches can no

9.5 A & B A horse that rushes, like this Spotted Saddle Horse, is usually "pushing" on the bit, using it to his own advantage (A). The rider's instinctual response is to tense up and take hard on the reins, which exacerbates the problem. The horse learns to work quietly by asking him to slow down using half-halts (see p. 159) with a regular "give-and-take" motion on the reins, then rewarding him for responding even a slight amount to this pressure (B).

longer propel the horse's body forward, and he quickly "loses steam." Your horse will probably move his hind feet; just maintain the rein pressure until he comes to a standstill. Reward him by immediately releasing the pressure and allowing him to walk off. Once he stops promptly each time you take on the rein, repeat the exercise to the left side.

After he understands the cue, repeat the exercise at least 30 times to each side, still starting from a standstill. Next, teach him to respond to the cue from a walk, and again repeat the lesson 30 times to each side. Progress up to a gait, and then a canter (if you feel safe enough and if it is appropriate to canter your gaited horse—see p. 167). Repetition is the key to success. Once the horse has mastered this move (or "not move"), practice it from time to time as a reminder.

The one-rein stop is your "emergency brake," and every horse should have one in case something ever frightens him enough to throw him into "flight mode." However, the goal with a rushing horse is not to teach him to *stop*, but to *teach him not to rush in the first place*. This is a very simple, straightforward lesson.

Solution: Release from Pressure

Mount up and ask the horse to move forward. Chances are, you won't have to ask very hard! Relax your seat, lengthen your legs, and let your horse move forward with no contact on the reins. Yes, your horse will rush. When he starts to pick up speed, perform a strong half-halt to ask him to slow (see p. 159). The instant he hesitates—even the slightest amount— relax and give him his head again (figs. 9.5 A & B).

He will rush off again…and again. Each time, use your aids to slow things down. You will find yourself doing a nearly constant "give-and-take" on the reins as you reward his responses by *releasing all pressure* on the bridle. Your horse learns to seek this reward by slowing down when you take on the reins; the faster your response is to his obedience, the faster he learns the lesson.

This lesson teaches you discipline as a rider because your instinctive response is likely to grab those reins and pull back hard. Now, your only job is to stay as relaxed as possible on top of the horse, and work with a soft give-and-take on the reins.

Sooner than you expect, your horse is going to slow down to where you can begin to teach him appropriate rein aids. You want to teach him how to drop his head and bend through his neck and body in response to the rein. As mentioned previously, a horse that is soft and supple through the body has a quiet, focused mind and is more attuned and able to respond to his rider's aids.

Solution: Serpentine Ground Poles

Horses don't actually get "hard mouths" but rather get "rigid necks," because a horse that rushes through the bit is necessarily stiff through the neck. Riding serpentine patterns around ground poles (see p. 177) is an excellent way to start working a stiff-necked horse, because it asks for a deep bend, especially in the neck, then allows him to straighten out between the poles before cuing him to bend in the opposite direction (fig. 9.6).

When doing this work, be sure that when you pull on one rein, you release pressure on the other so you're not inadvertently sending conflicting signals and once again giving the horse something to resist. Remember, this work needs to be done either in a jointed snaffle bit that will not pinch the horse's tongue or—since you cannot do direct-reined lateral work with a solid-mouth curb bit—in a curb with independent, pinch-free action from side to side, such as the Imus Comfort Bit™ (see p. 109).

Bring your inside rein back toward your knee. Keep it nice and low with a straight line from your hand to the horse's mouth. Firmly press your inside

9.6 Serpentines around ground poles are a good way to begin working a stiff, unresponsive horse laterally. When you take up rein on the inside of the bend, be sure to offer a corresponding degree of slack on the outside rein, or you will confuse your horse and make the problem worse.

leg against the horse's side at the girth, and take your outside leg back to prevent the hindquarters from swinging out. You want the horse's entire body to bend and soften.

After the horse begins to drop his head and bend softly in response to the reins, you can shorten your reins to begin describing smaller circles and figure eights around cones (see p. 174). This encourages even more softening and bending. Ten or 15 minutes of this work is all you should plan on. You're asking for athletic movement through the horse's whole body that he is not accustomed to—you don't want to tire, bore, or frustrate him. Finish the lesson while you both feel encouraged and refreshed. Repeat these lessons in an open area once the horse is responding well. Shortly thereafter you may take him out on the trail.

PROBLEM: Herd Bound

Horses who rush often are also "herd bound," meaning that they panic whenever there is any distance between them and another horse. For this reason, it's possible to solve rushing when working alone in a paddock or arena, but still have problems when out on the trail. So to complete this schooling you need to work with another horse and rider (see also Barn Sour, p. 204).

Solution: Play "Leap Frog"

When beginning the following exercise I recommend riding with no more than one other horse and rider. You and your companion will play "leap frog" with your horses to help your herd bound horse get used to going in a nice, soft responsive frame even when out on the trail with others riding ahead.

Ask the other rider to ride her horse far enough ahead of yours so your horse gets a bit worked up. Use the give-and-take technique on the reins to hold him back—but not for long—then move him toward the horse ahead. Do not allow him to stop once he's caught up; instead, pass the other animal and go on out in front for a ways. If the other horse gets excited, so much the better—you can use this game to retrain both animals. Leap frog down the trail, extending the distance between the two horses each time.

Before long, as he stops getting upset over the separation, you'll be able to ride your horse either in front or in back of the other horse with ease. A useful variation on this, especially when headed toward home, is that instead of "leaping forward," you "jump to the rear" by taking your horse from lead position, turning him around, and riding him in the opposite direction a ways before assuming the "behind" position. Hold him in the back until he gets excited, and then have the other horse reverse direction and ride back behind you, and so on. Once your horse works well with one horse, introduce another one or two to the game. After just a couple of rides you'll have a horse that is—as one recent clinic participant described her previously barging gelding—"soft as butter."

PROBLEM: Barn Sour

A "barn sour" horse is one that refuses to leave his barn or property or, should the rider manage to get away from home, pulls continually once turned back in that direction. As always, the problem may be discomfort; however, it may be that he's not been ridden away from home frequently enough to feel safe, or he's become too bonded with a stable- or pasturemate (see also Spooking and Balking, p. 205).

Solution: Lateral Exercises

The basic way to handle this is to practice the series of *lateral exercises* from chapter 8. A horse that has become soft and supple, and habituated to responding to his rider's cues, demonstrates far less resistance than one that is ridden infrequently and in poor form. Many such horses are half-trained, having only been taught to balance the weight of a rider and respond to basic rein cues. Such horses can be dangerous when confronted by a challenging situation.

Solution: Travel to Ride Elsewhere

Another suggestion is to truck your horse away from home several times and ride in unfamiliar places. Make the rides fun! Bring along companions, stop and let the horses graze, vary the gaits, play horsey games, go for a swim, practice your schooling exercises with your friends (most riders I know love playing around with the various schooling routines). I truly believe horses enjoy these kinds of activities as much as their rider. When a horse has nothing to look forward to out on the trail except lugging the rider up and down hills, or over flat sand, with little or no horse and human communication, what is his incentive for leaving the barn, where he can enjoy the playful companionship of other equines and eat to his heart's content?

After several interesting rides in a place where the horse cannot refuse to leave the barn, you most likely will have retrained him to respond to your cues, and go where he is directed. Problem solved.

PROBLEM: Spooking and Balking

Spookiness can be an inherent trait, or learned behavior. It's important to ascertain the reasons *why* your horse is exhibiting these behaviors, because that determines the most appropriate way to respond.

SPOOKING AS RESISTANCE

I have one mare that, if not ridden regularly, spooks hard at every little thing on her way out of the barn, refuses to pass logs on the side of the trail, and tries to whirl toward home every time she sees something "frightening." Yet this same mare becomes placid as an old plow horse on the way home. Once I realized her spooking and balking was actually caused by barn sourness, I dealt with her behavior very strongly.

ESTABLISHING AUTHORITY

In the above situation, the horse needed to understand she *could not* fool me, nor get away with the situation. I had to establish that I was the boss, in charge of where she could and could not go. (This, by the way, is a common problem—a timid rider can make for a troublesome horse.)

When she balked, I would see-saw on the reins, thump her with my boots, push vigorously with my seat and, if this didn't make her move forward, give her a good pop with the end of my reins. I persisted until the instant she took a step forward, then immediately rubbed her neck and told her, "Good girl!" For a while, she only took a step or two before trying her ploy again, so I repeated my negative and positive reinforcement as many times as necessary. Then I made sure she was ridden a few times every week so I didn't have to deal with that behavior on a regular basis!

FEARFUL SPOOKING

On the other hand, some horses are simply more sensitive and attuned to their environment. To treat such a horse in the above manner would likely turn him into a basket case, so at first you need to give the horse the full benefit of the doubt. One way to determine if your horse is truly frightened is to ride him away from, and then back toward the barn several times. It's best to ride him in the lead of a group so he doesn't get his "courage" from another calm horse going first. If your horse is resistant he will balk on the way out, and rush on the way home. A genuinely fearful horse will spook at the same things when ridden in both directions.

Solution: Desensitization to Objects at Home

The first order of business is to desensitize the horse to all kinds of stimuli. Introduce him to a tarp, first from a distance and then up close. Lay the tarp on the ground and let the horse graze near it. Or, if you're working inside, place a small amount of grain on the edge of the tarp, while you stand in the center of it to show that it is harmless. Gradually, ask him to walk over the tarp. At first he may try to dodge it, but if you remain calm he will likely be comfortable stepping on it within 10 or 15 minutes.

Now pick up the tarp, and move it around. (Be sure to wear hard boots, and keep yourself safe.) Aim for him to be so comfortable with the tarp you can lay it down on his back, or drag it along while leading him and riding him. Take this as slowly as necessary—you'll probably find the process quite fun!

Next, introduce him to floppy rain gear, to umbrellas opening and closing, and to popping balloons or paper lunch bags. Start this work from a distance away, and move in closer as he calms down. Be sure to repeat everything on both sides of his body, as it is true that you can train a horse to be nonresponsive to an object on one side, and when he's confronted with it on the other side, he'll still go ballistic.

I have a pool with a floppy cover in my backyard. I also have dogs, and a barbeque grill with another floppy cover. There are strange objects around, such as hoses, tables and chairs, and a large outdoor umbrella. I recently took a four-year-old gelding that was extremely spooky and walked him all around my backyard until he was comfortable eating grass right next to the pool. I then tied him to a sturdy rail on my back deck, right in the middle of all these frightening "gremlins." Within five minutes he had settled right down, one hind foot cocked, and his eyes half-closed. I stepped out on the deck immediately over his head, and he hardly gave me a moment's attention. An hour earlier, he'd have jumped right out of his skin. Exposure is the key.

The secret to success is to do this work routinely, so that frightening objects of all kinds quickly become "ho-hum." I tie balloons, flags, and feed bags to my pasture fences. It may not be particularly decorative, but people are always impressed by how calm-natured my horses tend to be. This is not an accident, but the result of some simple commonsense practices.

Solution: Desensitizing on the Trail

No matter how habituated a horse is to everyday objects around the farm, there may be times out on the trail when he is completely unprepared for something strange and unusual. Last year one of my horses was totally unnerved by a tree stand that we had to pass. Should this happen to you, all the schooling you've done pays rich dividends as you calmly cue your horse for a half-halt, or ask for extension and lengthening of stride. Gain his attention particularly on the side opposite the spooky item, and keep his focus on *you,* rather than on it. When the horse is totally unnerved—and this can happen—either have a calmer horse lead the way past, or dismount and walk him progressively closer to it. After he's calmed down, remount and ride on.

Oh, and what happened with that tree stand? I tied my horse near the foot of that tree and we broke for lunch!

> **There may be times out on the trail when your horse is completely unprepared for something strange and unusual.**

PROBLEM: Tongue over the Bit or Hanging out of Mouth

A fairly common problem with horses, especially young ones, is the tendency to place the tongue over the top of the bit, or else hang the tongue out one side of the mouth. A horse that puts his tongue over the bit can be annoying at best, and dangerous at worst, while riding a horse with a lolling tongue is unsightly enough to be embarrassing.

One young Mountain Horse gelding I trained started hanging his tongue out one side of his mouth after about a month of riding. I had his

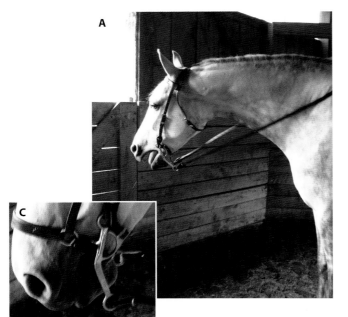

9.7 A–C On occasion a horse like this American Saddlebred gets in the habit of hanging his tongue out one side of his mouth, or he may play with the bit, getting his tongue over the mouthpiece or grabbing the shanks with his lips (A). A dropped noseband adjusted so the mouthpiece is "trapped" between the noseband and the corners of the horse's lips can quickly teach the horse to keep his tongue in place and go with a quiet mouth (B). Adjust the noseband so the horse can breathe freely, but cannot open his mouth wide enough to play with the bit (C).

teeth checked (always the first order of business with either of these issues), and no problems were detected. I realized he only did this when faced with a challenging situation, or when he became tired. It was his way of pacifying himself when stressed. It never ceases to amaze me how many ways horses communicate with us when we take the time to analyze and interpret their behavior.

Many gaited horses have been ridden—even started at a very young age—with a harsh bit that causes them to develop an aversion to contact with the bit. This may be why your horse exhibits this behavior; therefore, it is *extremely* important for you to use a bit that won't cause pain or discomfort, and to be as light with your rein aids as possible.

Solution: Dropped Noseband

Once it has been determined that there are no issues with the horse's teeth, and that he's comfortable with his bit, the solution to this problem is simple. Use a dropped noseband with a long brow piece and place it so the noseband is just below the bit, trapping the bit between the noseband and the corners of the horse's mouth. Adjust it snugly, but not so tight that it interferes with breathing (figs. 9.7 A–C). This prevents the horse from opening his mouth wide enough to work his tongue over the bit or hang it out one side of his mouth. Usually after several rides the horse learns to go with a nice, quiet mouth, and the noseband can be eliminated.

PHYSICAL ISSUES

PROBLEM: Locked Stifle

A common affliction among gaited horses is an upward fixation of the patella, otherwise known as a "locking stifle." The symptoms of this condition may be so subtle as to cause the horse owner many nights of restless, worried wondering, or so obvious that it seems an otherwise healthy horse has become functionally useless (fig. 9.8). The good news is that oftentimes these animals—even those with very pronounced signs—can be brought back to soundness using basic riding and conditioning techniques.

The stifle joint, equivalent to the knee joint in a human, is mechanically complex. Horses have the unique ability to rotate and lock the "kneecap" (patella) over a groove in the lower, protruding portion of the femur (large upper bone of the leg). A horse with his leg braced in place like this is able to stand while sleeping. This is a rather handy device for an animal of prey that may not have time to get his large body up from the ground to escape quickly when attacked. This locking mechanism also enables the horse to maintain a forward extension of the long, heavy hind limb with minimal effort, because the extended limb is temporarily braced into position during a certain portion of each stride.

The ability to selectively lock this joint in place is certainly useful. But on occasion this locking mechanism goes haywire and the patella is snagged—locked in place—over the protruding portion of the lower femur for an inappropriate length of time. This hinders freedom of motion. Symptoms of this mechanical glitch may be quite diverse, creating a great deal of confusion for both horse owner and veterinarian. While most veterinarians are acquainted with the problem, few are aware that it is especially prevalent among gaited horses. Therefore, a vet may not immediately consider this syndrome when evaluating a horse with varied and intermittent lameness issues.

SYMPTOMS OF A LOCKING STIFLE

Symptoms of a locking stifle include: chronic dragging of the toe of one hind foot; the horse's hind leg hitching up for several strides after the rider asks him to move forward; stiffness in one hind limb, particularly after a period of rest; a pronounced hitch or popping action in the horse's rear leg; the leg actually locking in place so that it drags behind the horse; the sudden sensation when riding that the horse's hind leg is giving out from beneath him; the hind leg swinging in an outward arc, rather than straight underneath the body; an inability or unwillingness to take up a proper canter lead; and/or shortening of hind leg stride.

To further confuse matters, any number and combination of these symptoms may be intermittent, seasonal, or subject to particular condi-

9.8 A horse with an upward fixated patella may have mild symptoms, such as a hitch in its gait, or his hind leg may lock up altogether.

tions. Young horses may exhibit dramatic and frightening symptoms, then simply grow out of it a season or two later. Some horses display distinct lameness after being confined to a stall or following periods of prolonged rest. Horses in northern climates may demonstrate problems during the first few spring rides after a long winter layover.

It's not uncommon for a horse to lock up while traveling down hills or at the end of an especially trying ride. The animal that refuses to take a correct canter lead, especially on a circle, might be suspect. The truth is this problem is so pervasive among gaited horses that the smart owner always includes it in their shortlist of possible causes when facing difficult-to-pin-down, hind-limb lameness issues.

Have you ever owned a motor vehicle that misfires or otherwise demonstrates problems at inopportune times, but runs like a clock when you take it to a mechanic for repair? This is fairly typical of what happens when a horse with upward fixation of the patella is examined by a veterinarian. A surefire diagnosis of this condition can be tricky!

CONTRIBUTING FACTORS

The causes of this syndrome include poor or weak supportive muscling in the horse's hind leg; too straight (post-legged) hind-leg conformation; and lax patellar ligaments. You might wonder why *then,* is the condition so much more common among gaited horses?

As I've said before, gaited horses are "quadridextrous" in nature—that is, they can move each leg independently of the others. In order to express such free, "loose" motion (how often have you heard, "That horse is a loose mover"?) the animal's ligaments must possess a high degree of elasticity. People with this kind of tissue elasticity are often called "double-jointed." The downside to being built this way is that excessively loose ligaments may allow so much freedom in the joint that when it's stressed, the joint pops right out of place. I learned this lesson firsthand as an athletic young person when my shoulders routinely popped out of joint.

An important contributing factor is the poor riding employed by many gaited-horse riders. Given the extra degree of inherent elasticity in the joint ligaments of many gaited horses, it becomes especially important that the muscles and tissues surrounding the joint be maintained in strong, dense condition in order to support the joint and eliminate excess laxity in the ligaments. Routinely riding horses in an uncollected, "strung out" form is extremely detrimental to the overall strength and soundness of the horse's hind leg structures. Yet this form of riding has long been the norm for gaited horses.

A pacing or step-pacing horse, for example, still has far too much body weight on each (hyper-extended) hind leg just before the foot is picked up. This not only stresses the joints and stretches those lax ligaments, but contributes nothing to the strengthening of the supportive muscles. This makes these gaits—smooth as they might be for the rider—a physically debilitating "double whammy" for the horse.

That's the bad news—and that's also the good news! Because just as poor riding form contributes to the syndrome, so can good riding and conditioning help to reverse the condition. This is often true even when the symptoms appear quite severe.

Solution: Surgery

On rare occasions a horse may be inherently so prone to a locking stifle that it becomes necessary to resort to a surgical solution. While surgery usually eliminates the problem with few side effects, it is always better to take a non-surgical approach whenever possible. When an owner is willing to make the effort to recondition the horse appropriately, surgery is seldom required. The most common and effective solution is to keep the muscles and ligaments surrounding the stifle joint in strong, dense condition. This can be accomplished through a program of regular exercise and by adding an appropriate supplement to the horse's diet. While I'm not generally a proponent of doing a great deal of supplementation for horses, this is one situation where I've found it can be useful.

> **Routinely riding horses in an uncollected, "strung out" form is extremely detrimental to the strength and soundness of the horse's hind leg structures.**

Solution: Ground Exercises

Round-Pen Work

A severely stifle-compromised horse should not be ridden until you've improved the condition to some degree through ground exercises and supplementation. With such a horse, position your round pen on a spot where the ground has a slight uphill elevation, and simply do your usual round-pen exercises so that he is forced to balance his weight properly. In this case, do not work the animal more than five minutes to either side, and *make sure the circumference of the round pen is at least 60 feet,* as working on a tight circle is stressful on the horse's legs. If you have no round pen, working on a very long lunge line is also acceptable. One rule: insist on an engaged, active walk. (See more on round-penning on p. 148.)

Line-Driving

Line-driving is another excellent way to help condition a horse that cannot be ridden. Line-driving on hills and over ground poles at least 4 inches in height is useful, as is working the horse through sand or deep grass. (See more on line-driving on p. 151.)

Solution: Riding Exercises

If your horse can safely be ridden—and the majority of "stifled" horses can—you can help strengthen the tissues surrounding the stifle joint by exercising over ground poles and performing frequent rein-backs and half-halts. Avoid working circles, figure eights, or any exercises that require a higher percentage of weight to be borne on the *inside* hind legs, as these exercises place extra stress on the stifle joints.

Hill Work

If you can ride up and down hills, use these to good effect, making sure your horse keeps his hind end well underneath his body going both ways. You can do this by stopping and asking for a rein-back as you approach a downhill slope, then maintaining moderate contact on the reins as your horse negotiates going down. However, you should avoid pulling the reins so hard that he actually lifts his head. His neck should be arched and his head slightly telescoped downward.

If your horse begins to "fall" downhill, stop and ask for another rein-back. While challenging, this is always a good idea in any case, as it helps the horse to balance his own and the rider's weight properly on tricky downhill terrain. This is especially important since a stifled horse is in danger of falling downhill when his hindquarters are not kept properly engaged. You need to assess the severity of your horse's condition to determine how steep a hill he can safely handle.

Maintaining balance and form is easier when the horse climbs uphill, as gravity naturally pulls his weight back over the haunches. Your job then is to insist on a very active, strong walk—do not permit your horse to slip into a canter or slow, lazy walk. The horse is being exercised for his own long-term welfare and cantering is easier than actively walking uphill, while dog walking offers no appreciable benefits.

All reconditioning on hills should be planned with your horse's current state in mind. Those with only slight, intermittent stifle problems may be expected to negotiate frequent, fairly steep inclines and be ridden for a relatively long period of time, perhaps as long as two hours. Animals that evidence stronger symptoms should be kept to lower climbs and ridden for shorter stints. A half-hour of light-to-moderate hill work might be the most such a horse should be expected to handle until his condition starts to improve. For some horses, ten minutes of work might be a good start. You walk a fine line between doing so little as to be ineffective, or so much as to be damaging. If in doubt about how much exercise is appropriate, consult your veterinarian.

Ground Poles and "Deep Going"

Ground poles are an excellent device for improving balance, form, and condition. To start, place ground poles that are 10 feet long and 4 to 6 inches high on the ground at 10-foot intervals. If your poles aren't that high, raise them off the ground. Ride your horse over the poles, performing half-halts as you approach them. Work at this for at least ten minutes to start. Stop often and ask the horse to back up in order to keep his weight over his haunches and strengthen the muscles and ligaments in the rear legs. Once he is accustomed to working over the poles, you can ask him to rein-back over them. However, do not perform serpentines around them.

Riding your horse through any kind of "deep going," such as sand, deep grass, or mud, is another useful exercise for the "stifled" horse.

PROBLEM: Hollow (Swayed) Back

The poor form in which gaited horses are commonly ridden predestines a high percentage of them to become hollow- or sway-backed. The results are saddle-fitting problems, long-term soundness issues, and too often, a horse that's (consequently) unhappy under saddle (read: sore, surly, and snappish). Many gaited-horse farms start backing their young horses at two years or younger, when their body is not yet equipped to carry a rider. This also contributes to the development of a sway back, as the immature ligaments that hold the back and torso muscles in place are stressed beyond capacity.

A hollow back in gaited horses has traditionally been considered an unsolvable problem, since gaited horse training methods have been based on the premise that our horses need to be ridden in a stiff, hollow frame in order to perform smooth saddle gaits. This is simply not true. What *is* true is that our horses need to be extraordinarily comfortable in their tack in order to gait in a functionally healthy way with a moderately "rounded-up" back. I fear that in the past there's been far too much emphasis placed on methods, when it would have been better from the horses' perspective to rethink the original flawed training premises.

You can practice simple ground techniques and riding exercises to help restructure and strengthen the back of even an older riding horse. Teaching your horse to stretch those unconditioned, stiff muscles is the first order of business. The work starts from the ground, and then moves to working under saddle.

Solution: Ground Lessons

Belly Lift

One useful ground technique for helping your horse to round up is the *belly lift*. If you go down on your hands and knees and stretch your back upward—like a cat—it involves tightening and lifting your abdominal muscles. This is what you want to encourage your horse to do because it lessens the compression on the disks between the horse's vertebrae while encouraging development of the abdominal muscles. As with humans, good abdominals make for a strong back.

There are two ways of performing the belly lift, depending on whether you work with a partner or alone. When the former, have the helper stand on one side of your horse while you stand on the other. Reach under the horse's barrel immediately behind the girth and link hands to lift up the horse's barrel so it feels as if you are trying to pick the horse up.

Be sure to bend at the knees and use your legs rather than your back (you don't want to hurt your back while healing the horse's!) If you observe the horse closely, you'll soon note a very slight rise to his back. Once you obtain this rise, release pressure. Repeat this exercise twice more, moving 6 inches back along the barrel each time.

When working alone, stand alongside your horse just behind the girth. Lay your hand flat underneath the horse's barrel so your fingertips can press the midline mark. Use your fingertips to press firmly upward while pressing the heel of your hand up into the horse's belly. Again, do the lifts from your legs and press until you notice a slight rise in the horse's back, which may be accompanied by a relieved sigh.

Reflexive Back Lift

The *reflexive back lift* is an extremely useful solution to the hollow-back problem that can be done by one person. Stand behind your horse, as closely as possible. (If your horse has any tendency to kick, do not do this exercise.) Place the tips of your fingers on both hands up toward the horse's point of hip. Press firmly (dig hard!) into the hip muscle while dragging your fingers downward. There is a point in the hip muscles—it is slightly different on each horse—that triggers an automatic response whereby the horse dramatically raises his belly and back. Experiment to locate this spot on your horse. Once you find it, repeat six or eight times. This technique should be practiced routinely at least once every day. When you ride, do it before mounting, once every hour during the ride, and again when you finish.

Other useful groundwork for a hollow back includes the head-lowering and neck-stretching exercises outlined on p. 178. Teaching your horse to stretch these unconditioned, stiff muscles is the first order of business.

Solution: Mounted Exercises

Tack Considerations

Just as most "people exercises" require certain types of gear, so too does this work. The first thing you need to do when starting this routine is to make certain there is no bridging in the saddle you ride in (see p. 138). By this, I mean that the bars of the saddle's tree lie flat along the entire topline on both sides of your horse's back, with *no gap* under the seat area.

On a hollow-backed horse, the weight of the rider is concentrated on either side of the shoulder and at the loins. As you might imagine, this creates a considerable amount of pressure-point pain and discomfort at these places. What often exacerbates this problem is that horses (like people) are asymmetrically built—that is, one side of their body is more developed than the other. This means that there is usually a greater degree of pressure on the shoulder and back area on one side. The horse's response is to try to "flatten" his back down away from the pain. If you can imagine walking in a shoe with a pebble in the heel—and another in the toe— you begin to get an idea of how this works (or rather, doesn't work) for the horse.

I offer the Have-a-Heart™ bridge-pad system to alleviate this problem. Its design allows you to perfectly fill in the hollow area(s) of the back so that the weight of the rider is properly distributed. With a sway-backed horse, you want to be sure the saddle bars are distributing your weight evenly along the entire topline. There are two layers of open-cell foam within the pad, so it can be easily adjusted to suit the degree of sway—and

> Horses (like people) are asymmetrically built—that is, one side of their body is more developed than the other.

possible asymmetry—as the horse's back is reformed using the techniques and exercises I discuss here. The goal is to eliminate, or reduce, the "hollow" that has developed in the horse's back. There are a number of other bridge pads on the market, as well. Whatever pad you use, remember the principle of *padding away from the pressure* (see p. 141).

Let it also be noted that your horse must be able to transfer action up forward from the loins through the back and neck, especially when performing a smooth saddle gait. If you want these back muscles to become healthy and useful, they can't be restricted by a saddle that acts like a stationery splint tied on and held firmly under the weight of the rider. Some of the horses I am called to work on have back muscles that feel like cardboard; there's very little resiliency left. This happens as a result of poor saddle dynamics. (Please pay particular attention to the information offered in chapter 6 on saddle fit and dynamics.)

Schooling Exercises

Once the horse is comfortably fit, practice the following mounted exercises I discuss in chapters 7 and 8:

- Head-Lowering and Neck-Stretching (p. 178)
- Half-Halts (p. 159)
- Conscious Collection (p. 180)
- Figure Eights (p. 175)
- Serpentines (p. 177)

All help develop *lateral* and *vertical flexion,* and if practiced routinely, recondition the muscles of the horse's back. While this effort is ongoing, avoid overworking the horse. A horse that becomes fatigued won't have the energy to move in good form. Riding beyond this point is self-defeating, so be prepared to be patient with the process.

I once conducted a clinic where a woman kept trying to get her horse to lift his back by leaning forward, pointing her toes down, and prodding her horse in the belly. This was ineffective, to put it mildly, but her trainer insisted this was the best way to improve her horse's condition and way of going.

This threw the rider into a poor, front-heavy position, and the prodding merely annoyed the horse. If you should ever receive this advice, please do your horse a favor and ignore it!

Whenever you complete a schooling session under saddle, take a few moments when you've dismounted to do some head-lowering and neck-stretching, as well as a few belly lifts and reflexive back lifts.

Some horses become so "low-backed" that the three ligaments that support the back are permanently compromised. While you can strengthen the belly and back muscles, *stretched ligaments* are another matter altogether. For this reason, while you can usually successfully reform the back of horses that have a light to moderate amount of sway, reforming a severely hollow-backed horse—whether aged or not—only meets with moderate success. Nevertheless, any improvement is beneficial to the horse and contributes to a longer career under saddle.

GAIT ISSUES

Now that you've successfully eliminated any behavioral and physical issues, it's time to tackle problems you may have with your horse's gaits or way of going. What follows are the most common issues I've seen in gaited horses and how to resolve them.

PROBLEM: Lazy Forward Motion

Many riders complain about their gaited horse's lack of forward impulsion. This isn't a horse problem so much as it is a challenge to the rider. If you want your horse to gait well, then the second thing you absolutely must do is teach him to actively move forward in a correct four-beat walk with energy generated from the haunches.

I say this is the "second" thing because—as you surely know by now—the first, most important thing is to make sure your horse's saddle, pad, and bit are well-fitted for a full range of comfortable motion. Assuming this is the case, then there is absolutely no reason nor excuse for riding a lazy horse.

While some folks point their finger with exasperation at the animal and claim he simply will not move forward with energy and consistency, I have yet to find a sound, well-fitted horse that couldn't be taught, in very short order, how to attain and maintain good forward action.

Solution: Encourage an Active Walk

The secret here is persistence and consistency on the part of the rider. To begin teaching correct impulsion, ride your horse on a straightaway or on a large circle with minimal rein contact. It's important not to take on the reins as you don't want to send the animal conflicting cues of "stop" and "go." He needs to be actively encouraged "on" without any restrictions of forward movement.

To cue the horse for an energetic walk, first "ask" your horse to move by deepening your seat and pushing into the saddle. Resist the urge to use your feet as most lazy horses have been poked and nudged so constantly by their rider's boots that they've tuned them out altogether. Continually riding with your heels poked into your horse's sides also makes for very a poor rider position in the saddle, which further inhibits the horse's desire and ability to move forward.

Your horse probably won't respond much to your initial request, so heat things up a notch by repeating the request, only this time use your seat, upper leg, and a voice cue to "Walk!" There's a better than even chance that the horse either ignores you altogether, or picks up the pace for one or two strides, then drops back down to a dragging walk. Please don't get upset at the horse about this, since it was most likely you who taught him how to get away with such lazy behavior in the first place.

Instead of getting riled up, be prepared for the animal to behave this way: Anticipate his action and the instant there is another drop in speed, give the horse a good pop with your riding crop, the ends of your reins, or use your (humane) riding spurs. When I say a "good pop," I mean a *good pop.* Many times riders simply substitute continual light poking with the feet with continual light tapping with a crop, with equally poor results.

I'm not suggesting you beat your horse, but do give enough of a "smack" to let him know you mean business and to act as a future deterrent to lazy action. If you have trouble deciding on where the line between effectiveness ends and cruelty begins, consider your horse's reaction. Every horse is different, and a whack that would drive one animal up a wall may hardly have any effect at all on a more stoic creature.

On a couple of occasions I've had clinic riders who absolutely couldn't bring themselves to put enough energy into this action to be effective with their horse. I helped them determine the appropriate level of firmness by using a riding crop on one of their legs. These people were a little shocked, to be sure! But they agreed that while my action definitely got their attention—and they wouldn't want it repeated—they were not actually injured by it. I'm almost certainly the only horse clinician in the country who gets away with "horse whipping" her clients, but as testament to the effectiveness of appropriate negative reinforcement, each one of these people immediately improved their horse/human communication skills!

Solution: Active Forward Motion

Until the horse is well conditioned to perform his own best four-beat gait in good form, a correct four-beat walk with impulsion is more difficult to maintain than a stiff, incorrect gait. Therefore, after the horse has picked up speed he's likely to initially stiffen up and break to trot, pace, or an inappropriate gait. Use your rein to check the horse out of the wrong action, and your leg or other riding aid to encourage continued active forward motion. At this point you must persistently insist on forward action. After you've asked twice, and insisted once, don't drop back to merely "asking." Keep using your riding aid vigorously to insist on continued active walking. The horse should move at a correct four-beat walk as fast as possible without breaking to another gait. Every time the horse stiffens up and breaks from a loose, flowing walk, check him in the bridle and at the same time use your forward aids to demand continued active forward motion.

This maneuver is tricky at first and may take a session or two to perfect. Remember what it was like when you learned how to drive a standard-shift car and your timing on the gas and clutch had to be perfected? This exercise is very similar in that you are *disengaging the incorrect gait,* while at the same

Until the horse is well conditioned to perform his own best four-beat gait in good form, a correct four-beat walk with impulsion is more difficult to maintain than a stiff, incorrect gait.

time *engaging the horse's "drive train."* Before long you and your horse will achieve correct synchrony, and he'll know that when you ask for a more active walk, it doesn't give him permission to stiffen up into an incorrect, lazy gait—and that you are ready and willing to demand that he maintain active forward motion. Once a horse understands you mean business, and there are negative consequences for inappropriate behavior and responses, you will seldom, if ever, need to be quite so forceful again.

The secret here, as mentioned before, is consistency. It will do you no good, and will in fact set you backward from your goal, if you give the horse a good "pop" one time and fail to follow up with another the instant he starts dragging along. I liken this to a child who asks his mother for candy, and she says "No," but he comes back again and again, insisting on a piece of candy, and she finally rolls her eyes, shrugs her shoulders, and gives it to him. That child has learned that "No" really means "Yes," if he only persists long enough. The same goes for your horse. When he has learned to slow down after only a few active steps, and you fail to persistently get after him for it, you've inadvertently reinforced the very behavior you're trying to eliminate.

For a few days plan to practice this active walking before moving on to the next stage of this exercise, which is Conscious Collection (see p. 180) while moving energetically forward. It should only take three or four riding sessions before moving with impulsion has become an ingrained habit for your horse.

Problem: "Camel Walk"

Some very long-strided horses with long backs have a very uncomfortable dog walk, which is called a "camel walk." There's an exaggerated rolling action through the horse's back that can be very hard on the rider's hips and back.

Solution: Reseat Yourself

You will have limited success at changing this characteristic, but there are a few things you can do to make a smoother ride. First, be sure you are seated forward, just behind the withers, rather than back toward the horse's loins. Riding forward places you over the horse's "hinge," where there is the least amount of 'back action." (See further discussion of this on p. 124.)

Solution: Maintain Collection

To avoid being continually "rocked-and-rolled" in the saddle, keep the horse lightly collected on the bridle, even when walking at slow speeds. It's the loose motion of the uncollected dog walk that causes so much rolling action. Collecting your horse shortens his frame, contains the action, and smooths out the walk.

PROBLEM: Stumbling

I'm always surprised at how many gaited-horse owners complain about their horse stumbling. Since the gaited horse always has at least one or more feet on the ground, he is inherently *more* surefooted than a non-gaited horse.

Solution: Schooling for Impulsion and Collection

As with lazy forward motion, stumbling is closely associated with poor saddle and bit choices, as well as lack of impulsion and collection, so the basic corrective measures are identical to those described under "Camel Walk" (see p. 222). Stumbling is an extremely dangerous habit, so along with impulsion and collection exercises, every time your horse stumbles you should snatch up sharply on the reins, push him forward, and say "Quit!" Then give him a pop with a crop or the end of your reins, just to let him know you mean business.

Horses that are rump-high are at a disadvantage, and especially so when they are structured in such a way as to be "daisy clippers" in front—that is to say, they have very little "lift" in front (see p. 93). This is the case when the horse has a very long, laid-back shoulder and a short, horizontal arm. If you don't already own a horse with this conformation, I advise against considering one for purchase. Teaching him to collect properly and lighten up in the front enough to increase the amount of leg lift can be a real challenge.

> Stumbling is closely associated with poor saddle and bit choices, as well as lack of impulsion and collection.

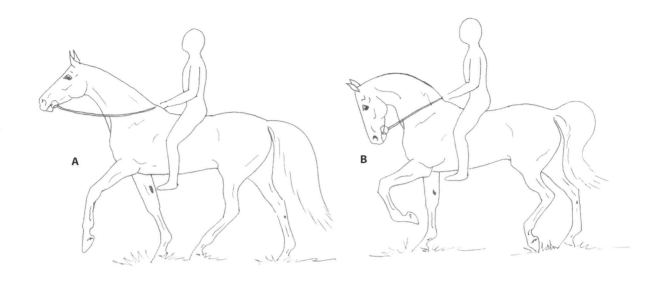

A

B

9.9 A–C A horse that is uncollected and "strung out" goes with an elongated frame, a hollow back, and places excess stress on his joints (A). The hind leg is hyperextended before the horse's weight comes off it. Horses ridden this way tend to pace or step pace. A horse may "over-tuck" his head and move with "false collection" (B). This does not take the excess strain of moving in poor form off his body, and he still tends to move laterally. A horse in good form generates impulsion from the hindquarters that is transmitted through his body and "collected" on the bridle (C). His entire frame is condensed, his back slightly rounded, and his and the rider's weight are correctly distributed over all four legs.

C

BBJ

Solution: Mechanical Aids

Sometimes a little mechanical aid is advisable if the horse persistently stumbles in spite of your best corrective measures. While this may seem converse, in such a case I suggest that the horse be shod with toe weights in front. The weights cause him to increase the amount of lift he has and decrease or eliminate stumbling. The weights need not be a permanent fixture: After wearing them for several weeks the horse develops muscle memory, so when the toe weights come off, the higher lift in front remains. It may be necessary to shoe him this way two or three times yearly in order to maintain the habit of increased forefoot action.

PROBLEM: Forging

Forging is especially common in horses that perform a natural running walk, since their long hind stride causes the hind foot to interfere with (strike) the same-side forefoot. Your horse may forge only when he's fatigued, or when he is due for a trim, but this is a full-time challenge for some horse owners.

Solution: "Squared-Off" Toes

I've had many people ask me how they should change the angles of the horse's feet to eliminate forging. I always explain that it is not wise to change the natural angles of the horse's foot, as doing so places undue stress on the delicate internal structures (see p. 234). What you might try instead is to have your farrier square off the front toes. This give the horse a little faster breakover in front without actually changing angles. Also, be sure to ride with plenty of impulsion. Sometimes horses that forge are simply too lazy to move well off their hind end and pick up their feet. You need to keep right on such a horse to get him to collect and move out as he should.

PROBLEM: Pacing and Step Pacing

Many gaited horses—indeed, it seems the majority—perform a straight pace or step pace as their preferred gait. While it's always your intent to encourage natural gait action, it is best to try to bring the strongly lateral, "pacey" horse as close to the center of the Gait Spectrum as possible, for his own long-term welfare (see p. 3).

Remember, a *pacing* horse is moving one set of lateral, (same-side) legs in perfect unison, creating an even two-beat gait, with a moment of suspension between one set of feet picking up and the opposite set striking the ground. The motion of the pace is from side to side, and because of the suspension, there's also some up-and-down movement. No fun for the rider!

The *step pace* is nearly identical to the pace, except that the hind foot sets down a split second before the same-side forefoot. This eliminates suspension and resultant concussion that occurs in a straight pace.

Often a step pace is a smoother gait for the rider, but any horse executing it is going in a strung-out manner that places too much weight over the front end and discourages proper balance and collection (figs. 9.9 A–C). In other words, the horse lands heavily on each front leg, while each hind leg is hyperextended behind him before the weight comes off it, placing excessive stress on the hocks and stifle joints. This can cause problems with the soundness of these structures. It also encourages a ventroflexed (hollow-backed) frame, making the horse hard to fit for saddle and weakened throughout his topline. Since the horse's back muscle *(longissimus dorsi)* is the largest muscle in his body, you should keep it strong and healthy for as long as possible.

Another problem with the step pace is that most horses can only sustain it at relatively low speeds—perhaps up to 5 mph or so. When the rider asks for greater speed in gait, step-pacing horses invariably revert to a jarring and uncomfortable straight pace.

This makes pacey gaits unfortunate for both horse and rider. The most common complaint I receive by far is from people who have a horse with extremely uncomfortable pace gaits under saddle. Many of these poor souls despair of ever being able to retrain their horse, yet are emotionally attached to him.

Other people do not realize there is a problem with the pace or step pace, and believe it is a correct saddle gait. One highly respected mainstream equestrian magazine ran a feature article on the subject of gaited horses, and every photo in the article showed horses, with widely grinning riders, performing fast pace or step-pace gaits! My staff administrator hung that photo in a prominent place in her office.

Solution: Detecting the Lateral Gait

Many riders mistakenly believe the comfortable step pace they experience is a rack, running walk, or other acceptable saddle gait. In fact, at clinic and expo presentations I sometimes have the audience inform a rider when her horse is performing a lateral gait because she simply cannot discern this for herself and refuses to believe it unless others confirm the gait for her.

Since you can't fix something that you don't know is dysfunctional, the rider must first learn how to detect a strongly lateral gait. One of the most telling signs is that the horse's head and neck swing from side to side, rather than up and down. Also, you might feel as though you are riding the proverbial "plank," since pacey horses are stiff through their body. Usually the head is quite high, though some horses "overtuck" their head in "false collection."

9.10 A–C The horse in A has become lazy, strung out, and "pacey." In B, the rider leans back, takes on the reins, and pushes with her seat and legs, performing a half-halt. The result is that the horse rebalances his weight in C and slips back into an easy-going, correctly timed fox trot.

A

B

C

Have someone record you riding on video, so you can study it to see what precise characteristics are evidenced when the animal's lateral (same-side) sets of legs are moving in synchrony, or nearly so. While watching, envision yourself in the saddle, and recall what your physical sensations were when riding this gait. Then, when you actually do ride, pay close attention to all of these indicators. You might ask someone on the ground to inform you when the horse turns pacey so you get the feel for that gait in saddle.

Solution: Retraining Exercises

It can be a real challenge to retrain an animal that has been allowed to pace or step pace. These gaits, while murder on the horse's body over the long term, require little effort. All the horse needs to do is stiffen through the body and shuffle his same-side sets of legs forward and back…forward and back…forward and back….

I repeat this so you get the feeling of the hypnotic effect such an easy-to-perform gait can have on the horse. It is outright addictive and, like any addictive behavior, the first order of business is total abstinence. The horse must not, under any circumstances, be allowed even one stride of pace or step pace.

As with any gait training, the primary riding exercise for retraining the extremely laterally gaited horse is to practice "working the walk" (see p. 164) with increasing speed and correct collection. Animals that have been permitted or encouraged to pace, however, progress much faster in their retraining if a few additional techniques are added to their riding routine (see below).

As you work the walk, when you sense the horse slipping into his lateral gear, the first thing to do is to get him to rebalance his weight over his haunches using correct halts, rein-backs, and half-halts (see p. 159). All of these simple maneuvers help get your horse gathered up and moving off his hind end (figs. 9.10 A–C). Yes, I'm talking about collecting and rebalancing. Again.

Ground Poles

An exercise I find especially useful for pacey horses is working over *ground poles.* You need at least eight, spaced 10 feet apart. You can finetune the distance to suit your horse after you practice crossing them for a short time.

When you bring the horse into the line of ground poles, give a strong half-halt and push him to go very vigorously over them (figs. 9.11 A–C). If he tries to dodge out to the side, keep your focus firmly straight ahead and use your legs to drive him forward. Or, if he starts hitting the poles with his feet, give a snatch on the rein and say "Quit!" or a sharp "Eh!" (Universal horse language, no?)

If your horse seems truly unable to clear the poles without hitting them after several rounds, vary the distance between them by a foot or so—shorter when your horse is short-legged, longer for a taller horse. The more poles you can work over, the better. Eight poles should be the minimum, and there is no maximum number.

When working over poles a horse is forced to "telescope" his neck and look down to see where he places his feet, which causes vertical flexion, and rounds and softens his back through the topline. It is also impossible for a horse to work lateral sets of legs over ground poles, so he is encouraged into a more evenly timed gait. At first, when you get past the last ground pole, bring the horse immediately back down to a walk to prevent him from slipping to a pace. Many times people are so encouraged by how well their horse gaits over the ground poles that they try to maintain the gait for too long past the last pole. This is rarely successful until later in schooling, as it takes time to develop neurological memory.

Once your horse has practiced clearing poles for 10 to 15 minutes, allow him to take just one or two regular steps past the ground poles, and bring him back to a walk, or halt. Over time you should be able to increase the distance, until the horse maintains the four-beat gait indefinitely.

9.11 A & B The Tennessee Walking Horse in A is resisting working over ground poles. The rider remains calm, focused, and consistent until the horse willingly crosses over the center of the poles in B.

9.11 C The result of these efforts is a horse with correctly timed saddle gaits, and a strong, respectful bond with his rider.

Rollbacks

Rollbacks (see p. 181) are also an excellent exercise for pacey horses. After you complete a rollback, the horse is working strongly over his haunches, which helps maintain a more evenly timed four-beat gait.

Lateral Exercises

Lateral exercises of all kinds are useful because a horse is rigid through the body when pacing, and lateral exercises keep a horse soft and supple. I especially like *spiraling in and out* (see p. 177). After completing a series of spiral exercises, many horses can be ridden in gait for several steps.

Uphill and Deep Footing

Working fast *when going uphill* is very useful, as it keeps more weight rearward. And in heavy or *deep footing*, horses find it difficult to maintain a two-beat gait, so riding through sand, snow, deep mud, or high grass is an excellent way to retrain the pacey horse.

Cantering

Another useful exercise for a pacey horse is to canter him, as this teaches him to use two diagonal pairs of legs—one set in unison, one set in opposition—and totally breaks up the lateral action of pace. However, I offer this advice with a stern word of caution. Horses with strong lateral gaits have a propensity to cross-canter, which is to take opposing canter leads on the front and rear legs. This is *extremely* dangerous because the horse may easily hit a front foot with a hind foot, resulting in a somersaulting fall, right on top of the hapless rider. So if you ask for a canter, and find yourself pushed forcefully up out of the seat with each stride, *immediately* bring the horse back down to halt, and begin again. You must always ask for the canter from the walk, or halt, and *never* from a pace or step pace. It may be that your pacey horse will not be able to canter until he's developed a much stronger ability for a collected, correct walk, which also breaks up the lateral action effectively, over time.

As I discussed on p. 167, a canter-challenged horse often does well when asked for a canter on an uphill incline. This is because the horse's weight is naturally shifted rearward, over his haunches, and the front end is lightened, making it easier for him to take a correct lead, both front and hind. If you use this technique, bring the horse back to walk at the top of the incline, rather than allowing the canter to deteriorate into a pace or cross-canter once you hit level ground again.

It is imperative as this training progresses to ride with people who are sympathetic to your cause. It will not work to spend a week, or three, teaching your horse how to move in a functional, "square" fashion, only to head out on the trail with friends who insist on riding at a clip that outstrips your horse's ability to keep up without breaking to pace. You'll soon find yourself back at square one. Believe me, this is as frustrating for your poor horse as it is for you!

PROBLEM: Trotting and Slick Trotting

There are a number of ways to deal with the diagonally oriented horse that tends toward the "trotty" side of the Gait Spectrum (see p. 3).

Solution: Half-Halts

If your horse consistently breaks to *trot,* ride him at the walk until he breaks to a slow trot. Then perform several light half-halts, taking more on first the right rein, and then the left rein, until the gait smooths back out. While a "pacey" horse needs to be kept *at* the breaking point without being allowed to break, the "trotty" horse does better when ridden just *past* the breaking point, and then brought back.

However, if it becomes apparent that the horse is inclined toward a fox trot, you can help develop this gait by slightly lifting the reins with each half-halt. This frees up the shoulders and allows for a slightly increased length of front stride. Once the horse begins to fox trot, you can lower your hands and ask for correct collection on the bridle.

Solution: Retraining Exercises

Downhill Work

The trotty horse does better when worked on downhill inclines, and under a heavier rider. Be sure when asking for speed downhill that you get the horse well balanced off his haunches first, to avoid the possibility of a downhill fall or stumble.

Lateral Work

Another useful tactic for the trotty horse is to cue for a shoulder-in or haunches-in (see pp. 187 and 188). Setting the front and hind feet on different tracks usually breaks up the trot very well; once a four-beat gait has been established, bring his forehand and hind end back into alignment.

Solution: Training Technique for Slick Trotters

When a horse *slick trots* the hind foot sets down an instant before the diagonally opposed forefoot. This is an uncomfortable ride where the rider feels the saddle cantle come up and forcefully "bump" her seat forward with each stride. It is extremely hard on the rider's back.

I had a mare that was prone to this gait, and I cured the problem by having my farrier square off her front feet for a faster breakover (though he did not change the natural angles of her foot). This meant that each front foot would set down an instant faster. Once she was warmed up, I let her gait full out for a few minutes, which helped her get back the natural "forefoot-first" rhythm of the gait. Then I gradually and softly collected her on the bridle with light half-halts, lifting lightly on the reins to help keep her shoulders "free," and she maintained the correct footfall pattern. Though her nose was slightly in front of the vertical, she nevertheless worked nicely off her haunches. When I asked her to shorten stride, I brought her back into correct collection with her head on the vertical, and at that point, she would once again execute the flat walk. Though she was a registered Tennessee Walking Horse, she never could go faster than a flat walk without breaking to a fox trot, but she could perform that gait at blazing speeds!

This is an example of how every horse is different. While I can offer techniques and suggestions for particular circumstances, what works for one horse may not be effective for another. It is my hope you will thoroughly familiarize yourself with the techniques outlined in this book, tailor your schooling to the needs of your individual horse, and have a lot of fun in the process!

APPENDIX A
Optimal Hoof Care for the Gaited Horse

Honoring the Horse's Natural Foot Conformation

Few issues have been as controversial in the gaited-horse industry as that of how to trim and shoe; the topic initiated a firestorm of opinion and debate that began over half a decade ago, and continues to the present day. Foot and leg abuses have long been rife in the gaited horse industry—particularly in the Tennessee Walking Horse show world (fig. A.1 and see p. 26).

Actually, as with horses of every kind, gaited horses should be trimmed and shod according to the natural angles of their feet and pasterns. Angle degrees should not be varied for the sake of improving their gait. Gait training is properly done from the saddle and not from under the horse's belly. When this policy is bridged even moderately, it all too often leads to unhealthy excesses.

Barefoot Trimming

Over the past few years I developed a cursory interest in learning how to transition gaited horses from

horseshoes to "bare" feet, even purchasing specialized boots to put on my horses for trail rides—with which I had little success. For that reason, I went back to shoeing in the traditional way. I assumed that going *au natu-*

A.1 "Big Lick" show horses (see p. 31) have such heavy shoes and stacks on their forefeet that metal bands are utilized to hold them on. Here you can see the unnaturally high angle of the stacked horse's foot, as well as evidence of chemical treatment of the pasterns prior to placing chains around them.

rale was simply not feasible for my horses because of our region's rocky trails and soft, moist pastures.

In the course of speaking to people who have extensive experience and knowledge, I decided to explore the topic of barefoot trimming further. As a result, I am convinced that horses that have successfully transitioned to a barefoot lifestyle are much better off for it. I am not yet prepared to declare it is the only "right way" to care for your horse's feet, but I am impressed enough by the literature and evidence (the number of success stories) to include the information here for you to consider.

In the pages that follow my intent is to offer a basic understanding of how a barefoot trim is executed, and how the barefoot horse's foot should appear when it is properly cared for. This is not intended, nor should it be referred to, as instruction on how to perform your own hoof trimming. If this topic is of interest, then I highly encourage you to do your homework and find a professional farrier who is competent and experienced to help you make the transition from shod to unshod.

HEED BAREFOOT "PIONEERS"

In order to be successful at keeping your horse barefoot, you need to gain a wealth of knowledge on the subject. Modern pioneers in the field of barefoot horses include Jaime Jackson, Pete Ramey, and Dr. Hiltrud Strasser, among others (see p. 240 for contact information). Recent university studies have concluded that, for a number of reasons not previously understood, a horse's overall condition is healthier and more comfortable when his feet are kept in a natural state.

BAREFOOT VS. SHOD

Natural Foot Improves Blood Circulation

The horse's foot is not a static object but is engineered to flex with each step. This action helps the foot to work as an efficient shock absorber but, equally importantly, it serves as an additional "blood pump"—the expansion and contraction of the foot with each step enhances the circulation of blood through the animal's entire body. When the foot hits the ground, the unshod hoof expands, pulling blood down the leg and into the hoof. When the foot is picked up, it naturally contracts, sending the blood back up the leg and through the body. These four corollary circulatory pumps lighten the heart's workload, which explains why barefoot horses have, on average, a 10 percent slower heart rate than shod animals.

The additional blood that flows into the foot upon concussion with the ground serves to cushion the joints, tendons, and ligaments in the foot and leg. In the process, these structures are richly nourished by that protective pool of blood, leading to healthy growth and strong, dense structures. When the foot is deprived of this natural source of nutrients, the nerves become numb, much like that of one of our limbs "going to sleep," and unsoundness can be masked for so long that a problem is critical before it becomes apparent.

Negative Effects of Shoes

Placing a metal shoe on the horse's foot has a number of negative impacts on the horse, aside from restricting the blood flow I just described.

- It increases the amount of vibrational concussion that travels through the horse's body with each stride, creating additional stress on bones, joints, and ligaments.
- It prevents the foot from wearing down gradually and evenly, according to the horse's natural conformation.

- Metal shoes contribute to contracted heels, hoof cracks, heel corns, seedy toe, white line disease, navicular syndrome, laminitis—and the list goes on. Many thousands of horses with "hopeless" cases of navicular syndrome or laminitis have been restored to complete health by simply giving them a natural barefoot way of life.

CORRECT "BALANCE" FOR THE FOOT

For years it was customary, even for those who didn't create exaggerated angles or participate in extreme trimming and shoeing practices, to balance the horse's foot by trimming the hoof so it was exactly level from front to back, and from side to side. This created a foot that was perfectly level when the horse was standing on level ground. Once the foot was thus balanced, a shoe was made to fit the hoof, and nailed on. (Unfortunately, too often farriers took the shortcut of shaping the foot to the shoe, rather than the other way around.)

It is largely the consensus of today's natural- or barefoot-trim farriers that the secret to a good hoof trim is to make certain the foot is balanced according to the conformation of the individual horse's foot and leg, which can vary significantly from horse to horse. An animal that has a predisposition toward toeing-out, for example (see p. 165), does not benefit from having the inward structures of the foot and leg forced into a "correct, upright, level-to-the-ground" balance. Rather, this causes undue stress for the horse, and exacerbates the problem over time.

Determining Correct Foot Angles

When viewing the horse from the side, it is important that the angle of his foot is the same as the angle of his shoulder and pastern (fig. A.2). The angle of the foot from 1 inch above the coronary band to 1 inch below the coronary band should be carried all the way down to the ground, and an imaginary line run from the center of the pastern joint to the ground should bisect the hoof (fig. A.3). If the angle of the hoof is too high or too low many kinds of issues can develop, not only in the foot, but throughout the horse's body. Excess stress caused by improper trimming creates chronic inflammation, arthritis, and encourages organisms such as thrush to thrive in the resultant unhealthy hoof tissues.

Assessing the Individual Horse

So we know what to look for insofar as the angle of the foot goes, but how does the trimmer know how to achieve the optimum angle, and foot balance, for the individual horse? Not visible in the hoof drawings included here is the underlying system of veins and nerves called the supercorium. The supercorium is "master central" to the horse's foot, not only carrying blood, but also "reading" all the circumstances and events that transpire in the foot. The supercorium then responds accordingly by causing

A.2 The primary structures of the horse's lower leg and foot.

A.3 In A you see a foot that is well balanced—you can draw a straight line from the center of the pastern joint down to the ground, bisecting the hoof. Drawing B shows a foot with an angle that is too steep, placing excess stress on the entire leg. Example C is very commonly seen in gaited horses: a very low angle, short heel, and long toe.

the foot to be nourished and grow according to its precise needs at any given time. This means, in the case of a natural barefoot hoof, that the sole and walls of the feet grow precisely in accord with the conditions and requirements of the foot, which in turn sends the supercorium information regarding its current environment. It is really an amazing system of communication and support!

The result of this symbiotic relationship is that the supercorium causes the plane of the sole to grow as appropriate for the conformation of the horse and the environment to which it is exposed. Subsequently, the sole plane is the perfect guide for establishing where the hoof wall ought to be trimmed.

Let's say a horse has a crooked pastern, and as a consequence the foot needs more support on the outside edge. The supercorium "reads" this condition as it receives stimuli from the horse's motion, and produces denser hoof sole where it is needed. In the wild, horses travel 20-plus miles per day over varied terrain, so their hoof walls do not outgrow the depth of the sole plane, and a perfect balance is maintained. Our domestic horses have far less freedom to roam, and are often kept in soft paddocks or bedded stalls, so the growth of the hoof walls cause the feet to become unbalanced (calling for intervention in the form of trimming). When the horse is trimmed regularly—every two to six weeks—then all that is required to maintain a perfectly balanced

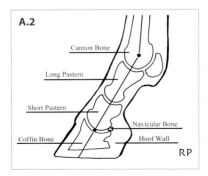

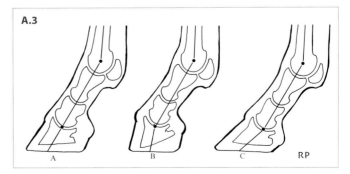

foot is to trim to the level of the live sole plane. Once this trim has been established, the wall should not be permitted to grow longer than $^1/_2$ inch beyond the plane of the sole.

PRIME CONSIDERATIONS FOR A BAREFOOT TRIM

• Trimming to the natural sole plane: To help establish the horse's natural sole plane there must be only slight trimming or scraping away of the dead matter on the frog and sole—just enough so the trimmer can see where the live sole begins. Under no circumstances should there be any trimming away of the live sole. Doing so thins the sole, and causes the coffin bone to adjust too close to the ground. The live sole plane has a fine, waxy surface that is white or yellowish—sometimes with gray lines—in color. It is easy to distinguish it from the dead, flaky matter that needs to be scraped off (fig. A.4).

• "Mustang roll": A wild horse that has naturally balanced feet also has a "roll," or bevel, that develops along the entire outside edge of the hoof wall. This is called a "mustang roll" and helps prevent the hoof wall from chipping or cracking, while creating an optimal environment for the laminae.

• "Toe rocker" and breakover: Many natural barefoot trimmers create a "toe rocker" at the front of the horse's toe. A toe rocker is a bevel to the front edge of the toe that enables a faster point of breakover (fig. A.5). Breakover is the point of the stride when the horse's foot begins to "roll over" prior to leaving the ground. The ideal point of breakover is at the tip of the coffin bone, over the toe callus. The farther behind this point the breakover occurs, the more stress is placed on the feet and legs. Traditional trimming methods do not include a toe rocker, and so cannot facilitate a

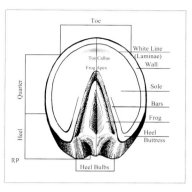

A.4 The parts of a healthy front foot (a hind foot will be slightly more oval shaped).

natural breakover point for the foot. Trims that include a toe rocker enable the horse to achieve a naturally more forward breakover, which relieves stress on virtually all the structures of the foot and leg, and helps keep the laminae strong and tight to the hoof wall. People who correctly trim their barefoot horses imitate these patterns of wear.

TRANSITIONING TO BAREFOOT

Proper Preparation

Through the course of my research, I discovered that you can't simply perform a customary "pasture trim" on a horse that you are trying to transition

A.5 This illustration shows how the point of breakover affects the foot and leg. The red line (A) shows how traditional trims cause the breakover to be toward the rear of the foot. The line at the tip of the toe (B) shows where natural wear occurs in wild horses, and the associated red line (C) shows how much more forward this places the breakover.

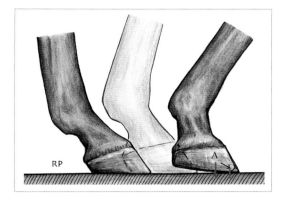

over to going barefoot. There are special considerations that have to be taken into account, including not only learning the specific trimming techniques I've already outlined, but also providing optimal nutrition and housing. The barefoot horse needs to have a life that is as close to that experienced in the wild as possible.

Responding to Initial Foot Tenderness

When a horse is transitioned to a barefoot trim, he may become especially tender-footed and exhibit problems not seen when he was shod. This is to be expected, as the hoof was numb (see p. 235) for as long as it was shod (and/or incorrectly trimmed), and underlying problems may not have been evident because of this. Also, it takes time for the horse's foot to "relearn" how to respond to a natural trim and environment, and to grow appropriate amounts of sole and hoof wall. The diminished veins and nerves in the foot need to be redeveloped, as well. All this takes time; a horse that has been shod for years cannot be expected to fully transition over a period of days, or even weeks.

For this reason many people use various kinds of hoof boots when they ride their newly barefoot horses. There are a number of types and styles on the market, and some experimentation may be required to discover what works best for you and your horse.

Ideal Environment

A horse that is going barefoot needs an environment that allows the sole to thicken and toughen; this can't happen on soft pasture or in confined paddocks. It can be accomplished by placing pea stone and gravel in protective run-in sheds, around feeding and watering areas, and wherever the horse travels or congregates with others. And travel he should!

To facilitate the transition to barefoot life, the horse is ideally left outdoors in a herd situation the majority of the time and encouraged to move about as much as possible. This might mean moving feeding sites some distance from run-in shelters, and watering tanks or buckets some distance from both of them—and then dumping gravel and pea stone along the paths between them. It can also help to place pea stone in your round pen and work the horse there for a period of time each day, with the appropriate amount of time being determined by the current condition of the horse's feet.

Nutrition for Optimum Foot Health

The horse's diet should not include artificial or added sugars. This means feeding natural grains and forage, without added molasses. An overload of simple sugars in the horse's system breaks down into toxins that interfere with the processes necessary for growing good, functionally sound feet. This is true whether the horse is shod, or unshod. (It also leads to hormonal imbalances and stomach ulcers.)

The Shod Horse

A barefoot trim is exemplary even when you decide you want—or need—to continue to shoe your horse. Those with a limited amount of turnout area may never be able to appropriately transition their horse to going entirely barefoot. The horse should, nevertheless, spend a period of time each year (at least three months) unshod, in order for the foot to have optimal health and strength. There are special shoes on the market that allow for a rocker toe, and some shoe materials that enable the foot to maintain its natural flexibility.

The old saying, "No foot, no horse," is more true than many of us ever imagined. If we are to ensure the long-term health and safety of our gaited horses, it is imperative to educate ourselves on the most reliable methods for achieving and maintaining strong, well-functioning feet and legs.

APPENDIX B
Resources

BREED ORGANIZATIONS

American Saddlebred Horse Association
www.saddlebred.com

American Walking Pony Registry
478-743-2321

Florida Cracker Horse Association
www.floridacrackerhorses.com

Galiceño Horse Breeders Association
817-389-3547

**Kentucky Mountain Saddle Horse Association /
Spotted Mountain Horse Association**
www.kmsha.com

**McCurdy Plantation Horse Registry &
Association**
www.mccurdyhorses.com

Missouri Fox Trotting Horse Breed Association
www.mfthba.com

National Show Horse Registry
www.nshregistry.com

National Spotted Saddle Horse Association
www.nssha.com

National Walking Horse Association
www.nwha.com

The Nokota Horse Conservancy
www.nokotahorse.org

North American Peruvian Horse Association
www.napha.net

Paso Fino Horse Association
www.pfha.org

**Pure Puerto Rican Paso Fino Federation of
America**
www.puertoricanpasofino.org

Racking Horse Breeders Association of America
www.rackinghorse.com

Rocky Mountain Horse Association
www.rmhorse.com

**Spotted Saddle Horse Breeders and Exhibitors
Association**
www.sshbea.org

**Tennessee Walking Horse Breeders' and
Exhibitors' Association**
www.twhbea.com

Tennessee Walking Horse Heritage Society
www.walking-horse.com/twhheritagesociety

**Tiger Horse Association (Appaloosa Coat
Patterns)**
www.tigerhorses.org

**The Tiger Horse Breed Registry and Members
Association**
www.tigrehorse.com

United States Icelandic Horse Congress
www.icelandics.org

**United States Mangalarga Marchador
Association**
www.usmarchador.com

United States Peruvian Horse Association
www.uspha.net

United States Trotting Association (Standardbred Horses)
www.ustrotting.com

Walkaloosa Horse Association
www.walkaloosaregistry.com

ANIMAL WELFARE ORGANIZATIONS AND EVENTS

Friends of Sound Horses / The Sound Horse Conference
www.fosh.info
www.soundhorseconference.com

The Humane Society of the United States
www.humanesociety.org

Unwanted Horse Coalition
www.unwantedhorsecoalition.org

Stop Soring
www.stopsoring.com

United States Department of Agriculture
www.usda.gov

TRUSTWORTHY GAITED HORSE TRAINERS AND CLINICIANS

Gaits of Gold (Brenda Imus)
www.gaitsofgold.com
(Check out the community message board:
www.gaitsofgold.com/wowbb)

WillBeGaitin Ranch (Chris and Crystal Larsen)
www.willbegaitin.com

Howe They Walk Farm (Anita Howe)
www.howetheywalk.com

Four Square Horse Ranch (Tara Flewelling)
www.foursquarehorse.com

BAREFOOT TRIMMING INFORMATION

Barefoot for Soundness
www.barefoothorse.com

Heal the Hoof
www.healthehoof.com/conventional_treatment.html

The Horse's Hoof
www.thehorseshoof.com
(See Barefoot Hoof Care Resources at
www.thehorseshoof.com/resources.html)

Gwenyth Browning Jones Santagate
www.barefoottrim.com

Dr. Hiltrud Strasser
www.strasserhoofcare.org

Jaime Jackson
www.jaimejackson.com

Pete Ramey
www.hoofrehab.com

TACK & EQUIPMENT

National Bridle Shop (Gaited Horse Tack)
www.nationalbridleshop.com

Trafalgar Square Books (Horse Books and DVDs)
www.horseandriderbooks.com

Index